TALENT
TALKER

60 Conversations to Unlock Talent and Potential

Yolanda Lacoma & Martin Sutherland

kr
publishing

First published in 2018

ISBN: 978-1-86922-747-0 (Printed)
ISBN: 978-1-86922-748-7 (ePDF)

Published by KR Publishing
P O Box 3954
Randburg
2125
Republic of South Africa

Tel: (011) 706-6009
Fax: (011) 706-1127
E-mail: orders@knowres.co.za
Website: www.kr.co.za

Printed and bound: Tandym Print, 1 Park Road, Western Province Park, Epping, 7475
Typesetting, layout and design: Hugh Sutherland
Cover design: Hugh Sutherland
Editing and proofreading: Helena Nell
Project management: Cia Joubert, cia@knowres.co.za

Contact PeopleTree Group
E-mail: info@peopletreegroup.com
Website: www.peopletreegroup.com

TalentTalker.com

Click, Coach and Develop

Talent Talker was originally written as a handbook for developing people. It forms the basis of the talent assessment and development work that we do for companies across the world.

But like any book, it is linear in nature and the information you are looking for might not always be that easy to find. So we wanted to re-imagine it as a resource that would always open to the page you needed, when you needed it and provide you with the most relevant development conversation.

TalentTalker.com does just that. It quickly helps you find the best conversation, for the right situation, in the shortest possible time.

When we asked our clients if their managers had good development conversations, nearly all of them said "No". We wanted to find out why?

It wasn't that managers didn't want to have development conversations, or that they didn't see value in having them. They just didn't feel like they "spoke that language". If you've ever tried to learn and speak a foreign language, you'll know how awkward and incompetent you can feel when you first try to express yourself. If you can avoid it, you usually do.

Getting managers to have development conversations is one of the most important drivers of unlocking talent and potential in your organization. This book, and the TalentTalker.com application, makes it easy for any manager to sit down and have a development conversation.

Those conversations can be about improving performance, managing a career, developing leadership skills or formulating and executing new business strategies. Talking connects people, people who feel connected are more engaged, engaged people deliver exceptional results.

If you want to build a company of great people developers, we'd like to be a part of that journey.

You can find us at www.peopletreegroup.com, email us at info@peopletreegroup.com or call us on +1 786 245 5258.

Table of Contents

Table of Contents

Acknowledgements

First of all I thank Katherine Fitzgerald, who is a brilliant woman and a great mentor. Throughout the course of writing this book, Martin Sutherland, my business partner and harshest critic, helped me to shape the content coherently. I owe him a debt of gratitude because his feedback had a huge impact on the content.

Helena Nell, the editor, was heroic in cleaning up my writing. She was patient, tireless and meticulous in polishing the chapters and getting the book ready for print.

Because this is my first book, I naively thought I just had to write it. It could not be further from the truth! Pat and Hugh Sutherland helped me to make decisions about critical issues related to the binding, layout, margins, fonts and everything needed to create the book you now hold in your hands.

My son, Ander Limia, helped me to find the quotes used in every chapter. Most importantly, his maturity and independence made it easy for me to stay glued to my computer without worrying about having a teenager in the house.

I would like to thank Zulma Bianchi and Isabel Antol'n for their excellent translation work in the Spanish version.

Thanks also to Quentin Duncan for his awesome and creative ways of capturing my ideas and transforming them visually.

I would like to thank the many clients around the globe who have chosen me as their executive coach. Their questions and insights have challenged and strengthened me. Their work and life experiences have been the real inspiration to write this book, and their simple suggestion to Çplease write something practicalÓwas the best advice I ever received.

While writing this book, I suffered from serious health problems which brought me great physical and emotional pain. I thank this book for keeping my mind distracted when just getting through the day seemed an impossible task.

The Art of a
Great Conversation

Books are usually read alone, but we would encourage you to read this book with someone. The art of conversation is dying as technology replaces face to face interactions with short text messages and emoticons. Businesses are continually looking to automate processes, increase efficiency and embed technology as a panacea for people management and development.

As a technology company, we are certainly not technophobic, but we do think that designing technology to increase and improve human interaction should be a fundamental principle. It is way too easy to value efficiency over effectiveness.

If you are managing people, then you cannot avoid talking to them. It may be face to face, over the phone, via video conference or email. It may be many times a day or a few times a week. But now think about what that interaction says about how you view that person.

If your style is depersonalized and directive, you can expect people to do what they are told and wait for instructions. If you only focus on what you need, you can expect the other person to do the same. If you avoid talking about certain topics, you can expect people to fill in the gaps with their own (usually inaccurate) assumptions.

Talking to people communicates a lot more than just what you say. It communicates how you feel about them, what you value, what motivates you, how much they should trust you, and many other clues that define your relationship with them. If you don't think developing people is important, then go to Chapter 20 : Develops People before continuing, but if you do, then let's take a look at what leads to great development conversations.

1. **Start with a Purpose**: Before having a development conversation with someone, you need to explain why. There are many reasons to have a development conversation, and most people think it's because they have done something wrong. Because development conversations are often avoided, it's a little like your partner saying "We need to talk", and nothing good usually comes from that. So be clear that the purpose is to help them achieve a goal or overcome a problem that is important to them.

2. Ask lots of questions: Before jumping to a solution on how to fix something, it's a good idea to explore when, where, why and what actually happens. The starting point of a development conversation is not only to accurately identify what the ineffective behavior looks like, but also to understand when it happens (e.g. when they are under pressure), how the person normally reacts (e.g withdraws), who tends to amplify the response (e.g. senior executives), how they feel (e.g. anxious).

Each answer can help the person to understand their response better and more accurately identify the reason for the behavior that doesn't work. You'll see in each chapter there are strategies for action, they are the most common reasons people display ineffective behavior. Identifying the underlying reason will personalize the development plan and help the person understand how to rethink, or "re-feel", in order to be more effective.

3. Strive for consensus: We only change when we take ownership of the need to change and responsibility for making a change. One of the most common mistakes with development conversations is pushing your agenda to hard. You may feel that you know exactly why someone does what they do, and how they should fix it, but they are the ones that have to change. What you want to look for are specific actions that the person can, and is willing, to take and find out how you can support them.

4. Secure a commitment: Much like new years resolutions, it's easy to say you will, but harder to actually do anything when it comes to changing behavior. Ultimately it is the person's responsibility to make the change, but getting commitment to specific actions and timeframes creates a "social contract", a promise between you and the other person to act. It also helps to highlight unrealistic commitments ("I'll go to gym 2 hours a day, 5 times a week) and identify required resources ("I'll need a gym contract and a personal trainer") and see if those resources are available.

Why be a Talent Talker?

Great people developers take an interest in others, they recognize that they didn't get to where they are on their own, and they want to "pay forward" the time that others have invested in them. Helping others unlock their talent and potential is an enormously rewarding activity, and it doesn't take very much time, just the right attitude. If you look back on your own career and recognize a talent talker in your past, you owe it to them to become one yourself. If you don't see a talent talker in your past, you need to look harder, because no one can make it on their own.

The Evolution of the Talent Genome
Why a different model?

Development vs recruitment

The creation of a behavioral competency model sets off from either a recruitment or development mind-set. Models with fewer competencies have generally been developed for selection purposes because of the need to limit the number of questions that can be asked in interviews. Similarly, models with more competencies have generally been developed to enhance or improve performance.

The PeopleTree model is a development-based model, because we believe it provides greater insight into the complexity of effective leadership behavior. To manage the interview process, PeopleTree has created questions for clusters of competencies to simplify the process and interview for several competencies simultaneously.

Long vs short definitions

Our experience of using behavioral competencies to assess individuals over the last 12 years has highlighted the difficulty raters experience when too many behavioral statements, or constructs, are used to describe a single competency.

The PeopleTree competency definitions are deliberately shorter to reduce the confusion and ambiguity of too many constructs, while emphasizing the core behavioral characteristic that is being assessed.

Accuracy of titles

After studying raters' behavior, we realized that a large proportion of individuals providing feedback did not read the full definition and used only the title of the competency to make an assessment.

The PeopleTree competency titles have been specifically created to take this factor into account by using easy-to-understand language and capturing the essence of the definition in the title.

Updating of the language

Many of the more ubiquitous models have their origins in the '80s and '90s, and there has been difficulty to update and create a more relevant language.

The PeopleTree model and definitions use more recent and contemporary language to explain and describe behavior, taking into account the impact and influence of technology, shifting values and social culture.

Removal of redundancies

This relates to the use of longer definitions and models with fewer competencies of which the definitions tend to have overlapping constructs or concepts. It leads to the rater feeling as if they have "seen it before" or are assessing the same behavior.

The PeopleTree competencies, with their shorter definitions and focus on clear, unambiguous core characteristics, reduce this sense of redundancy.

Reductionism vs emergence

Most competency models, specifically the selection-based ones, tend to group too many concepts together in one competency, which restricts the ability to break down, recombine and explain the diversity and complexity of human behavior — an approach that tends towards reductionism.

The PeopleTree competencies were created as a set of basic building blocks that can be combined to create more complex concepts. This approach acknowledges that it is not just the mix of competencies but their strength that ultimately cause particular behavior to emerge. An example would be hydrogen and oxygen, which are both gases in their natural state. But when they are combined in a particular way (H_2O), they create water with a set of emergent properties that neither element possesses independently.

Time spent on assessment

Because of the compound definitions or multiple levels in the majority of competency models, we have frequently encountered the complaint that the assessment process can become time-consuming and cumbersome. This usually results in the shortening of the model, in other words, not using all the competencies needed for assessment.

We have timed individuals providing feedback on the full set of PeopleTree competencies and the average time it has taken is between 9 and 14 minutes. This does not reduce the quality of feedback, as we have noticed a much higher level of consistency between raters.

Is the model integrated with other tools or processes?

- Development advice
  A full set of development tips and coaching advice has been developed for each of the competencies. The advice is practical, focused, and easy to read and apply.

- Interview questions
  Interview questions have been developed for the competency clusters. They allow an interviewer to probe multiple competencies simultaneously.

- Translatable into other models
  PeopleTree has translations for a number of popular models and can develop translations for company-specific models.

- Integration with business strategies and capabilities
  PeopleTree has also developed the Organizational Genome, which translates strategies into capabilities and leadership competencies.

How was the model created?

- The purpose of the model was to develop a "periodic table" of human behavior, in other words, to identify a set of behavioral attributes that, when merged in different combinations, determine an individuals's effectiveness in a particular context

- This model has created a non-biased, culture less, context-free set of attributes that can be used as basic building blocks to configure individual effectiveness in any context

- Sixty two of the most research-based competency models that have been correlated with performance across diverse contexts, such as position levels, industries, job types and cultures, were used as references to identify the competencies in the model.

talent
genome

How to use this book

Definitions

The competencies' definitions serve as the compass that identifies the behavior you want. They provide a specific language to communicate with others, identifying strengths (Well Developed, points right), areas for improvement (Underdeveloped, points down), and strengths used excessively (Overdeveloped, points up) both for yourself and the people you supervise.

Instructions:

Read the Definitions and become familiar with the descriptions for Well Developed, Underdeveloped and Overdeveloped behaviors. Take time to reflect on how well the Definitions apply to you and those you supervise.

Overdeveloped

As we all know, too much of a good thing can become problematic. For example, an individual who is excessively composed could also be seen as detached, indifferent and lacking in empathy.

Instructions:

If you have identified the Overdeveloped behavior as the area in which change is needed, you want to go to the end of the chapter.

One cannot become "less good" at a competency. To create a balance, you must develop so-called Stabilizer Competencies to tone down the Overdeveloped one. Identify one or two of these Stabilizer Competencies, find the appropriate chapter and follow the Strategies for Action that would lead to development.

(a)

How to use this book

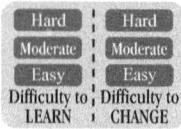

Hard	Hard
Moderate	Moderate
Easy	Easy
Difficulty to **LEARN**	Difficulty to **CHANGE**

Difficulty Indicators

The level of difficulty in developing specific behaviours is determined by two factors. The first factor is how difficult it will be to LEARN. Some behaviors are complex and involve the factoring in of many variables, such as not receiving immediate feedback, acting with minimal information and not having a clear understanding of cause and effect. No one is born with these behaviors well developed; mastering it requires practice.

The second is how difficult it will be to CHANGE. Some competencies are strongly associated with personality characteristics or belief systems. If you have these characteristics or a belief system that supports the behavior, it will seem natural to you to demonstrate the Well-Developed behavior. If you do not, the Well-Developed behavior will feel unnatural and provoke a strong emotional response.

Test yourself

Before you start developing the competency, ensure it really is something you need to work on. Each competency will have a set of behavioural anchors, which are listed in the Test Yourself box. If your answer is "true" to most of the behaviors listed, it indicates that this is not a competency you need to work on now. If your answer is not True to several of the behaviors, it indicates room for improvement and that developing the competency will be time well spent.

NOTE: Assessing yourself is a starting point, but self-assessment is known as the least accurate of all methods. Feedback from others provides a richer and more textured picture and will identify areas for development more accurately. The PeopleTree feedback methodology is designed to collect subjective perceptions from multiple sources — people who know you — aggregate those views and look for overlapping or recurring patterns. These patterns identify strengths as well as areas for development. The methodology is non-judgmental and reduces bias, or what is know as the "horns and halo" effect, by shaping a balanced view of each person. For more information on how to use the PeopleTree assessment process, contact PeopleTree Group at info@peopletreegroup.com.

The self-test can also be used during and at the end of your development period to gauge your level of improvement. The more items you can confidently tick off, the greater the level of skill you have achieved in that competency.

How to use this book

Instructions:

You should tick off the items that apply to you most of the time. Be as honest as you can with answers. If you are unsure about an item, get feedback from trusted peers.

Strategies for Action

The Strategies for Action guide involves a method based on three steps to help increase the likelihood of change in the development process:

(a) Identifying with a statement (I think or feel this now)

(b) How could I Rethink or feel differently and

(c) What could I do to change (React).

We behave the way we do for many reasons, and our thoughts and feelings about a particular issue usually drive our behavior. Each statement you select has an accompanying narrative to help you explore the risks of your perception and the rewards associated with changing it.

This will help you to consider other ways of thinking or different perspective (Rethink)

You will then want to look at suggested action items, based on the statement with which you identify, and incorporate some or all these actions into you behavior (React).

Instructions:

Select the statement with which you identify the most or that most describes your feelings. Find the corresponding number and read the Rethink and React strategies. Possibly, you will identify with more than one statement; if that happens, select the Actions that best suit your present environment.

(c)

1. Achiever

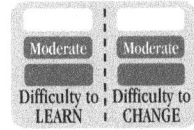

> "The results you achieve will be in direct proportion to the effort you apply"
>
> Denis Waitley

Well Developed
Consistently achieves results and meets goals and targets

Underdeveloped
Lacks the energy to push for results and often misses performance targets

Overdeveloped
Pushes for results at the expense of people, processes or procedures and causes damage to the organization

Instructions

Read the definitions on the left. If the Underdeveloped definition applies, go to the Strategies for Action section.

If the Overdeveloped definition applies, go to the end of the chapter.

Test Yourself

True	I set clear goals for myself and know my performance targets
True	I want to do well and set a high standard for myself
True	I expect setbacks
True	I consistently meet my performance goals
True	I do not let my energy get drained by obstacles
True	I know how to step back and recharge before tackling tasks that appear insurmountable

Note

Are you sure you need to develop this competency?

If the answer is "True" to most of the statements on the left, you probably do not need to develop this competency.

Achiever

1

Strategies for Action

Most ineffective behaviors have an underlying thought or emotional pattern. By identifying these patterns, you can understand the impact they have and design strategies to counteract them.

① I put off working on things I do not want to do/I leave things for the last minute

② I spend so much time making sure I get the "right" results that I do not get results

③ I feel burnt out/I lack motivation

④ I have so much going on I cannot meet my targets

⑤ I am not good at taking risks/What if I am not successful?

⑥ I am unclear about what must get done/Expectations at work are ambiguous

Instructions

1. Read and select one or more of the ineffective ways of thinking/feeling to the left.

2. Find the corresponding number below that will help you to rethink this pattern and identify specific and practical actions that you can take.

---

1 | I put off working on things I do not want to do/I leave things until the last minute

Rethink

If you tend to put things off until the last minute, it will be difficult to deliver quality results consistently. It is hard enough to meet deadlines under normal circumstances, but it is even harder with the added pressure that procrastination brings. Your assignment is not going to go away if you ignore it and, unpleasant as it may be, your challenge is to adopt strategies to help keep you on track.

Your work habits may be producing results but, likely, there is room for improvement if you are always doing things at the last minute.

React

(a) As a rule, first do the things you do not want to do. You will have to do them anyway, and often they prevent you from working productively because you spend too much energy trying to avoid these few tasks. Write down what they are and enlist a co-worker to keep you on track.

(b) Focus on doing the things that matter most so that you spend your time wisely. If time overtakes you, you will at least have taken care of the items that have the most impact. Be specific about what these things are and create a priority list. Confirm with an appropriate person that you have prioritized accurately.

(c) Tackle the task in palatable increments. Work on things during breaks you may have between your commitments and appointments. It will ensure the amount of work is manageable and you will see increasing progress.

(d) Anticipate that everything will take longer to complete than you expected. Whatever the deadline, subtract time from it to give yourself impetus to start. Reward yourself every time you meet the deadline.

(e) Take action immediately. Limit the time between getting the assignment and starting to work. Sitting still too long without taking action can harm your motivation.

(f) If you perform best or are motivated by working with others, recruit peers with whom you can collaborate to get you started. They will also be able to help keep you on track, especially if your performance is tied to others'.

2 | I spend so much time making sure I get the "right" results that I do not get results

Rethink

Wanting to get things done right is a great beginning, but being able to follow through and get results is the ultimate goal. If you are a perfectionist, you will find yourself constantly tweaking things to make them slightly better. But there is a point at which improvements' value is insufficient to justify your tweaking. Although it is counterintuitive, knowing when to stop improving will actually help you to better your performance.

React

(a) Limit the time you spend on a given assignment. Set points at which you will confer with your superior for feedback on the level of detail you should be achieving. This will help to keep your expectations of yourself realistic.

(b) Reframe your expectations. Aim for completing a task or assignment well, not making it perfect.

3 | I feel burnt out/I lack motivation

Rethink

There are many reasons why you may be feeling burnt out. You may have been keeping up an unrealistic pace, not finding enough ways to decompress, or have an unrealistic workload. Whatever the reason, it is key to recognize burnout and not ignore it by doing things as usual. Burnout inevitably leads to poor performance.

React

(a) Build flexibility into your schedule so that you can tackle a particular project at a time that makes sense for you. Many people mark specific time blocks off to work on an assignment, but if you are burnt out this may backfire because your inspiration and motivation will be inconsistent — they cannot be scheduled. Take advantage of the times you feel ready to work on a project, even if it is just for a short period. Conversely, move on to something else if you are not producing anything. Spinning your wheels will build frustration and increase negative associations with the work at hand.

(b) Review and reward your progress continually. Break down the project into smaller tasks and reward yourself every time you accomplish a step.

(c) Be honest with your superior. They may be able to assist you by doing something simple such as helping you to delegate some of your work. Often, people do not like to inform their superior of problems because they do not want to appear as if they cannot handle the situation. Inevitably, though, burnout will show in your performance, so act before it does.

(d) Shake things up — if you are chronically feeling burnt out it may be time to look for another position within the company or try something completely new. Spend time to investigate your options and set your goal.

4 | I have so much going on I cannot meet my targets

Rethink

Typically, there are multiple tasks and demands vying for your attention at work and in your private life. At any moment, a person may have a long list of things outstanding that must be done. The reality is that, at work, few people have the luxury of having enough time to get everything done. Using your time wisely is particularly critical to producing results, and this means you must recognize the non-essential activities in your day-to-day schedule and limit them. The challenge is not to work more, but to work smarter.

React

(a) Focus on doing the things that matter most. Be specific about what they are and create a priority list. Confirm with your superior that you have prioritized well and accurately.

(b) Which activities take up most of your time? Create a list of your activities and assign the approximate times you are spending on each category. Then divide the categories into "essential" and "need to do". What does your time allotment look like?

(c) Are you delegating appropriately? In which tasks can you involve others?

5 | I am not good at taking risks/What if I am not successful?

Rethink

Some assignments will require you to enter unchartered territory and push ahead boldly to get results. If you are not comfortable taking risks and pushing the envelope, you will be tempted to take the path of least resistance, even if it is not the best way to achieve results.

Undoubtedly, you will experience failures in your career, but remember, it is more risky for your career not to take on challenges. If you do not rise to challenges, you will have less opportunity to prove your abilities and sharpen your skills. And, it is likely that future assignments may not be entrusted to you.

React

(a) Slowly raise your risk comfort level by taking on smaller assignments that require you to extend yourself.

(b) View mistakes as opportunities to learn and reflect. Every time you make a mistake, write a list of the benefits of having made the mistake — the specifics of what you have learned, who you met in the process and so forth.

(c) Read biographies of business or public leaders who you admire. Look for a common theme of risk taking among them.

(d) You may have taken more risk than you have thought or given yourself credit for. Document your accomplishments. What risks did each of these accomplishments involve? Write them down, regardless how small the risk was. Ask people who know you well to help you. The objective is to show that all careers are based on a combination of challenges to which we are continuously called upon to rise. You may already be more of a risk taker than you think.

6 | I am unclear about what must get done/Expectations at work are ambiguous

Rethink

An unclear destination is difficult to reach. You may be a dedicated high performer, but if you do not understand where to focus your efforts or the expectations others have of you, it will negatively affect your ability to reach your potential. If you are not sure about either your expectations or what is expected of you in return, you may believe you are performing well when, in fact, your standards may be below average.

We typically inflate our perception of our accomplishments and performance, so it is important to have a proper yardstick by which to measure them.

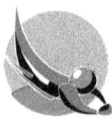

React

(a) If you do not have a work plan yet, meet with your superior to develop one with specific goals and targets for each year. Agree to reassess your work plan occasionally to make any changes necessary.

(b) Be prepared to ask your supervisor and peers about your performance and whether you are meeting their expectations.

(c) Take a cue from peers that are known high performers. Compare your standard of work to theirs — do not rely on your own perception. Use their assessment as a yardstick to measure your level of accomplishment.

Overdeveloped

Research has shown that strengths can become weaknesses because you can, in fact, do too much of a good thing. You cannot become less good at a competency in which you excel, but you can balance the behavior by developing a few Stabilizers to tone down an excessive strength.

Stabilizer	Overdeveloped
22 Diplomatic	Pushes for results at the expense of people, processes or procedures and causes damage to the organization
24 Empathetic	
26 Ethical	
28 Fair	
30 Global Thinker	
34 Listens Well	
43 Motivates People	
47 Patient	
58 Trustworthy	
59 Unifies People	

Instructions

Read the definition. If it applies to you, choose a few Stabilizers and develop them by selecting the relevant chapter and following the Strategies for Action.

For more instructions see the How To Use This Book section.

2. Adaptable

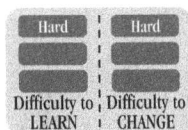

> "The most important trip you may take in life is meeting people halfway"
>
> Henry Boyle

Well Developed

Adapts behavior to the interpersonal style and needs of others

Underdeveloped

Has only one style of interacting and seems unwilling or unable to adapt to others' communication needs

Overdeveloped

Adapts too readily to others' interpersonal styles and is seen as unpredictable or too accommodating

Instructions

Read the definitions on the left. If the Underdeveloped definition applies, go to the Strategies for Action section.

If the Overdeveloped definition applies, go to the end of the chapter.

Test Yourself

True	I can identify suitable styles that work better with different people
True	I can identify the style needed to work in different situations
True	I understand there is more than one way to act around people without losing my authenticity
True	I adapt to others so that they can relate to me
True	I feel comfortable among diverse groups of people

Note

Are you sure you need to develop this competency?

If the answer is "True" to most of the statements on the left, you probably do not need to develop this competency.

Adaptable

2

Strategies for Action

Most ineffective behaviors have an underlying thought or emotional pattern. By identifying these patterns, you can understand the impact they have and design strategies to counteract them.

① People must accept me as I am

② Differences are not that important/I just assume that others are like me

③ I just cannot get along with some people

④ I believe changing my behavior is the same as being manipulative

Instructions

1. Read and select one or more of the ineffective ways of thinking/feeling to the left.

2. Find the corresponding number below that will help you to rethink this pattern and identify specific and practical actions that you can take.

1 | People must accept me as I am

Rethink

You do not want to compromise who you are for the sake of others. On the surface, this sounds like a noble approach which promotes authenticity. But it points to a level of inflexibility that can cause you problems in your personal life and at work. At its most extreme, this attitude risks alienating people.

The workplace has become increasingly diverse. You can count on some exposure to people who are very different from you. Even those with similar backgrounds have varying personalities and motivators. Why not take the initiative and adapt in whatever way you can so that you can understand others better and be understood? It is also possible that "the way I am" needs some improvement. For example, you may think of yourself as a candid and straightforward person, but your sensitive colleagues may perceive you as borderline rude or insulting.

It would be more productive to adapt your behavior slightly to accommodate others than to hope they will accept you as you are. Remember that your flexibility sets the tone for how flexible others will be towards you.

React

(a) Become a better observer of other people's behavior. Try to mimic the behaviors of the group or other person. For example, if the person appears withdrawn and quiet, tone down your behavior. Lower your voice and be reserved and composed instead of energetic and animated, until you get to know them better. The key is to pay attention to the other person too, not just yourself.

(b) Research the group with whom you will be interacting. Knowing people's backgrounds can provide much information about their styles.

(c) Ask others what you need to do differently to improve your relationship with them.

(d) Be honest about being unsure about whether your style could be offensive in any way. This applies particularly if you are working with groups from other nationalities. People will appreciate your concern.

(e) Does your behavior fit the organization's values or expectations? Try to define what these are and consider how suitable your behavior is.

2 | Differences are not that important/I just assume that others are like me

Rethink

Superficially, many people appear alike, especially if you have limited exposure to people from different backgrounds. We tend to project our values and views on others. The golden rule implores you to treat others as you would like to be treated, but it is better to stick to the platinum rule: treat others as they would like to be treated. To do this, you must first be able and willing to recognize the differences between people.

Research undertaken by Birkman International over the past 30 years has shown that people's everyday behavior can be drastically different from their needs, which are hidden. Awareness of differences becomes increasingly important as you progress through your career and is needed to manage others. Managers are often unaware of the full range of possible interpersonal and leadership styles, and that these styles are influenced by a variety of factors such as personality, culture, preference and genetics.

Well-known personality constructs include the four ego functions as described by Carl Jung, namely sensation, feeling, thinking and intuition, and the Myers-Briggs personality tests. The Hex model, for example, developed by K. David Katzmire, is an expansion of the four-styles model and is one of numerous personality theories. Raising your awareness of people's different styles will help you to value the importance of adapting to others to maximize your effectiveness and reach your goals.

React

(a) Investigate different interpersonal styles to recognize the types with whom you interact.

(b) Consider the person's background and discipline or field and how these may differ from yours. If you are interacting with accountants, for example, they may prefer to keep the conversation quite structured and may want you to share more details.

(c) Gauge the emotional state a person might be in: sad, irritated, nervous etcetera. It is important to respect people's mental state and accommodate it.

(d) Consider first how the person may be different from you and only then look for similarities. This will help you to avoid projecting on others.

(e) People's reactions and body language can help to guide your behavior. Look for changes in facial expression, tone of voice, posture. You can adapt accordingly.

(f) Some of us have a natural talent for picking up clues about others. If you think you cannot read other people, think again. The key is to really observe them —- how they communicate, their demeanor, expressions, body language. Clues about people and who they really are, are written all over them and you can use these clues to help you adapt to their interpersonal needs. Simply raise your level of awareness.

(g) Get to know people on a personal level. There is no better way to understand people than to spend time with them.

3 | I just cannot get along with some people

Rethink

Are you quite flexible with most people but seem unable to adapt to a particular person or group? Flexibility is easier with those with whom we share something in common, but the challenge lies in remaining flexible with people outside this group. It is not necessary to be friends with individuals to maintain a productive work relationship. The key is to adapt your behavior sufficiently to establish a relationship built on mutual goals and respect.

React

(a) Identify the mutual goals among you and the person or group and use that as the bridge to common ground.

(b) Get to know the person better to challenge your assumptions about them. Typically, meetings in social settings away from the pressures of work give you a fresh perspective of others, so try to arrange them, if possible.

(c) Lack of flexibility on your part might stem from bias towards a group. Consider the hidden biases you may harbor and try to challenge the assumptions on which they are based.

(d) Recognize the other person's interpersonal style and its strengths and contributions, even if it is different from yours. For example, you may be dealing with someone who is forward and talkative, very different from you. But these traits may add real value in, for example, the sales role with which you are uncomfortable.

4 | I believe changing my behavior is the same as being manipulative

Rethink

Being able to manipulate is different from an ability to adapt to others. By definition, manipulation involves control or influence over somebody or something, in an ingenious or devious way. It entails changing or presenting something in a way that is false but personally advantageous. By contrast, adaptability represents a conscious choice to achieve mutually beneficial goals. If you are adaptable, you do not change who you are. Instead, you are able to draw from your individual well of complexity, experience and empathy to remold yourself in ways that help you to relate to others. In turn, other people can relate to you.

React

(a) Try to put yourself in the other person's shoes.

(b) Consider the pros, for both of you, of adapting your behavior.

(c) Ask yourself whether you would like someone to do the same for you. More than likely, you would appreciate such an effort.

Overdeveloped

Research has shown that strengths can become weaknesses because you can, in fact, do too much of a good thing. You cannot become less good at a competency in which you excel, but you can balance the behavior by developing a few Stabilizers to tone down an excessive strength.

Stabilizer	Overdeveloped
1 Achiever	Adapts too readily to others' interpersonal styles and is seen as unpredictable or too accommodating
16 Decisive	
17 Demonstrates Good Judgment	
13 Courageous	
35 Manages Conflict	
12 Confident	
39 Manages Time	
58 Trustworthy	
48 Plans Work	
50 Problem Solver	

Instructions

Read the definition. If it applies to you, choose a few Stabilizers and develop them by selecting the relevant chapter and following the Strategies for Action.

For more instructions see the How To Use This Book section.

3. Ambitious

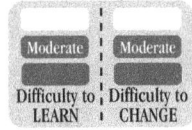

"Intelligence without ambition is a bird without wings"

Salvador Dali

Well Developed
Is motivated to achieve career advancement

Underdeveloped
Is reluctant to accept new challenges or take on the increased responsibility promotion requires

Overdeveloped
Comes across as overly ambitious and acts out of self-interest, not for the team's benefit

Instructions

Read the definitions on the left. If the Underdeveloped definition applies, go to the Strategies for Action section.

If the Overdeveloped definition applies, go to the end of the chapter.

Test Yourself

True	I am confident that I can succeed in a role or position other than mine
True	I am clear about what I need to do next for a promotion
True	I am taking the necessary action to work towards career advancement
True	I am aware of the opportunities available for advancement in my organization
True	I have discussed my future plans with my boss or mentor
True	I am interested in being promoted

Note

Are you sure you need to develop this competency?

If the answer is "True" to most of the statements on the left, you probably do not need to develop this competency.

Ambitious

③

Strategies for Action

Most ineffective behaviors have an underlying thought or emotional pattern. By identifying these patterns, you can understand the impact they have and design strategies to counteract them.

① I do not have what it takes/I do not think I am capable

② I do not feel motivated/I do not see opportunities for advancing in the organization

③ I do not really think about the future/I focus on success in my current position/I like what I do

④ I am too exhausted to consider a promotion

⑤ I do not want too much responsibility

⑥ My work will speak for itself/I will get promoted when my work is noticed

Instructions

1. Read and select one or more of the ineffective ways of thinking/feeling to the left.

2. Find the corresponding number below that will help you to rethink this pattern and identify specific and practical actions that you can take.

1 | I do not have what it takes/I do not think I am capable

Rethink

Ambition is difficult when you do not believe in yourself and your capabilities. Why not take ownership of your strengths and weaknesses and start working with what you have? There is only one guarantee that you will not succeed, and that is if you do not try.

Taking on new challenges allows you to test your potential through both mistakes and successes. Remember, you are part of a team and it is unlikely that you will be given new responsibilities without some support from your supervisor and peers.

You cannot step into a new role knowing everything about it and having all the capabilities needed for the job. Most people will agree that they learned their job while doing it, and did not come to the position already equipped with the necessary skills and experiences.

People who demonstrate ambition and willingness to test their capabilities are rewarded in an organization. Do not get left behind because of self-doubt.

React

(a) Every day, visualize the things you want in your life and career. A growing movement believes in the power of visualization to "attract" what we need in our lives. Read *The Secret* by Rhonda Byrne.

(b) Positive affirmation can help to rewire your thinking. Be vigilant against negative thoughts about yourself and practice to replace them with positive ones immediately.

(c) Identify a few people who you admire for their self-confidence and talk to them about their views on the world. Note the differences in your thinking styles.

(d) Do not give mistakes more importance than they deserve. Write down the worst-case scenarios and analyze them. Unless your life or someone else's is at stake, the worst is never as bad as you might think.

(e) Read about people who have made mistakes but still succeeded, such as Thomas Edison. It took 10 000 failures to make the light bulb!

(f) You do not need to have all the answers. Work the part of your plan that you can, and ask for help with the rest.

(g) Extend your comfort zone. You are building confidence every time you take on a new challenge or task. Keep score of the new challenges you have overcome.

(h) Understand what your challenges will be if you were to move to a new position or role. List the things you are potentially uncomfortable doing. It could be managing people for the first time, networking more than usual or learning more about a specific technical area. Be as detailed as possible with your list. Which items on the list are perceived challenges and which ones are real? For example, you may not have supervised people before but work well with others, are approachable, patient, manage conflict well etcetera. All these behaviors point to your likely success as a manager of others.

(i) Learn more about the position you are interested in by spending time with the incumbent or someone in a similar role. Find out what they regard as the greatest challenges of the position. The more you know the better equipped you will be to start the job without being blindsided by unexpected demands.

(j) If you believe you truly lack the skills critical to getting a promotion, talk to your supervisor about devising a development plan that involves key assignments and experiences to help build your skills set. Make sure you communicate both your interest and your concern about shortcomings.

(k) In the end, no amount of preparation will guarantee you are 100% ready for a position. If the opportunity is available and you want to do it, stop thinking and take action.

(l) If you find that your lack of self-confidence is affecting your ability to function and advance in your career, seek the help of a professional coach or counselor as part of your development plan. A trained therapist can help you to challenge deep-rooted thinking patterns.

2 | I do not feel motivated/I do not see opportunities for advancing in the organization

Rethink

Do you have a vivid picture of what success means to you? It is your responsibility to step back every so often to reconsider your overall career goals. You may not feel motivated about your current assignment or project, but no assignment lasts forever. Knowing what you are working towards gets you through the hard times, because the reality is that much of our workdays are filled with routine and boring, yet necessary, activities.

Motivation is something you often stumble across when you least expect it, so keep moving forward and explore your possibilities one day at a time. Typically, many more opportunities than the ones you are aware of exist in an organization.

React

(a) Revisit your career goals. Are you still on track? Is your lack of motivation due to your current assignment or another temporary circumstance, or is the problem your position itself?

(b) Identify the specific needs that are not being met by your position. Assessment tools such as the Birkman method scrutinizes individuals' less obvious needs that are not met in their work environment and professional relationships. Other factors may be more obvious, such as salary, your relationship with your boss or a lack of challenging assignments. The PeopleTree Group's Talent Management system has a motivation survey which addresses motivational areas.

(c) Talk to your supervisor about the role you envision for yourself and how the opportunity can be created. Be honest — your supervisor may be thinking you are perfectly content with your situation.

(d) It is important to keep the momentum going when you are unmotivated. Identify three actions to complete in the next month that could help you to regain interest in your career.

(e) Try to visualize yourself doing something new. What would be your dream position in the organization? It makes sense to create a vision of your future then focus strategically on how to get there.

(f) Continue to look for opportunities within the company by networking and trying new roles until you find a project, assignment or job that motivates you.

3 | I do not really think about the future/I focus on success in my current position/I like what I do

Rethink

Most people focus their efforts on day-to-day issues in their jobs and can quickly become so buried that they cannot see the wood for the trees.

Although it is a priority to meet or exceed your performance targets in your present position, it is just as necessary to keep an eye on your future to sustain a healthy and rewarding career.

Keep abreast of your developmental needs to position yourself as a visible and viable candidate for promotion. Even if you enjoy your position now, create an opportunity to discover responsibilities you may enjoy even more.

React

(a) Put a plan in place for your career advancement. Let your supervisor help to identify the competencies, experience and technical skills you will need to get promoted.

16

(b) Take the initiative to find out about positions open in your company.

(c) Become knowledgeable about the skills considered scarce in your industry. Companies make extra efforts to retain employees with these skills.

(d) Try to visualize yourself doing something new. What would your dream opportunity in the organization be? It makes sense to create a vision of your future then focus strategically on how to get there.

(e) Make time to network. Talking to people and getting more exposure increase your chances of discovering new ways to raise your visibility and advance your career.

(f) Take growth one small step at a time if you are not comfortable with drastic changes or do not really know which step to take next. Experiment with new assignments that test different skills. It may surprise you to discover other things at which you are really talented. You will find yourself getting more comfortable doing different assignments the more diverse your experiences become.

(g) Inquire about short-term opportunities in your company, perhaps in a new department, if this could help you to advance towards your long-term goals.

(h) Read *The Leadership Pipeline* by Ram Charan and Stephen Drotter, which describes the competencies necessary to function successfully throughout different organizational levels.

4 | I am too exhausted to consider a promotion

Rethink

You may be feeling burnt out and believe a promotion will only create further imbalance in your life. But there are many successful people in leadership positions who lead balanced lives. Specific factors may be influencing your situation and contributing to your burnout, but they may no longer be an issue with a promotion. Similarly, certain disturbing factors within your control could change, but you have not been able to slow down enough to address them. For example, with a promotion you may have access to greater resources to conduct business, or you could delegate more. You may be able to negotiate less travel or move to offices that are closer to home.

Instead of denying yourself a good opportunity that may be available in the near future, invest effort and energy to implement positive changes that balance your life with your work habits. Your hard work has gotten you this far, and noticed, so use your talent to get your needs met.

React

(a) Can you pinpoint the reasons why you are feeling so burnt out? Which things within your control can change and which cannot? You will be surprised to see how changing one or two factors can provide the room you need to re-energize. Get feedback from family, peers or a coach about what those factors could be. Sometimes we find it hard to see what seem obvious to those around us.

(b) Is your workload reasonable and realistic? Talk to the relevant people about your work distribution if that contributes greatly to your burnout.

(c) Make sure you recharge daily with exercise or a hobby that helps to take your mind off work.

(d) Which aspects of the opportunity being offered do you like and which ones put you off? Which terms are negotiable? Typically, there are ways to tailor a promotion to better fit your needs.

(e) Observe successful people in your organization who have demanding jobs but keep a balance between their professional and private lives. Learn how they do it.

(f) Take a breather before making a decision. Take some time off to relax and think clearly. Whatever your decision upon your return, it will be based on a better perspective.

5 | I do not want too much responsibility

Rethink

You may not show interest in advancing your career because of the added responsibilities it entails.

Career advancement does not necessarily mean more work, though, rather a different set of responsibilities.

Examine the emotional, financial and personal costs of not extending beyond your current level of responsibility. Passing up too many opportunities means that, eventually, you may be overlooked altogether or become pigeonholed indefinitely.

React

(a) Write down the pros and cons of staying in the same position.

(b) Identify a position that truly piques your interest and for which you would be willing to make sacrifices. Keep searching if you cannot identify something now.

(c) Even if you are not ready for a promotion, keep discussing possibilities with your peers and supervisor to demonstrate your interest.

(d) Talk to people in other positions a level or two above yours. Ask how they like their jobs and what the principal benefits are.

(e) Find out as much as possible about the position under consideration. It is common to make incorrect assumptions about the responsibilities a position entails. Talk to the incumbent, if possible, or others who have been in a similar role.

(f) Engage a coach to examine in depth the reasons why you are not interested in taking on more responsibility.

6 | My work will speak for itself/I will get promoted when my work is noticed

Rethink

It is risky to assume your hard work will give you enough visibility to advance in your career. You may be highly productive and competent, but still get caught off guard during performance reviews and bonus time. Or you may be overlooked for promotion because you have failed to invest time in authentically promoting your accomplishments. With a little initiative you can ensure that your important contributions are noticed.

If you feel your values are compromised by focusing on climbing the corporate ladder, remember that promotion exists to reward hard work and talent.

React

(a) Approach your self-promotion like you would any other business endeavor and create a personal marketing plan. Establish the actions you will undertake and hold yourself accountable weekly.

(b) Create a weekly status report to inform your boss about your accomplishments.

(c) Communicate your efforts to all your stakeholders, not just your peers or manager. If appropriate, consider informing your clients, senior management and business network.

(d) Learn to create a brief statement that communicates the highlights of your success without providing unnecessary details.

(e) Be wary of being too modest. Are you deflecting praise too quickly? Accept well-deserved praise graciously and with pride.

(f) Do not accept blame too quickly. You are accountable for your actions, not other people's mistakes. Taking blame when it is undeserved dilutes perceptions of your contribution.

(g) You may be more comfortable promoting your group's effort, which gives you a chance to highlight your role but share the accolades.

(h) Prepare well for your performance reviews. You must be able to highlight accomplishments and provide supporting documentation for the less obvious goals you have met.

Overdeveloped

Research has shown that strengths can become weaknesses because you can, in fact, do too much of a good thing. You cannot become less good at a competency in which you excel, but you can balance the behavior by developing a few Stabilizers to tone down an excessive strength.

Stabilizer	Overdeveloped
26 Ethical	Comes across as overly ambitious and acts out of self-interest, not for the team's benefit
20 Develops People	
44 Networked	
34 Listens Well	
49 Politically Astute	
43 Motivates People	
47 Patient	
52 Self-Aware	
59 Unifies People	
7 Collaborative	

Instructions

Read the definition. If it applies to you, choose a few Stabilizers and develop them by selecting the relevant chapter and following the Strategies for Action.

For more instructions see the How To Use This Book section.

4. Approachable

Moderate
Easy
Difficulty to LEARN | Difficulty to CHANGE

"Always hold your head up, but be careful to keep your nose at a friendly level"

Max L. Forman

Well Developed
Is friendly and easy to approach

Underdeveloped
Appears aloof and disinterested in others, and struggles to make conversation

Overdeveloped
Avoids unpleasant interaction and is overly concerned about being likable

Instructions

Read the definitions on the left. If the Underdeveloped definition applies, go to the Strategies for Action section.

If the Overdeveloped definition applies, go to the end of the chapter.

Approachable

4

Test Yourself

True	I enjoy talking or listening to others
True	I share similar experiences I have had when people talk to me
True	I make time for people when they need to talk
True	I can build good rapport, even with strangers
True	I appear friendly even if I am in a bad mood or stressed
True	I allow people to express themselves without interruption
True	I keep judgment or criticism of others to a minimum

Note

Are you sure you need to develop this competency?

If the answer is "True" to most of the statements on the left, you probably do not need to develop this competency.

Strategies for Action

Most ineffective behaviors have an underlying thought or emotional pattern. By identifying these patterns, you can understand the impact they have and design strategies to counteract them.

(1) My workload keeps me very busy

(2) My mind is preoccupied with too many things/ I worry too much

(3) If there is no reward attached to the relationship, I tend to be uninterested in people

(4) I am introverted or shy

(5) I tend to be critical/I tend to focus on the negative aspects

Instructions

1. Read and select one or more of the ineffective ways of thinking/feeling to the left.

2. Find the corresponding number below that will help you to rethink this pattern and identify specific and practical actions that you can take.

1 | My workload keeps me very busy

Rethink

Are you constantly running from one meeting to the next, always checking the clock, never stopping long enough to have a real conversation? Perhaps you wish you could be friendlier, but you just do not have the time.

Nobody wants to step in front of a moving train, and people find it difficult to approach a person who hardly has the time to get their own work done.

Demanding work schedules are difficult, but being friendly and making the time to show interest in the people behind the issues is not an impossible task.

You can do many things to be more approachable that require little time and effort. If you are inaccessible, people will be reluctant to request your direction or support. If you slow down enough to think about it, you may very well find that your hectic pace is more self-imposed than you realized.

React

(a) Be aware of acting frenzied or disorganized in your day-to-day duties. If you constantly complain about all the meetings you have and the work you cannot get done, you send out a signal that you should not be disturbed.

(b) Be realistic about your schedule. Are you overbooking yourself? Identify the activities that would be good to do, versus those that are critical. Some people enjoy the thrill of a hectic pace, but cutting corners both exhausts you and makes you unapproachable.

(c) Take one or two breaks a day to check in with people, not their tasks.

(d) Remember humor. Use your sense of humor to make light of your impossible demands and encourage others to share their woes.

(e) Improve your composure. Remaining calm and attentive, even under pressure, sends the message that you are available when people need you. It sets a great example to show you are approachable, even in stressful situations when people may need you the most.

(f) Are your values and behavior compatible? If you value being friendly and approachable, consider whether you are prioritizing accordingly.

(g) What does your body language signal? For example, if your eyes dart around when someone talks to you, you send a message that you are disinterested or have better things to do. Be aware of fidgeting or looking at your watch.

(h) Delegate effectively, especially if you are in a management position. You may be mired in tasks that could be delegated instead of focusing on your most important role: providing direction and vision for others.

2 | My mind is preoccupied with too many things/I worry too much

Rethink

Do you walk down the passage without noticing who you have passed? Perhaps you cannot focus when someone is talking to you, because paying attention is competing with all the other things on your mind. Perhaps you are consumed by thoughts about what is to come and cannot be bothered with day-to-day details, including people. If you recognize any of these scenarios, you are likely living in your own world too much. This leaves little room for relationships or realizing their value. Others receive the message that they are less important than what is on your mind, that you are annoyed with them, or too stressed to be bothered.

Relationships play a key role in life and work. They provide a sounding board for our thoughts and an outlet for our feelings, and are instrumental in helping us gain assistance to complete tasks and attain goals. Relationships provide emotional support and encouragement.

One study of five million people, conducted by Gallup Consulting and Tom Rath, a psychologist from the University of Michigan, concluded that "people who work with friends or make friends in their workplace tend to be happier, more proactive and more efficient, not only in the office, but also when they are not at work". But the benefits of strong relationships can only be realized if you nurture them on an ongoing, consistent basis. It means you must be willing to step outside your world and make yourself accessible to others.

Managers need information about what is going well, what is behind schedule, who is producing the goods and who is not, whether morale is up or down, and so forth. A manager who is cut off from informal communication with subordinates will eventually fail.

Taking your work seriously is important, but it must be put into perspective to alleviate unnecessary stress on yourself and others. Taking your work or yourself too seriously will not guarantee more productivity and is likely to make you less pleasant and approachable.

React

(a) Find a balance between interaction with others and time on your own. Because making time for others will not come naturally to you, schedule "people breaks" during the day in which you make yourself available to simply chat.

(b) Try to stay in the present and mentally engaged during conversations with people. Restate what the person has told you and show interest by asking questions and providing feedback.

(c) People cannot instinctively know which information you need or whether they are bothering you with issues they could handle themselves. Explain the information you require and when would be a good time for them to approach you with problems.

(d) Be aware of the signals you may be sending out that keep people at bay. Avoid frowning all the time; make direct eye contact and smile.

(e) Ask yourself when was the last time you actually asked after someone's welfare? If you cannot remember, it has been too long.

(f) Do you have friends at work? Cultivate friendships and give yourself a well-deserved break by spending time with these colleagues.

(g) Openly acknowledge and celebrate others' personal milestones such as birthdays and anniversaries. Be sure to attend such events, if only for a few minutes.

(h) Try to lighten up and approach your world less seriously. You may have a lot on your mind, but you can share it with others with some humor. It lets others know that even though you are busy, you are willing to make the time to laugh at yourself and share your worries. When possible, share funny stories about things that have happened to you.

(i) Try laughter therapy, which claims beneficial effects from the use of positive emotions associated with laughter. The benefits of laughter are well documented, yet a study showed that preschool children laugh up to 400 times a day, while adults laugh only 17 times a day on average. Research has shown that laughing can help to reduce blood pressure and stress hormones, trigger endorphins, the body's natural painkiller, boost immune function by raising levels of infection-fighting T-cells, increase muscle flexion and produce a general sense of wellbeing. Take advantage of all these benefits by injecting some laughter into your workday.

(j) Chances are that if you are too serious at work, you are too serious at home. Do more things that help you to relax in your personal life. Watch more comedies, play games with your kids, do more things that make you laugh, get away from daily stress by taking frequent breaks.

(k) Spend time with people who have a positive attitude. We model much of our behavior on that of our peers and people with whom we spend time.

(l) Breed a culture of humor in the workplace by encouraging people with a sunny disposition to share their humor with everyone.

(m) Smile as often as possible. Studies show the positive effects of smiling occur whether the smile is fake or real.

(n) Meditation brings stillness to the mind. Try to build meditation time into your daily routine with practices such as mindfulness, a method that focuses on awareness of the here and now. There are many workshops and books available to help you get started.

3

If there is no reward attached to the relationship, I tend to be uninterested in people

Rethink

Does your level of friendliness and interest depend on what the other person can do for you?

Are you approachable when you need assistance or support during a project, and nowhere to be found once it has been given? There is no harm in actively seeking professional relationships that benefit your interests and promote your goals. People do this every day, networking inside and outside of the organization. But that is different from behavior that leaves people feeling used once they no longer serve a purpose. Such behavior is unfair and inauthentic and will quickly cause others to lose the trust and respect they have for you.

The most approachable leaders in any organization are the ones considered to act authentically. You will be rewarded with the trust and respect of your peers and subordinates – and that is priceless.

React

(a) Maintain an open-door policy for everyone at all times. If it is not a good time to converse, schedule another appointment and keep it.

(b) Stay in touch with people to check how they are, and not just when you need a favor.

(c) Schedule a set time in the office during the week when you will be available for anyone to come and talk to you. Ensure you have cleared your schedule and can offer your undivided attention.

(d) Practice management by walking around. Commit yourself to spending a dedicated amount of time with employees on the floor or in various offices each day, in essence walking through the organization to find opportunities to make positive comments and receive input or feedback. This approach permits direct access to you and promotes the exchange of ideas. Make sure you do it authentically, in other words, be yourself and do it in your own unique way.

(e) Find ways to help others. Volunteer without being asked. Do not help others just because they have helped you.

4 | I am introverted or shy

Rethink

For some people, interaction with others is energizing and comes naturally, but those who are introverted find it difficult and possibly draining. You may be just as approachable as the next person, but introverts are often perceived as disinterested or aloof. You may be seen as not being a team player when, in fact, you are just less comfortable in group settings.

Being overly shy can pose many challenges, especially if you manage people, but introverts can be very empathetic and listen well, which characterize approachability.

Become creative about how you make yourself available to others. Let them know who you really are and what your knowledge entails.

React

(a) Maximize your opportunities to interact with people one on one. Schedule a set time during the week when you are available for anyone to come and talk to you. Drop by people's offices to talk one on one at least once a week.

(b) Use humor to break the ice and bond with others.

(c) Do you have friends at work? Just one or two close relationships can help to bring you out of your shell, especially if your friends are more extroverted than you.

(d) Attend some work-related social activities. It gives people a less formal opportunity to get to know you and gives you a chance to nurture friendships.

(e) Be aware of the signals you may be sending out that keep people at bay. Make direct eye contact, smile as much as possible, uncross your arms.

(f) Show interest in others' lives and ask them to tell you about themselves. Most people like to talk about their lives, which takes the pressure to talk off you.

5 | I tend to be critical/I tend to focus on the negative aspects

Rethink

Imagine every time you approached peers, they told you what was wrong with your idea or why their problems were bigger than yours.

Being overly negative or critical is a surefire way to put people off. There may be truth in your criticism, but approachable people make others feel as if they have gained something positive from talking to them. If someone is approaching you for help or advice, negativity does not add any value. And remember, people do not necessarily want solutions — sometimes people just need an impartial, non-judgmental sounding board to provide some perspective. Also be aware that the most critical people are often those who are unhappy in their own lives.

React

(a) Let people finish expressing themselves before you interrupt with an opinion or solution.

(b) Always respond with a positive comment or observation, for example, "It is good that you are thinking about this", or "I know it seems like an impossible task but I have confidence in you, how can I help?", or "There are always challenging people you must work with. Are there other team members with whom you get along?"

(c) Spend time with people who are positive and upbeat. Just like negativity, optimism is contagious.

(d) Keep a journal about the positive things in your life. Small or big, raising your awareness about these things on a daily basis can prompt you to think more positively.

(e) Try to recognize and limit the following: blaming, defending, judging, stonewalling, excluding and being unforgiving.

(f) Ask peers, friends and family members whether they think you are generally negative. Sometimes we are unaware of how negative we are or the impact it has on others.

(g) Engage a coach or therapist to identify the areas in your life you might be neglecting or which leave you feeling unfulfilled.

Overdeveloped

Research has shown that strengths can become weaknesses because you can, in fact, do too much of a good thing. You cannot become less good at a competency in which you excel, but you can balance the behavior by developing a few Stabilizers to tone down an excessive strength.

Stabilizer	Overdeveloped
12 Confident	Avoids unpleasant interaction and is overly concerned about being likable
13 Courageous	
35 Manages Conflict	
38 Manages Underperformance	
39 Manages Time	
23 Directs People	
42 Monitors Work	
37 Manages Negotiations	
29 Focused on Priorities	
1 Achiever	

Instructions

Read the definition. If it applies to you, choose a few Stabilizers and develop them by selecting the relevant chapter and following the Strategies for Action.

For more instructions see the How To Use This Book section.

5. Balances Personal Life and Work

Moderate	Moderate
Difficulty to LEARN	Difficulty to CHANGE

"Even nectar is poison if taken to excess"
~ Hindu proverb

Well Developed
Balances the need to meet work responsibilities with factors that ensure a quality life

Underdeveloped
Allocates too much time or energy to either personal or work issues

Overdeveloped
Places too much emphasis on balance and is unwilling to make a sacrifice for either work or personal issues when necessary

Instructions
Read the definitions on the left. If the Underdeveloped definition applies, go to the Strategies for Action section.

If the Overdeveloped definition applies, go to the end of the chapter.

Test Yourself

True	I participate in a hobby or activity outside of work that helps me to relax and recharge
True	My family members accept my work schedule
True	I regularly prioritize what really needs to get done now versus that which can wait
True	I utilize my vacation time rather than let it accumulate
True	When I am away from the office I am not stressed about work
True	I am comfortable delegating or asking for assistance if my workload is too great
True	I continually keep my boss up to date about my workload
True	My goal is to do the best I can, not to be perfect
True	Occasionally I am willing to spend some personal time to meet a work target

Note

Are you sure you need to develop this competency?

If the answer is "True" to most of the statements on the left, you probably do not need to develop this competency.

Strategies for Action

Most ineffective behaviors have an underlying thought or emotional pattern. By identifying these patterns, you can understand the impact they have and design strategies to counteract them.

(1) I am passionate about my work/It is what makes me the happiest

(2) Work helps me to forget about other problems/It makes me feel good about myself

(3) I have to work overtime because my days are not long enough to get my work done

(4) I want to prove myself/I want to get ahead ahead in my career

(5) I rather do things myself/I am a perfectionist

(6) I do not want to let other people down/I feel pressured by others' expectations

(7) Success requires dedicatiton to either work or personal life

Instructions

1. Read and select one or more of the ineffective ways of thinking/feeling to the left.

2. Find the corresponding number below that will help you to rethink this pattern and identify specific and practical actions that you can take.

1 | I am passionate about my work/It is what makes me the happiest

Rethink

Increasingly, as the key to happiness, we are all encouraged to find work that fulfills us and about which we are passionate. There are countless self-help books that offer methods and insight about your search for the perfect job. So if you feel you have found such a calling, what is wrong with dedicating yourself fully to it?

The problem comes when there is no balance between the time and energy given to work versus all the other aspects of your life that deserve equal commitment. Work can provide a rush of adrenaline when a major project is accomplished or a target is met, and for many people this translates into an addiction, just like gambling or drinking. But unlike those types of addictions, society does not discourage people from working too hard.

On the contrary, leaders are sometimes expected to sacrifice themselves for the benefit of their organizations. The prolonged physical and mental stress associated with overwork, whether your job is your passion or not, is well documented as being damaging to your health and personal relationships.

With regards to the health of your organization, as a leader you set the model of behavior for the company. Make sure your best talent does not get burned out trying to follow your example.

React

(a) Set an alarm clock to mark the time to leave the office and make a commitment to do so when it goes off. Ask a colleague or assistant to check in with you to ensure that you have left.

(b) Do not bring your computer when you are traveling with your family for leisure. If you have to stay connected, agree with your family on a set time daily during which you will check and respond to e-mail.

(c) Use your vacation time, no matter what. Schedule your vacations at the beginning of the year. Inevitably, something will always come up, so ignore it and go ahead with your plans.

(d) Talk to your family about your schedule and make sure you reach an acceptable compromise about it. You may be assuming that your schedule has not affected anyone because no one has brought it up.

(e) Find other interests and activities that make you happy and which you can share with your family or friends. Remember, work is not the only thing that could possibly give you the rush you seek.

2 | Work helps me to forget about other problems/It makes me feel good about myself

Rethink

You may find that, at work, you are able to attain a sense of personal worth or accomplishment, which you cannot achieve outside of it. For example, at work you may have been able to gain a level of respect or sense of control that you do not experience readily outside the office walls.

Whatever the gap work fills, recognize the risks associated with tying your self-worth primarily to your job. To the extent that feeling good about yourself is always specific to context or environment, you become a slave to the context: people who have defined themselves solely by their careers have a difficult time reinventing themselves when their careers cease to exist. They also tend to suffer greatly in adapting to retirement.

Hiding behind work is also not any solution, be it temporary or permanent, to serious or chronic problems in your personal life. Unresolved problems outside of work will affect your performance. You may be irritable with your co-workers, find yourself depressed and unmotivated or, eventually, experience burnout.

When you think about who you are, make sure that your career is not the only aspect of your life that comes to mind and that work has not become an unhealthy coping mechanism.

React

(a) Diversify your interests and apply the same strengths to them that you exhibit at work. For example, get involved in volunteering. If you are detail-oriented or a great planner, you can help to organize a major fund raising event. Take up hobbies that you have thought you might be good at but never pursued.

(b) Participate in stress-releasing activities such as exercise or meditation.

(c) Never underestimate the importance of a supportive group of friends. You may have shut yourself out from close relationships if you have been buried in your job. Reconnect with old friends or take the time to meet new people with whom you enjoy spending time.

(d) If you know you have been avoiding personal issues for a long time by escaping in work, seek professional counseling.

3 | I have to work overtime because my days are not long enough to get my work done

Rethink

There will always be something that simply must get done at work. But is the project really going to fall apart if you do not stay that extra hour? Are you putting too much effort into perfecting your work? There is a point of diminishing returns after which productivity declines greatly because you are tired or have not had a break.

If you are continually playing catch-up, you must stop and assess the cause — or you will risk experiencing burnout.

React

(a) Prioritize your workload. Some things are simply more important than others, so spend your time wisely and get the important tasks done first. You will feel less pressure if the things you have not managed to do are of less consequence. Identify and write down the activities or tasks that take up most of your time. You will be surprised how much time gets spent on following up issues that are not important. Can your assistant help you with those tasks?

(b) If you feel you are constantly behind and cannot get your work accomplished in the allotted time, are you (or your boss) setting unrealistic expectations? Check your progress periodically. Your boss can add resources to assist you or can help to gauge whether you are setting realistic expectations for yourself.

(c) When you are feeling overwhelmed, talk to a trusted colleague. Talking things through with a peer will provide a reality check and a much-needed break from worry. Other people are usually good at giving us a better perspective about what really needs to get done.

(d) Are you a perfectionist? Not all tasks require equal attention or polishing. To which tasks can you give less attention because they will not have much of an impact on your bigger objectives? Always assess the amount of energy and time you put into your assignments and check whether it is really necessary.

(e) Consider taking time management courses that are available through the company or elsewhere.

Rethink

Being a workaholic does not necessarily help you to get ahead. Instead, your excessive work schedule may be perceived as poor time management or a lack of delegation.

Leaders lead by example, and workaholic behavior establishes a culture of excess and burnout in the organization. Joan Gurvis and Gordon Patterson from the Center for Creative Leadership point out in their book *Finding Your Balance* that balance is an ongoing process of making choices that support your values.

Making continual adjustments along the way is also part of the process of being balanced. Being 100% dedicated to work should not preclude success in other areas of your life. And, as a manager of people, demonstrating the value of balance will be one of your greatest organizational achievements.

React

(a) Are you asking for more work than you can handle, biting off more than you can chew? Being ambitious is commendable, but being overly ambitious can harm your performance and your health. Compare your workload to that of others to get a realistic gauge of how much should be on your plate.

(b) Keep track of the hours you work. This will give you a realistic picture of the time you are investing away from home.

(c) Talk to the relevant people if you have concerns about meeting their expectations. You are likely to be harder on yourself than anyone else. Sometimes, all people need to hear is reassurance that they are on track and meeting or exceeding expectations.

(d) Say no to work you cannot handle. Do not accept more work because you think it will reflect poorly if you say no. It will reflect more poorly when you cannot get the job done. It is okay to be honest about your workload. It is not going to cost you your career if you clearly have too much on your plate. Discuss your responsibilities with the person who reviews your work.

(e) Write down everything you want to accomplish personally, in your private life, as well as the things you would like to achieve professionally by the time you retire. Look at the list once a week to remind you of the things that constitute your life and interests outside of work and for which you need to make time.

(f) Find a mentor who has balanced a successful career with personal priorities. How did they manage to accomplish both?

5 | I rather do things myself/I am a perfectionist

Rethink

Perfectionism can lead to workaholism, and quickly. Many tasks do not require perfection, they just need to be done. Consider whether the extra work you are putting into a project is adding tangible value. It may, in fact, be slowing you down or preventing you from working on more critical tasks, which means your efforts are no longer cost-effective.

React

(a) Be judicial about what really needs your attention and how much work is necessary to accomplish the purpose of the assignment. Set completion deadlines for tasks.

(b) Let go of tasks that others can do and delegate these. You will not learn to rely on people until you delegate and give them a chance to prove themselves.

(c) Observe the realistic expectations others set for their work.

(d) Take advantage of the resources in the company and those outside available to you to get your work done more efficiently. Consider outsourcing work, if that is an option.

6 | I do not want to let other people down/I feel pressured by others' expectations

Rethink

Sometimes, imbalance in our lives is created by the demands others place on us, not those we place on ourselves. Chasing other people's agendas is an exhausting game that never ends.

You cannot realistically expect to please everyone or meet their expectations. So, if this is your approach, you can bet you will begin to feel exhausted — if you are not feeling that way already.

Others are not likely to put your needs above theirs, so why are you? Also, be careful about placing less value on your own priorities. They are just as important as everyone else's, so why would you not you manage them as such?

React

(a) Engage a life coach, if possible, to get clarification on your personal priorities and goals.

(b) Assess how much on your plate involves taking care of others. Whether it is helping co-workers with their projects or doing favors for friends, where do your interests and needs fit into the picture?

(c) Get comfortable with politely saying no. Do not explain why, just state that you have other commitments. Practice turning down small commitments on people with whom you are comfortable and move on to people you find difficult to turn down.

7 | Success requires dedication to either work or personal life

Rethink

It is possible to achieve balance between your work and life commitments. What may not be possible — and in reality is unlikely — is that, at any single point in time, you are able to dedicate equal amounts of energy and focus to conflicting demands.

There may be an important work project that lasts several months, or an illness in the family that pulls your attention elsewhere for an extended time. As stated in the introduction to this chapter, balance is about dedicating the appropriate amount of time at the appropriate point to the appropriate priority. And why treat demands in your personal life and those in your career as competitors?

Both aspects of your life provide outlets that help to re-energize you when one's demands are greater than the other. One aspect is not more important than the other because they both contribute positively to your wellbeing and sense of self.

React

(a) Keep an eye on the big picture. Each month, take a step back and review how much time you have spent on your work versus your personal life. If you are starting to notice one area taking over, make a point to increase your focus on the other area. You may do this every couple of months, but do not go too long without assessing your commitments.

(b) When you are starting to feel burnt out because of too much work or too many personal demands, immerse yourself in the opposite realm.

(c) Talk to individuals who you know are successful at work. Ask them how they balance their work and personal demands. You may be surprised to find that many of these individuals do, indeed, juggle their life commitments without compromising their work, and vice versa.

(d) Be clear about the things that matter most to you and that keep your personal and work lives happy and healthy. Be sure to honor these commitments and juggle the less important ones. For example, opt out of happy hour for professional networking if it is your child's birthday. You can also opt out of a dinner engagement with friends because the dinner with the company head was rescheduled for that same night. Honor what is truly important and use good judgment.

Overdeveloped

Research has shown that strengths can become weaknesses because you can, in fact, do too much of a good thing. You cannot become less good at a competency in which you excel, but you can balance the behavior by developing a few Stabilizers to tone down an excessive strength.

Stabilizer	Overdeveloped
8 Comfortable With Uncertainty	Places too much emphasis on balance and is unwilling to make a sacrifice for either work or personal issues when necessary
3 Ambitious	
54 Takes Accountablity	
17 Demonstrates Good Judgment	
50 Problem Solver	
46 Open-Minded	
29 Focused on Priorities	
2 Adaptable	
55 Takes Initiative	
35 Manages Conflict	

Instructions

Read the definition. If it applies to you, choose a few Stabilizers and develop them by selecting the relevant chapter and following the Strategies for Action.

For more instructions see the How To Use This Book section.

6. Bright

"Intelligence is quickness in seeing things as they are"

George Santayana

Well Developed
Can deal with complex intellectual and cognitive concepts

Underdeveloped
Has difficulty grasping complex concepts or ideas, oversimplifies them and lacks the necessary depth of understanding

Overdeveloped
Intellectualizes issues, seems arrogant and struggles to simplify complex ideas for others

Instructions

Read the definitions on the left. If the Underdeveloped definition applies, go to the Strategies for Action section.

If the Overdeveloped definition applies, go to the end of the chapter.

Test Yourself

True	I can restate complex ideas
True	I am routinely asked for assistance with difficult problems
True	I tend to understand concepts quicker than most
True	I am able to devise multiple ways to solve problems
True	I consider things carefully and thoroughly
True	I am described as sharp or smart by others
True	I am open to new ideas and ways of thinking
True	I remain level-headed and composed when dealing with sensitive issues
True	I understand the technical aspect of my business sufficiently to talk intelligently about it

Note

Are you sure you need to develop this competency?

If the answer is "True" to most of the statements on the left, you probably do not need to develop this competency.

Bright

6

Strategies for Action

Most ineffective behaviors have an underlying thought or emotional pattern. By identifying these patterns, you can understand the impact they have and design strategies to counteract them.

① I do not process information as quickly as everyone else/It takes longer for me to grasp concepts

② I can get overly sensitive or emotional when dealing with issues

③ I tend to guard my opinions strongly/I have difficulty to accept new options

④ I do not remember information/I am forgetful

⑤ I rely mostly on my people skills because they have served me well so far

Instructions

1. Read and select one or more of the ineffective ways of thinking/feeling to the left.

2. Find the corresponding number below that will help you to rethink this pattern and identify specific and practical actions that you can take.

---

1 | I do not process information as quickly as everyone else/It takes longer for me to grasp concepts

Rethink

Comparing yourself to others is senseless, because some people will always seem more or less bright than you. Everyone has strengths and weaknesses in different areas, so it is unhealthy to define yourself according to others' capabilities. It is also an unproductive use of your energy.

If you are self-conscious about a lack of knowledge, you may be reluctant to speak up or ask for further explanation when you need it. If you do not grasp concepts as quickly as others do, you should realize that there are many ways of learning and your environment may not be the most conducive to learning for you. If you are new in a job or lack experience, you will not necessarily be able to understand complex concepts as quickly as colleagues who have been there longer.

A learning curve always follows exposure to new environments and it can take as long as a year to get comfortable in a new job. And, while some people are naturally more agile in certain cognitive areas than others, research shows that you can continue to improve your cognitive skills. Studies also indicate that you lose some degree of intelligence if you do not put it to use, so it is good practice to continually sharpen your skills and not allow yourself to become intellectually lazy.

Many so-called bright people are actually just disciplined about learning and work hard to continually stay on top of their game.

React

(a) Focus to identify and improve the areas most challenging to you, especially if they are relevant to your career advancement.

(b) If the problem seems too complex to comprehend as a whole, divide it into smaller parts and tackle them one at a time. Let one solution lead to the next.

(c) Keep your mind sharp by incorporating mental puzzle materials into leisure time. Do crossword puzzles or games such as Sudoku at night before going to bed, or while you are waiting in a queue. They are fun and keep your mind nimble.

(d) Explore problem-solving techniques such as visualization, storyboarding and worst-case scenario development. Having several tools on which to draw is particularly helpful when you need to see things from different perspectives.

(e) Are your thoughts organized? The more complex the problem or issue, the more important it is to be able to organize it into manageable and understandable components. Use techniques such as mind mapping, flowcharting and checklists to clarify the concepts in your head.

(f) Ensure you define the nature of the problem well. Quite often, people tackle problems head-on, only to realize they have wasted time analyzing the symptoms instead of the problem itself. Are you oversimplifying the problem or making it more complex than it actually is?

(g) If you do not understand something, be sure to let others know. They may have to explain numerous times in different ways, but the alternative is to fall behind even further, which will make it even more difficult or impossible to catch up in future.

(h) Ask for a patient explanation and verbalize how you would best understand the information. For example, you may be more visual and require diagrams, or you may need information to be organized in a particular way.

(i) Be realistic and give yourself time to become more experienced in a new job.

(j) Not working in your first language can make it challenging to understand others or follow their train of thought. Get a language coach to help you. Let others know that they may have to repeat things or talk slower. Ask for as much information as possible before meetings to give you a head-start.

② | I can get overly sensitive or emotional when dealing with issues

Rethink

Have you ever noticed that the angrier you get, the more you lose perspective, the more nervous you get and the less clearly you think? Being overly emotional interferes with the calm and clarity needed for good decision making.

You cannot act completely independent of your emotions, but it is important to recognize when they begin to influence negatively your logic.

It is common to become stressed when a problem appears too difficult to solve. A stressed state is not a productive one and often leads to bad or irrational decisions.

React

(a) Try relaxation techniques that can help you to control your emotions, such as meditation and breathing exercises.

(b) Identify your emotional triggers and ensure you are aware when you react to them instead of the facts.

(c) Ask a trusted peer for feedback about the issues. They can provide you with valuable perspective and let you know when you are overreacting.

(d) Step away from a situation or move on to another issue. Giving yourself enough time to reconnect with your logical self can bring much needed clarity to a situation.

(e) Put the problem on paper. Mapping out the issues and a possible course of action helps to engage logic, rather than emotion.

3 | I tend to guard my opinions strongly/I have difficulty to accept new options

Rethink

Bright people seldom apply the one-size-fits-all solution, so check whether you often use words such as "never" or "always" when referring to issues or solving problems. Generalizations like these are an indicator that you limit your thinking.

You can greatly sharpen your insight and ability to process complex information by being open to new experiences and information, and by temporarily relinquishing what you already know. New information helps you to question existing ideas and generate new ones.

Exploring new topics and issues stimulates the brain and helps one to make different connections. And, a touch of humility allows you to listen well and learn from others. If you think you know everything, it is a good indication that you know much less than you think.

React

(a) Challenge what you know. Expose yourself to fresh ideas and points of view. Subscribe to trade magazines, read the newspaper, attend seminars, talk to experts in your company and encourage productive debates among peers.

(b) Look for hidden biases in your thinking, because they prevent you from accepting other possibilities.

(c) Challenge your beliefs by playing devil's advocate. Support the "other side" in an issue, if only for the sake of considering all options. Once you start to defend new turf, you may find yourself thinking quite differently.

(d) Refrain from interrupting others and jumping to conclusions before all the facts have been presented.

(e) Do not assume you know better than others. Even if you are an expert in your field, you may be missing some context or information that could change the solution entirely.

4 | I do not remember information/I am forgetful

Rethink

Have you ever wondered why some friends can remember what they did when they were six years old, yet you have trouble to remember events from last week? People's long- and short-term memory recall differs greatly, and many factors can influence it. For example, as a person becomes older, changes in the brain occur that makes it more difficult to recall certain information.

In recent years, there has been an increased focus on attention-deficit issues. With ever-growing demands at work, individuals are required to process, manage and store enormous amounts of information. It is therefore not surprising that complete recall is sometimes not possible. This also influences how much information you filter and store in your head.

Although a good memory is not a function of brightness per se, poor memory is often perceived as a lack of intelligence. Luckily, recall can be managed and even enhanced with some effort.

React

(a) Establish a system to help you remember things. Different methods work for different people, but something as simple as carrying a small notepad at all times to record items is more than adequate. The important thing is to have a system and stick to it.

(b) Use online tools such as Microsoft Outlook to help you remember events and meetings. Ask your IT department to familiarize you with all the tools available.

(c) If you are notoriously forgetful, rely on a good assistant to notify you about your commitments.

(d) Do not wait until later to jot down notes or reminders. When you record information immediately, there is no chance of forgetting.

(e) Ask people to follow up with e-mails and reminders.

(f) Keep your memory sharp with memory games. They are available online and there are many books on the topic as well.

(g) Ensure you get enough rest and do not burn the candle at both ends. Tiredness can make you forgetful.

(h) Examine your workload. If you constantly struggle to get things done, you may need to delegate or seek additional resources.

(i) Watch your stress level. Chronic stress can affect your memory. Ensure that you have built in enough time to relax and recharge.

Rethink

People with high emotional intelligence and above-average interpersonal skills often rely on these gifts to conduct business and steer through tough situations. Although emotional intelligence is an important component of leadership and work performance, like any other skills set it can be overused.

When charisma is used to replace substance and knowledge, it becomes a crutch and can lead others to distrust or lose respect for you. You may be the first person with whom people like to socialize, but the last one they consult on problem solving or depend on to get things done. Interpersonal skills are generally more difficult to develop than subject knowledge, so if you are naturally gifted with people skills, develop your knowledge to give you the advantage of having both types of smarts.

React

(a) Identify the operational and technical knowledge you should improve to conduct your business more intelligently. Prioritize gaining knowledge in the areas that will have the greatest impact on your ability to conduct business now.

(b) Engage a coach or manager to formulate a development plan, with specific actions aimed at increasing your functional knowledge and exposing you to requisite experiences.

(c) Raise your business acumen by subscribing to publications in your field. Read them to stay abreast of trends and increase your general knowledge.

(d) Exploit your social nature by attending conferences and association meetings where you can gain new insight about your business.

(e) Ask peers to send you literature and articles they have found particularly insightful.

(f) During discussions, focus less on your and other people's feelings and more on solving the problem.

(g) Work on your motivational smarts, that is, how driven you are to grow in challenging areas and achieve your goals.

Overdeveloped

Research has shown that strengths can become weaknesses because you can, in fact, do too much of a good thing. You cannot become less good at a competency in which you excel, but you can balance the behavior by developing a few Stabilizers to tone down an excessive strength.

Stabilizer	Overdeveloped
4 Approachable	Intellectualizes issues, seems arrogant and struggles to simplify complex ideas for others
60 Works Well with Boss	
24 Empathetic	
15 Customer-Centric	
33 Inspires a Future	
22 Diplomatic	
34 Listens Well	
43 Motivates People	
47 Patient	
7 Collaborative	

Instructions

Read the definition. If it applies to you, choose a few Stabilizers and develop them by selecting the relevant chapter and following the Strategies for Action.

For more instructions see the How To Use This Book section.

7. Collaborative

Easy | Moderate
Difficulty to LEARN | Difficulty to CHANGE

"None of us are as smart as all of us"

Japanese proverb

Well Developed
Is cooperative and handles collaboration well

Underdeveloped
Is too competitive or unwilling to cooperate with others

Overdeveloped
Relies too much on outside input to accomplish tasks or make decisions

Instructions

Read the definitions on the left. If the Underdeveloped definition applies, go to the Strategies for Action section.

If the Overdeveloped definition applies, go to the end of the chapter.

Test Yourself

True	I look for common goals among myself and others
True	I like to share what I know
True	I use opportunities to learn from others
True	I share credit for accomplishments and ideas
True	I try to accommodate my co-workers' needs and pace
True	I do not withhold resources or information to gain advantage over my team members

Note

Are you sure you need to develop this competency?

If the answer is "True" to most of the statements on the left, you probably do not need to develop this competency.

7 Collaborative

45

Strategies for Action

Most ineffective behaviors have an underlying thought or emotional pattern. By identifying these patterns, you can understand the impact they have and design strategies to counteract them.

1. I am very competitive/I want to be the best

2. I do not like the people with whom I work/ I cannot identify with them

3. I rather work on my own/I get more done

Instructions

1. Read and select one or more of the ineffective ways of thinking/feeling to the left.

2. Find the corresponding number below that will help you to rethink this pattern and identify specific and practical actions that you can take.

---

1 | I am very competitive/I want to be the best

Rethink

An overly competitive nature can hinder your ability to work well with others. Healthy competition helps to keep people at the top of their game, but being too focused on standing out and getting to the finishing line first usually alienates peers and team members. Ironically, teams who work together tend to obtain greater resources, recognition and rewards than individuals.

Differentiating yourself does not have to come at others' expense. Why not think of yourself as part of the best team? This approach prompts you to succeed, encourages collaborative behavior and allows a spotlight that is big enough for all.

React

(a) Make a point of crediting others. Acknowledge each time the group or person has done something well.

(b) Share information freely. Consider what you have withheld or felt possessive about previously, and why. How would you feel if important information necessary to get your job done was kept from you?

(c) Delegate or share work so that others can get credit for their efforts too.

(d) Gauge your competitive behavior by asking yourself whether your actions primarily serve you or the organization.

2 | I do not like the people with whom I work/I cannot identify with them

Rethink

Not each person or every team with whom you work will share your opinions or approach an issue from your perspective. Throughout your career, you are likely to work among people with diverse and different opinions, working styles and interests.

Whether you like someone or not, it should not prohibit you from working collaboratively — only your attitude can. In the end you may be surprised to discover you have more in common than you anticipated. Differentiate between the people and the problem: regardless of the parties involved, the problem remains the same, so use your energy to solve it instead of trying to like everybody.

React

(a) Explore any hidden bias you may have. List what makes you uncomfortable to collaborate with a person or group. Is it an individual, something he or she has done, or something that you associate with the person? Do you base your negative feelings on fact or opinion?

(b) Start by getting a consensus about the common goal. It is a powerful way to build unity despite differences.

(c) Focus on similarities rather than differences among the parties involved.

(d) Make a list of the strengths and resources that will be brought forth by working with this particular group. It will help you to see the added value.

(e) Do not assume people are the same and give a new person or group the benefit of the doubt. You may have had a bad experience before with people from a specific group — perhaps someone dropped the ball or your work styles were incompatible — but start with an open mind.

(f) If the opportunity exists, get to know the people you work with on a personal level.

3 | I rather work on my own/I get more done

Rethink

Individuals who perform well on their own or who are highly skilled are often hesitant or impatient about working with others. Collaborative work creates its compromises, in terms of time or control, for example, but there are many advantages as well.

From a personal development perspective, working with others helps to sharpen your communication skills. It provides exposure to new ideas and information, gives you the opportunity to work on more complex assignments, exposes you to other areas of the business and raises your visibility in an organization. The compromises are usually inevitable and worth the trouble.

React

(a) Practice your collaboration skills by working with small groups at first. Tackle projects with one or two people and build up to bigger taskforces or committees.

(b) To work with others may take more time, but consider the quality of the outcome and what you may learn as a result of your collaboration.

(c) When a group effort is completed, take time to think about what you could not have accomplished on your own.

(d) Offer your help to others. Helping others benefits the whole and, invariably, at some point you will find yourself needing their assistance.

(e) Work on being accessible. A warm interpersonal style can do much to ease people's tension and defuse emotions. If you seem too independent and disinterested in other people, you will have to fight that perception when the time comes to collaborate with them.

(f) Practice asking others their opinions instead of telling them how things should be done. Be the first one to listen and the last one to comment.

(g) Take the opportunity to mentor or work with someone who struggles or is less experienced than you.

Overdeveloped

Research has shown that strengths can become weaknesses because you can, in fact, do too much of a good thing. You cannot become less good at a competency in which you excel, but you can balance the behavior by developing a few Stabilizers to tone down an excessive strength.

Stabilizer	Overdeveloped
12 Confident	Relies too much on outside input to accomplish tasks or make decisions
13 Courageous	
35 Manages Conflict	
16 Decisive	
23 Directs People	
39 Manages Time	
37 Manages Negotiations	
29 Focused on Priorities	
1 Achiever	
54 Takes Accountability	

Instructions

Read the definition. If it applies to you, choose a few Stabilizers and develop them by selecting the relevant chapter and following the Strategies for Action.

For more instructions see the How To Use This Book section.

8. Comfortable With Uncertainty

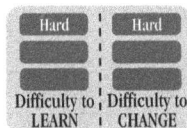

"Sit down before fact as a little child, be prepared to give up every preconceived notion, follow humbly to wherever or whatever abysses nature leads, or you will learn nothing"

Thomas H. Huxley

Well Developed
Is comfortable working in a changing and uncertain environment

Underdeveloped
Requires a high level of predictability and stability to function well

Overdeveloped
Creates unnecessary uncertainty and discomfort for others

Instructions

Read the definitions on the left. If the Underdeveloped definition applies, go to the Strategies for Action section.

If the Overdeveloped definition applies, go to the end of the chapter.

Test Yourself

True	I am optimistic that things will work out, even if the future is uncertain
True	I think typically change is positive and exciting
True	I am prepared to test new approaches
True	I can make decisions and take action without knowing all the details
True	I can change my course of action quickly
True	I consider multiple scenarios at once when devising strategies
True	I thrive in an unstructured environment

Note

Are you sure you need to develop this competency?

If the answer is "True" to most of the statements on the left, you probably do not need to develop this competency.

Comfortable With Uncertainty

8

Strategies for Action

Most ineffective behaviors have an underlying thought or emotional pattern. By identifying these patterns, you can understand the impact they have and design strategies to counteract them.

① Shifting gears all the time is difficult for me/ I like a structured environment

② I must be precise/I need to know all the details before I feel certain of my decision or work

③ I prefer to do things in a familiar way/I know what has worked in the past

④ I do not have the necessary skills or knowledge/I am not confident doing what I am required to do

⑤ I feel pessimistic about the future/I am not motivated

Instructions

1. Read and select one or more of the ineffective ways of thinking/feeling to the left.

2. Find the corresponding number below that will help you to rethink this pattern and identify specific and practical actions that you can take.

1 | Shifting gears all the time is difficult for me/I like a structured environment

Rethink

The good news about a highly unstructured environment is that you have room to be creative. The bad news is that you may have to function in controlled chaos and continuously shift gears.

Are you exhausted, overwhelmed or stressed most of the time? Do you feel you spend so much time in transition from one thing to the next that your work suffers? You may even stall regularly with certain assignments and ignore responsibilities that are just as important, or expect direction but feel you never quite get enough of it.

Juggling the demands of a dynamic, unstructured environment can be tricky. You will have to manage the hundreds of e-mails, messages, meetings and calls typical of such workdays, and would likely become a jack of all trades and master of none.

Surviving or thriving in an unstructured environment requires the ability to switch efficiently between tasks and roles, topics, problems and relationships, yet maintain a clear head. Adaptability at all levels is the key. Research from the Center for Creative Leadership points to three elements of adaptability: cognitive flexibility — the ability to use different thinking strategies and mental frameworks; emotional flexibility — the ability to vary your approach to dealing with the emotions of others and your own; and dispositional flexibility — the ability to remain optimistic and realistic at the same time.

Becoming skilled at adapting quickly will help you to stay afloat in a dynamic, uncertain environment.

React

(a) Tell your boss and colleagues that you prefer a framework in which to operate, or when a greater amount of guidance is needed. They cannot read your mind and may be operating on the basis of their own needs.

(b) You cannot bring structure to everything, so focus on the areas where you can. Make a list of the things that are structured in your workday and you will see that not everything is beyond your control.

(c) Have systems in place that allow you to quickly make the transition from one task to another without forgetting where you left off. Even a simple list can help you.

(d) Ensure your approach to people and issues is adaptable. A "one size fits all" approach does not work in a multifaceted work environment, and it will be exhausting to try to get things done your way all the time.

(e) Accept that you will have to stop and go continuously. Shifting gears does not mean you will not get things done. It simply means your attention will be shared among concurrent demands. You can always get back to what you had started earlier.

(f) Do not try to deal with each and every aspect of an issue or achieve complete solutions before moving on to something else. Most things cannot be resolved at once. It is acceptable to tackle things partially and move on, then return and resolve them properly. Reward yourself for taking the next logical step and not just for completing the task as a whole.

(g) Practice effective transition by doing multiple activities for a limited period of time, all in one day. Select activities that require a change of skills or frame of mind and do not try to complete any one assignment at once. For example, reply to a few e-mails, then provide assistance to someone you supervise, followed by tackling a section of a proposal or document. Then stop and make a few pending calls, and so forth. Keep practicing this and observe the different hats you must wear to move forward. Take pride in the number of activities in which you were able to engage instead of how many you completed from beginning to end. Notice how much quicker you are able to address multiple tasks.

(h) Observe a colleague who handles ambiguity successfully. What is different about your attitude and approach?

(i) Take relaxation breaks throughout the day, particularly when you switch between projects or major tasks, by doing a few moments of deep-breathing exercises or getting away from your desk for a while.

(j) Ensure you reflect on how things might have been easier in a particular situation, had you been able to switch gears more quickly and effectively.

(k) If you are chronically stressed and unhappy about your environment, investigate other opportunities to work in a more structured setting within the organization.

---

2 | I must be precise/I need to know all the details before I feel certain of my decision or work

Rethink

Do you feel the only way to reduce uncertainty and work effectively is to gather all the information or details beforehand? There is logic to that, but three other factors must be taken into account.

One, not all details are equally important. Quantity does not trump quality. Two, many decisions must be made under pressure and the priority may be to act swiftly. Many decisions are made under time restrictions, so the time spent on gathering data must be carefully weighed. How much time can you afford to spend on an unnecessary detail? Three, intuition is an effective tool in decision making.

Typically, intuition alone is not a strong enough basis for decisions, but there is much you already know instinctively to guide you through uncertainty. Remember, more often than not deliverables and decisions need to be good enough, not perfect. It is good to be deliberate and precise in your work, but in a rapidly changing environment you must maintain a flexible approach.

React

(a) Try to separate critical data from less important information. What is the minimum detail needed to understand enough to proceed with the project?

(b) Although you may find it difficult, focus on improving the speed with which you get through a project rather than how well it is done.

(c) Work on projects or tasks up to a point and then, before it is 100% complete, pass it on to someone else to review or take over.

(d) Before tackling any task or assignment, rate how important it is to get it done perfectly. Never give something a score of 10 because nothing can be done perfectly. Get feedback if you are unsure, particularly from your manager.

(e) Set a time limit for collecting information and gathering data before you actually tackle a task.

(f) Reflect on past projects in which you were involved. Which details were irrelevant in the end?

(g) Compare your expectations with those of your team and manager. Ensure you understand exactly how much effort or time they expect you to invest in the project.

(h) Trust your decisions. You will have to make many of them throughout your career.

---

3 | **I prefer to do things in a familiar way/I know what has worked in the past**

Rethink

Why question that which you know works? Remember, experience is an asset, but relying on what has worked in the past can become too restrictive an approach. You may find it difficult to accept criticism of tried and tested ideas or methods. Do you often tell others "I know what I am doing" or "Let's just do what's worked before"? Or often think that change will be too difficult?

Although familiar solutions provide a sense of security, they restrict us from entertaining new possibilities and being open to change. And that is a problem, because change is a constant in most work environments. Resisting change also puts you at risk of becoming obsolete. If you played a large part in creating a process, it is difficult to see it replaced with something new. But change is inevitable, so take pride in the part you have played and get ready for your future contribution.

React

(a) Consider whether conditions and assumptions in the current situation are the same as previously. What has changed? Do the differences warrant a new way to proceed which you should examine?

(b) First consider how things could be done differently, then add the standard way of doing them to the mix. Brainstorm ideas before reaching a conclusion.

(c) Ensure there are mavericks or forward-thinking people on your team. Their input will counteract yours and add balance.

(d) Remain open to all options. It is easy to become defensive and territorial when you are trying to defend the standard way of doing things.

(e) Remember both the good and bad about your standard procedure. List its pros and cons to create a realistic picture of how well it has worked.

(f) Experiment for the sake of it. You can practice getting more comfortable with new approaches outside the work environment. Try one new thing a week, from ordering an unknown item from the menu to taking a different route home. Satisfy your curiosity about a place and take a trip there. Exploring should be fun and part of your approach to both your life and work.

---

4 | **I do not have the necessary skills or knowledge/I am not confident doing what I am required to do**

Rethink

Many people worry about their ability to adjust their skills levels rapidly enough to meet the rate of change in their position, organization or industry.

If you expect to have extensive experience or in-depth technical knowledge about everything on your plate, you are setting yourself up for significant frustration and stress. In ambiguous settings, the ability to function productively despite a lack of experience is highly valued.

Ambiguous environments require that people continually reinvent themselves in order to manage their rapidly changing roles. Not knowing is not a weakness in itself. What matters is how you handle your lack of knowledge.

The more comfortable you are with learning throughout your career, the more effectively you will function in a variety of situations. No doubt, changing environments will test your existing strengths and require you to develop new ones quickly.

Handling uncertainty well will mark you as a leader. Do not assume that your lack of experience will necessarily prevent success, and remember everyone has talents that can be useful, regardless of the nature of the assignment.

React

(a) Admit it and deal with it. You may have to improve some of your skills, but worrying or comparing yourself with others will not produce any results or change the situation. Engage a coach to set up an individual development plan to help you work on areas that need attention.

(b) Instead of focusing on everything you do not know, concentrate on what you really have to know to complete the next task.

(d) Remind yourself of other situations in which you were a beginner and felt overwhelmed. How did you get through those experiences? Think of what you have learned to get where you are now.

(e) Consult a peer or mentor skilled in the area you need to develop and get their support when necessary.

(f) Ensure your expectations of yourself compare to those of your boss or supervisor. We tend to be hardest on ourselves and, likely, you need to know less than you think.

(g) Be patient with yourself and your mistakes. Success comes with experience, which is built on lessons from mistakes.

(h) Be resourceful when information is unclear or you do not know how to proceed. Find out who can help you with particular tasks, examine work that was done in similar projects and secure the reference materials and resources available to get you up to speed. Be an investigator and start asking questions.

5 | I feel pessimistic about the future/I am not motivated

Rethink

Is everything a big effort? Were you once energetic and positive, stomping at the bit to tackle challenges and change, but now it does not seem worth your while? Although this attitude will affect most people at some point in their careers, it can stifle your progress if it becomes a chronic state of mind.

A lack of motivation has a negative effect on your energy levels and your ability to champion change. It also has consequences for the people around you, because pessimism is contagious. Most people approach uncertainty or change with an amount of anxiety, and your negative attitude will only heighten your colleagues' apprehension. Even those not easily influenced by anxiety will have to deal with the demoralizing effect of your attitude. You risk the possibility of losing key talent who may want more energetic leadership.

A lack of enthusiasm is particularly harmful when it comes from someone in a leadership position, especially during times of change.

React

(a) Before speaking, always consider whether your comments could demoralize others. If they could, refrain from sharing your opinions or try to deliver the news in a more positive manner.

(b) Examine which components of work you enjoyed before your interest diminished, and what has changed. Are the changes self-imposed? Would talking to relevant people about changing the situation help to revive your interest? Would you regain your enthusiasm if you were involved in other assignments? Try to find options that will recharge your work energy.

(c) Examine your definition of your value to the organization. If you feel change in the organization will diminish your value, try to reinvent yourself. Identify the skills you need to enhance to remain competitive. Consider new assignments that could mark a new chapter in your career.

(d) Ensure you do not communicate your negative attitude by withholding support, encouragement or information.

(e) Encourage optimistic discussions about the future. Let people share their vision and hopes for the organization's future, and refrain from pointing out the downside of what they have shared. Do this in every meeting.

(f) Forget about the old days and how much better they were. Reflection is productive, but only as a means to analyze how to improve in future.

(g) Ask a mentor or coach to help you examine what has led you to your frame of mind, and which changes can be made before you become the last person with whom people want to work. Or worse, before you become obsolete.

Overdeveloped

Research has shown that strengths can become weaknesses because you can, in fact, do too much of a good thing. You cannot become less good at a competency in which you excel, but you can balance the behavior by developing a few Stabilizers to tone down an excessive strength.

Stabilizer	Overdeveloped
43 Motivates People	Creates unnecessary uncertainty and discomfort for others
2 Adaptable	
56 Technically Competent	
51 Recognizes Talent and Potential	
32 Informs Others	
18 Detail-Orientated	
33 Inspires a Future	
48 Plans Work	
29 Focused on Priorities	
49 Politically Astute	

Instructions

Read the definition. If it applies to you, choose a few Stabilizers and develop them by selecting the relevant chapter and following the Strategies for Action.

For more instructions see the How To Use This Book section.

9. Communicates Well (Verbal)

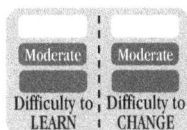

"The greatest reward is to know that one can speak and emit articulate sounds and utter words that describe things, events and emotions"

Camilo Jose Cela

Well Developed

Clearly explains a point of view and its reasoning in both one-on-one and large audience situations

Underdeveloped

Struggles to get a point across, is easily misunderstood and seems nervous around people

Overdeveloped

Could be too eloquent, with more style than substance

Instructions

Read the definitions on the left. If the Underdeveloped definition applies, go to the Strategies for Action section.

If the Overdeveloped definition applies, go to the end of the chapter.

Test Yourself

True	I am confident when speaking to others
True	My thoughts are well organized when I speak
True	I understand my audience before I start talking to them
True	I limit unnecessary tangents during discussions
True	I adapt how I communicate depending on the situation
True	I consider the level of complexity depending on the audience
True	I am usually able to add to a conversation
True	I provide enough context (make sure others are on the same page) when I start a discussion

Note

Are you sure you need to develop this competency?

If the answer is "True" to most of the statements on the left, you probably do not need to develop this competency.

Strategies for Action

Most ineffective behaviors have an underlying thought or emotional pattern. By identifying these patterns, you can understand the impact they have and design strategies to counteract them.

① I feel self-conscious when talking/I am nervous when doing a presentation

② I find it difficult to express myself in a concise manner/I struggle to organize my thoughts

③ I seldom adapt my style of communicating

④ I cannot express myself well when I get emotional

⑤ I often cannot find the words to express myself/I do not have anything to say

⑥ I have physical reasons that affect my general sense of confidence/I struggle with my accent

Instructions

1. Read and select one or more of the ineffective ways of thinking/feeling to the left.

2. Find the corresponding number below that will help you to rethink this pattern and identify specific and practical actions that you can take.

---

1 | I feel self-conscious when talking/I am nervous when doing a presentation

Rethink

Few people feel entirely comfortable when the spotlight is on them. Even the most prepared person can struggle during a presentation when overcome by nerves. Public speaking is ranked as one of the most common fears people have and comes close to the fear of dying. So, know that you are not alone and that managing your fears should be approached just like any other developmental opportunity.

The body's typical response to fear is a release of the adrenaline hormone, which is produced by the adrenal gland. This stimulates the heart rate and dilates blood vessels and air passages, among other things. Adrenaline is produced naturally in high-stress or physically exhilarating situations, and the term "fight or flight" is often used to characterize the circumstances under which adrenaline is released. It is an early evolutionary adaptation to allow humans to cope better with dangerous and unexpected situations. With dilated blood vessels and air passages, the body is able to pass more blood to the muscles and get more oxygen into the lungs in a timely manner, increasing physical performance for short bursts of time. But when this happens, oxygen to the brain is reduced, which impairs a person's ability to remain clear headed. In other words, it does not serve us well when trying to think straight and remain composed during a presentation.

Understanding the physiological side of fear is important, but it is more instructive to know that there are strategies to mitigate these responses. As you advance in your career, your visibility will increase, and as a leader in an organization you will have to present to others more frequently. Managing this issue has great rewards, both emotionally and for your career.

React

(a) There are many strategies you can practice daily to help you relax and give you better control of your body's physical reaction to stress. Explore, for example, relaxation techniques such as deep breathing and meditation. Practicing daily makes control of your responses more automatic and it will become like anything else in which you invest time and diligent practice — you will improve.

(b) Your alarm response in presentation situations is based on irrational and disproportionate fear of the situation at hand. Your body does not know this, so your mind must provide perspective. Use positive self-reinforcement to address irrational negative thoughts. For example, replace "What if I don't know how to answer a question?" with "I can't possibly know everything". Then find a balanced solution, such as "I will get back to the person with the answer later". Pay attention to and become aware of negative reinforcement.

(c) Use the visualization technique to get you more comfortable with the pending presentation, in other words, imagine yourself having a successful presentation. Try to go through the details in your mind. Make the experience as real as possible. Do this repeatedly until you start to believe what you visualize.

(d) Remain objective about your purpose: to communicate and engage people in conversation. If, in the process, people agree with you and like you and you are able to answer every question, that is simply a bonus, not your objective. Until you are more comfortable with presentations, remove unnecessary pressures and simply aim to effectively deliver the information.

(e) Join organizations such as Toast Masters, which helps you to practice gaining confidence to speak and present effectively in public because it provides experience in a non-threatening setting.

(f) Read some of the hundreds of books on effective public speaking, such as *Public Speaking for Success* by Dale Carnegie.

(g) Become intimate and comfortable with the subject matter. The more you know the more self-confident you will feel. You may need to do supplementary reading or talk to experts to help you.

(h) Use prompts such as note cards and PowerPoint presentations, but only as guides. Reading notes verbatim during a presentation makes it dry and you will not be perceived as adding value. It also discourages you from relaxing and letting your personality shine through.

(i) Act the part until you believe it. Speak confidently, even if you are not. No one knows you are uncomfortable unless you let it show. Look at your audience directly and speak up so that everyone can hear you. Avoid justifying or apologizing for everything you say, or fidgeting unnecessarily, because it will signal that you are nervous and lack confidence.

(j) Consult a professional counselor for relaxation techniques and anxiety reduction. Breathing exercises, bio-feedback and visualization are just a few of the tools you can use.

Rethink

Time constraints at work make it imperative for people to supply and receive information in a manner that is concise, clear and succinct. It is important to respect other people's time by being well organized and not elaborating endlessly when someone is listening to you.

Short, substantive talk is always more significant than long, meaningless chatter. And regardless of time constraints, always assume that people have short attention spans. One of the principal goals when trying to articulate your point is to avoid external and self-imposed distractions. Get to the point before it is lost on people.

React

(a) You do not need to be scripted to present well or hold a discussion eloquently, but if you tend to lose track easily, spend some time to organize your thoughts beforehand. Create a logical flow for communicating your ideas. Map what you want to communicate and ensure there is order to your ideas. Share the outline with a peer to see if it makes sense. Try using software such as MindJet Manager to map ideas beforehand or as they are discussed.

(b) Use prompts to help you stay on track. Draw up an agenda and make sure you do not veer from it. Ensure the agenda states the goals of the meeting or presentation. Even less formal discussions can benefit from an agenda. Prepare visual aids such as a PowerPoint presentation or simple note cards with the key points you must address by the end of the discussion. Your tendency might be to "wing it", but the necessary preparation will be to your advantage.

(c) Manage the amount of detail you provide when talking or presenting. Too much detail makes it difficult for people to remain focused on your point. Always ask yourself while talking whether the detail you are providing is critical to the conversation, or simply added information.

(d) Limit the amount of tangential conversation and personal anecdotes you introduce to a conversation. These departures from the topic can waste much time and distract your audience. Ask a trusted peer to point out when you are digressing. Being aware of the frequency with which you do this can help you to adjust your conversation style.

(e) Know your stuff! Although you cannot be an expert on everything, the more you know about a topic the more likely you are to provide relevant information.

(f) Do not assume that everyone is like you. Some people need you to get directly to the point and others want all the details. Are you getting cut short quite often? Do people tend to avoid asking you questions? Try to read the person's reactions or ask them whether you are providing too much information.

(g) Are you easily distracted? Always anticipate that you will be interrupted or asked questions when trying to make a point. If the question is not relevant, table it and, as tempting as it may be, avoid pursuing unnecessary digressions.

(h) To the extent that you can, make a conscious effort to minimize distractions in your environment beforehand. Schedule meetings in quiet places far from activity, ask people to turn off their phones and be conscious of minimizing distractions, and involve the appropriate number of people in meetings — the number should maximize input but limit distractions that will interrupt your focus.

(i) Try not to jump from thought to thought or topic to topic without closure or sufficient introduction to a new topic. Some people may be able to follow your communication, but others think linearly and need the conversation to be more organized.

(j) Do not forget to provide sufficient context for people when you start a conversation. Recap briefly where things stand and make sure people know what you are talking about before jumping to details.

3 | I seldom adapt my style of communicating

Rethink

Being articulate requires you to adapt your message in such a way that your audience understands it. For example, your audience may expect to hear a motivational speech about the future of the company and well-crafted words to inspire them, but instead you focus on presenting data.

You should adapt your style to different audiences or risk being misunderstood. No matter how organized, prepared or confident you may be delivering your presentation, if you have not understood your audience and crafted your message accordingly, the chances of getting your point across will be greatly reduced.

React

(a) When doing a presentation, it is easy to get caught up in the message and forget the listener. Stay in touch with your audience. For example, routinely ask whether they are following the point, hearing you well, or whether you need to talk slower. Keep gauging where they stand and whether you have to adjust your communication style. Be sure to get feedback at the end of the presentation to identify where there is room for improvement.

(b) What does your audience need to hear or see to remain engaged? Details, visuals, business cases? Perhaps you should cover more bases if you have a diverse audience.

(c) If you are presenting to people of a specific cultural group, become knowledgeable about their sensitivities and norms. Talk to a consultant, read about the culture and ask others who have had experience with that group.

(d) When speaking one on one, consider the individual's personality. Is the person more people oriented, analytical or reserved? Craft your message with the individual's personality in mind.

(e) Consider the complexity of your message. The audience's level of understanding of the subject will determine the information you provide, in other words, how complex or simple the message must be. If the people you are talking to are not experts on the subject, try to avoid technical jargon or unnecessary information that will leave them confused or frustrated.

4 | I cannot express myself well when I get emotional

Rethink

It is hard to get a point across articulately if you are overcome emotionally. Your most well-considered argument is unlikely to be heard if people are focusing on your emotional behavior. It is essential to remain level-headed in a professional setting. Often, you will need to rise above a provocative situation and continue to try to communicate your point, despite your feelings or circumstances such as an unfair attack. Your goal is to get your point across and arguing with someone or becoming defensive will not get you there. Staying composed will help you to get your message across.

React

(a) Recognize your "hot buttons" and when they are being pressed. Take a deep breath and give yourself time to calm down before responding. Remind yourself of your purpose — to have your point both heard and understood. It may require a great deal of patience.

(b) Ask for some time to collect yourself. You may need to leave the room, which is preferable to losing your focus entirely.

(c) Try to stay objective and patient. You do not have control over people's moods or their lack of respect. How is getting emotional going to improve the situation?

5 | I often cannot find the words to express myself/I do not have anything to say

Rethink

Do you feel like an outsider when people gather together to talk about work or current events? Perhaps you have something to say but cannot find the right words to express yourself. This is particularly common among people with a strong technical focus, who have not had the opportunity or need to communicate to those outside their field.

As people move up the career ladder, they are exposed to an increasingly diverse group of constituents and will need to express themselves in different ways and cover a wider variety of topics.

React

(a) Do supplementary reading on the relevant topic before going to a meeting or gathering of people.

(b) Read the newspaper as often as possible to stay knowledgeable about current events.

(c) Expose yourself to different methods of expression. Try to read diverse types of literature, for example, fiction, business journals, poetry and white papers. Take note of the vocabulary use, metaphors and analogies that you can incorporate into your communication.

(d) Attend a storytelling workshop to help you understand how to express yourself and optimally engage your audience.

(e) Spend time with peers who are effective communicators. Which topics do they cover? How do they manage small talk?

6 | I have physical reasons that affect my general sense of confidence/I struggle with my accent

Rethink

Communicating well is challenging enough, but if you have the added concern of a speech or physical impediment it can be downright frightening. Non-native speakers may find it frustrating and difficult to communicate if they have a strong accent. Remember that everyone has some form of personal hurdle to overcome — for some it is just less visible or obvious than others.

Your physical challenge does not define your abilities or intelligence. Do not be surprised if those around you are more self-conscious than you are because they do not know how to act towards you or how you wish to be treated. Physical challenges often give you an unique perspective on life that can add value to your relationships and interaction with others.

React

(a) Instead of ignoring your condition, address it upfront so that others know it is not a taboo subject and can move on to the relevant issues.

(b) If you are comfortable doing so, use humor to break the ice about your particular circumstances.

(c) Focus on the things over which you have control — how well you know the topic and how prepared, personable and approachable you are.

(d) Seek a voice coach, therapist or voice clinic where you can find support and learn techniques to deal with speech issues.

(e) Engage a native-language teacher to help with your accent.

Overdeveloped

Research has shown that strengths can become weaknesses because you can, in fact, do too much of a good thing. You cannot become less good at a competency in which you excel, but you can balance the behavior by developing a few Stabilizers to tone down an excessive strength.

Stabilizer	Overdeveloped
40 Market Aware	Could be too eloquent, with more style than substance
56 Technically Competent	
6 Bright	
34 Listens Well	
30 Global Thinker	
50 Problem Solver	
53 Strategic	
57 Technology Savvy	
31 Improves Processes	
33 Inspires a Future	

Instructions

Read the definition. If it applies to you, choose a few Stabilizers and develop them by selecting the relevant chapter and following the Strategies for Action.

For more instructions see the How To Use This Book section.

10. Communicates Well (Written)

> "I didn't have time to write a short letter, so I wrote a long one instead"
> Mark Twain

Well Developed
Writes accurately and professionally in multiple formats, with the correct amount of detail

Underdeveloped
Struggles to communicate accurately and professionally in writing

Overdeveloped
Uses written communication when verbal communication may be more appropriate. Writing is too clinical, lacks emotion or takes too long to craft

Instructions

Read the definitions on the left. If the Underdeveloped definition applies, go to the Strategies for Action section.

If the Overdeveloped definition applies, go to the end of the chapter.

Test Yourself

True	I rarely need to clarify what I have written
True	I adapt my writing style to suit the recipient
True	I have a good understanding of basic grammar
True	I always correct or edit my writing before sending it
True	I can get my point across in few words

Note

Are you sure you need to develop this competency?

If the answer is "True" to most of the statements on the left, you probably do not need to develop this competency.

67

Strategies for Action

Most ineffective behaviors have an underlying thought or emotional pattern. By identifying these patterns, you can understand the impact they have and design strategies to counteract them.

① The content is more important than the grammar or style of my writing

② I often have to clarify what I meant in my writing /I struggle to organize my thoughts

③ I do not adapt my writing style to cater for different readers

④ I often write based on what I feel at that moment/I respond impulsively

⑤ I often cannot find the right words

Instructions

1. Read and select one or more of the ineffective ways of thinking/feeling to the left.

2. Find the corresponding number below that will help you to rethink this pattern and identify specific and practical actions that you can take.

1 | The content is more important than the grammar or style of my writing

Rethink

Ultimately, the goal of any form of communication is to get your message across. How well you get that point across could depend on your ability to communicate it through good writing.

A poorly written message or response creates frustration and confusion. It can also waste both your and other people's time because the recipient is forced to seek further clarification. Poor writing is typically perceived as unprofessional and can create misperceptions about your intelligence.

Ensure that you invest the time and effort necessary to develop this vital skill.

React

(a) Always reread and edit what you have written. Mistakes are easy to make when you write something quickly and a simple review will catch them.

(b) Let a second pair of eyes look at your writing — a peer or an assistant can review important information you are sending out. It is remarkable how many mistakes another person catches. Try to improve the amount of mistakes you make.

(c) Do not assume people know what you are talking about, particularly if your writing style is quite concise. Ensure people have the appropriate context in which to understand your message.

(d) If you have the tendency to write as you speak, you may be using jargon or associate too freely in your writing. Conversations and written communication are very different methods of articulation and should not be confused in a professional setting.

② | I often have to clarify what I meant in my writing/ I struggle to organize my thoughts

Rethink

These days, we are highly dependent on written correspondence because e-mail has become the principal form of communication in the workplace. Whole projects can be carried out via e-mail, and in the global economy entire teams are managed remotely through written communication and instructions. Your thoughts may be clear in your head, but the challenge is to communicate these thoughts and ideas accurately and effectively.

React

(a) Organize your thoughts thoroughly before you start writing. Outline the points you want to make and ensure they are presented in a logical sequence. Review them with a peer to see if they make sense. If you are not naturally good at writing, use your other strengths to organize your thoughts beforehand. For example, if you are visually inclined, try software such as MindJet Manager to map and organize your ideas, or create your own drawing or illustration. If you are a verbal person, voice your thoughts out loud or make a recording of your proposals, then put them in writing.

(b) Do not provide unnecessary detail which will confuse or distract people from your written message. Which supporting information does the reader have to know? If the recipient is unfamiliar with the topic or subject, provide enough context to clarify your communication. Preferably, add attachments or provide supporting reference material to which the person can refer. Your basic message should provide the highlights or a brief historical summary only.

(c) Pay attention to formatting, especially when you need to communicate numerous points. Good formatting makes it much easier for the reader to follow your thoughts. For example, separate different points with paragraphs or appropriate titles or spacing, instead of all the information running together. Highlight in bold important points to which you want to draw attention. Although it may look somewhat dry and overly formal, use numbering or bullet points to order your writing.

(d) Poor grammar can make the simplest e-mail message hard to grasp. Ensure you understand the basic principles of punctuation. Use the spellcheck feature your software provides, but do not rely on that alone. Reread your work. *Eats, Shoots and Leaves* by Lynn Truss is an entertaining and insightful book about the perils of poor grammar.

(e) Curb repetitious statements or points that confuse your readers and sap their attention. You should not be repeating your point numerous times, except once in your summary. Reread what you have written and delete unnecessary statements — clear the "noise" from your writing. This sounds simple, but it is not done often enough.

(f) Ask others if they have difficulty reading your work and understanding your message, and exactly what confuses them. Use their feedback to enhance your writing skills.

3 | I do not adapt my writing style to cater for different readers

Rethink

It is easy to get so caught up in your message that you completely overlook the manner in which you are delivering it. Just like you would adapt your message when speaking to different audiences, good written communication must be molded for the specific reader.

Your writing style and tone are critical: it may be formal, direct and concise when updating your boss on a project's progress, but your communication to your subordinates about the same project would probably have to elaborate and could be less formal or include something to motivate them.

You will connect with people more successfully if you can adapt your message to them. They will hear what you are trying to say and your communication will have served its purpose.

React

(a) Consider the reader's personality. Write for the reader, not for you. Is the reader sociable or reserved, analytical or full of humor? Craft your message with the person's personality in mind.

(b) How well do you know the reader? Unless you know the person relatively well, use more formal communication. Ensure your writing style is appropriate for both the message and the reader.

(c) Take a cue from others' writing style. For example, if they respond with brief one-liners, you should know to write succinctly as well.

(d) Keep cultural differences in mind when writing. People from Latin countries, for example, tend to expect less formality in their communication than those from the Orient. If you correspond regularly with a particular cultural group, it is worth it to do some research and become knowledgeable about their sensitivities and norms. Ask a consultant, read literature about the culture, ask people who have had experience with that group.

(e) Consider the reader's level of understanding of the subject. If the person is not an expert, avoid technical jargon and use analogies or explanations to which they can relate.

(f) Ensure your vocabulary is appropriate to your readers. Ceremonious language use with the wrong audience can irritate and distract them, and you could be perceived as arrogant.

(g) Be conscious of the reader's position and status relative to you. Those in upper management have to read great volumes of information, so respect their time by writing succinctly and clearly. Focus on distilling your information down to the critical points.

4 | I often write based on what I feel at that moment/ I respond impulsively

Rethink

Emotional writing is appropriate in some situations, but rarely in a professional setting. In fact, it is risky to do so. Once your message is delivered the content and tone cannot be retracted, and apologies will not change that.

Lashing out impulsively in your writing, even if it is well deserved, only serves the purpose of letting you vent. Emotionally charged writing allows your feelings to overshadow a message that could have led to productive action.

React

(a) You may be inspired to write when you are emotional. Do put your thoughts into words, but do not distribute the message or document until you are feeling less affected. Give yourself time to read it again in a less emotional state and use the opportunity to edit the content and tone of the message. If possible, allow a day or two to pass, then revisit your thoughts and writing.

(b) Show what you have written to a trusted peer or two and get their perspective on whether it is appropriate.

(c) Try to identify your so-called red buttons. Self-awareness can help you to recognize when you react too sensitively and give you a chance to modify your message. Keep a log of the types of comments, situations or people that put you on edge and learn from it.

(d) If you must respond immediately, take a deep breath and try to calm down. While you write, remind yourself that the purpose of communication is to get your point across. Do so in an objective manner and try to understand the recipient's point of view. It may require a great deal of patience, be warned!

(e) If you are sensitive about a subject and wish to communicate your feelings, preferably arrange a personal meeting. Writing is often not an easy medium through which to express your emotions calmly and clearly.

5 | I often cannot find the right words

Rethink

You know what you want to say, but you cannot seem to find the right words to express yourself properly. This is particularly common among people with a strong technical focus, or those who have not had the opportunity or need to communicate much outside their field. Perhaps you are not working in your first language and struggle to find the right words or phrases. Whatever the reason, there are many ways to improve with just a bit of effort from you.

React

(a) Read as much as possible. Increase the amount of time you spend on reading — it is the only way to expose yourself to different styles of expression and enhance your vocabulary. Try to read diverse types of literature, for example, fiction, business journals, poetry, white papers. Take note of the vocabulary, metaphors and analogies which you can incorporate into your communication.

(b) Practice writing. Like any skill, it needs repeated application to improve. Keep a journal at home to get you in the habit of expressing your thoughts in writing, or take a creative writing course to stretch your imagination and abilities.

(c) Immediately consult the dictionary when you come across unfamiliar words. Memorize them and incorporate them in your written communication from now on. A good dictionary is an essential tool in every office, regardless of your position.

(d) Keep a Thesaurus close by to help you identify alternative words to use. There are many online Thesauruses and dictionaries available, but as a rule they are not as comprehensive as their printed counterparts.

(e) If you are not writing in your first language, ask a native speaker to help with phrases and word choices and how to translate what you mean.

Overdeveloped

Research has shown that strengths can become weaknesses because you can, in fact, do too much of a good thing. You cannot become less good at a competency in which you excel, but you can balance the behavior by developing a few Stabilizers to tone down an excessive strength.

Stabilizer	Overdeveloped
1 Achiever	Uses written communication when verbal communication may be more appropriate. Writing is too clinical, lacks emotion or takes too long to craft
15 Customer-Centric	
17 Demonstrates Good Judgment	
32 Informs Others	
35 Manages Conflict	
39 Manages Time	
4 Approachable	
45 Open	
49 Politically Astute	
9 Communicates Well (Verbal)	

Instructions

Read the definition. If it applies to you, choose a few Stabilizers and develop them by selecting the relevant chapter and following the Strategies for Action.

For more instructions see the How To Use This Book section.

11. Composed

> "Do not lose your inner peace for anything whatsoever,
> even if your whole world seems upset"
>
> St Francis de Sales

Well Developed

Remains calm under pressure

Underdeveloped

Becomes emotional when under pressure

Overdeveloped

Is seen as unemotional and cold, or unable to relate to emotional decisions or excitable situations

Instructions

Read the definitions on the left. If the Underdeveloped definition applies, go to the Strategies for Action section.

If the Overdeveloped definition applies, go to the end of the chapter.

Test Yourself

True	I do not take it personally when someone is upset
True	I do not show my emotions even if I am upset
True	I stay calm and collected even when under a lot of stress
True	People come to me when there is a crisis
True	I never have tantrums or become overly emotional in public

Note

Are you sure you need to develop this competency?

If the answer is "True" to most of the statements on the left, you probably do not need to develop this competency.

11 Composed

Strategies for Action

Most ineffective behaviors have an underlying thought or emotional pattern. By identifying these patterns, you can understand the impact they have and design strategies to counteract them.

① I am a very emotional person

② I lose my composure mostly when I am under too much stress or pressure

③ I have a short fuse/I get angry or defensive easily

④ I think it is important to let people know how I feel/I want to be honest

Instructions

1. Read and select one or more of the ineffective ways of thinking/feeling to the left.

2. Find the corresponding number below that will help you to rethink this pattern and identify specific and practical actions that you can take.

1 | I am a very emotional person

Rethink

Some people are very emotional and may want to cry when they are overcome with feelings. Women, in general, tend to be more affected by this and quicker to show their emotions than men. This generally applies to their personal lives, but it can spill over into professional settings.

Being highly emotional can help a person to be more empathetic, but it can also make it harder to remain emotionally neutral. Regardless of gender, being overly emotional in the workplace clearly has drawbacks. Even though you may be more sincere and open by displaying your emotions, it is likely to make people uncomfortable, for example, if you start to cry during an intense meeting or rant endlessly after you have been overlooked for promotion.

Being overly emotional distracts people from the issue at hand and, typically, marks the end of a productive discussion. Reacting with excessive emotion can also leave a bad impression of you that is difficult to undo. It becomes difficult to judge in which situations you can be counted on to remain composed. It can affect your credibility as a professional or as a person able to handle the pressures of leadership.

React

(a) Try to think more with your head than your heart. If you feel your emotions welling up, imagine how an emotionally detached person would approach the situation.

 (b) If you are feeling overwhelmed by your emotions, politely ask to take a quick break to collect your thoughts. Step outside the room or phone back in a few minutes. It is better to do this than break down in front of others.

 (c) If possible, take a day off to get perspective and let your emotions settle. It is remarkable how differently we see things after we have stepped away from the situation for a moment.

 (d) Focus on controlling your breathing by taking deep breaths. This is a very effective way to calm yourself.

 (e) Consider carefully to whom you are talking in a given situation. Not everyone expresses themselves through emotion or may be comfortable around people that are emotionally expressive. Instead of getting sympathy or support, you may put people off.

 (f) Make sure you have outlets for your feelings outside of work. Trusted friends, family members, a coach or counselor can provide you with a productive outlet for your emotions.

2 | I lose my composure mostly when I am under too much stress or pressure

Rethink

A person can be the picture of composure when their environment is under control, but when the pressure is on their behavior changes drastically. Stress can bring out the worst in someone very quickly, for example, snapping at others, irritability, bossy or controlling behavior and making illogical decisions. Staying calm and composed allows you to stay focused on solutions.

 Certain professions depend on the ability to stay composed under pressure. Emergency-room doctors and firemen, for example, who must face life-or-death situations, must stay clear-headed and make quick decisions despite the stress. Likewise, people in organizations look for direction from — and respect — individuals who can remain composed when things seem to be at their worst.

 It may not be possible to control a situation, but you do have a choice in how you react to the problem.

React

(a) When you feel you are losing your composure, try deep-breathing exercises, an effective way to slow down the body's adrenaline response to stress. There are many techniques for breathing that you can practice daily.

(b) Research has shown that stress can negatively affect the clarity of our thinking. Sometimes it is necessary to get away. Take a short break to clear your head. Take a walk or go to lunch, whatever is necessary to leave the situation behind. This will not change the situation but will give you a chance to collect yourself.

(c) Take action. Write down the steps that must be taken to resolve the problem. Focus on the priority items.

(d) Ask for help before you blow a fuse. Under stress we often forget that there are other resources available. Do not assume you have to do it all yourself. Engage other people to help. Just talking to someone about the stress you are under can be cathartic.

(e) Model your behavior on that of a respected peer or person who is skilled at staying calm under pressure. Ask them how they succeed in doing it.

(f) Use a tool such as the Birkman personality assessment.The information it provides delivers insight into your underlying needs and associated stress behavior, based on 11 behavioral components. Just being aware of these reactions allows you to adopt better attitudes and more productive behavior. A certified consultant can help you to interpret the results.

3 | I have a short fuse/I get angry or defensive easily

Rethink

Protecting ourselves is innate to being human, a coping mechanism for defense from perceived threat or attack. But when this emotion is mismanaged it becomes disruptive and possibly even hazardous in the workplace.

Lacking insight about situations or people predisposes a person to react with anger or ways that are disrespectful to others. Leaders must be able to talk about differences rationally and, when conflicts arise, they must remain composed by drawing on their insight to enable positive cooperation.

React

(a) Give yourself a few minutes before speaking to consider the consequences of your reaction. You may feel like you have evened the score or brought justice to the situation, but once you have said hurtful or unfair words the damage cannot be undone, only forgiven.

(b) Apologize for your outburst immediately. This is difficult to do while you are angry, but if you recognize that your behavior was inappropriate and take responsibility for it people are usually willing to continue engaging with you.

(c) Consider your attitudes and expectations of others and situations. If they are inappropriate or unrealistic, you are setting yourself up for emotional frustration and, possibly, conflict.

(d) Even when the other person makes it difficult for you to respect them by provoking you, you will need to disengage yourself from their comments and value the person. Unless you do so, you will never be able to re-engage them in cooperative behavior.

(e) When you are provoked, first try to put yourself in the other person's shoes. Whether the accusation or situation is fair or not, try to understand the reasons or motives behind the comments. Use comments such as "I understand how you might feel that way" to defuse the situation and calm both of you.

(f) Adopt some form of daily relaxation technique to manage your tension and frustration. Exercise, meditate, do yoga or get a hobby that brings you peace.

(g) Share your thoughts and talk your issues through with a trusted peer or friend. This has great therapeutic advantages.

(h) Identify the particular triggers that make you defensive or produce an anger response. Know that you will need to remain particularly patient when exposed to those situations, people or topics.

(i) Try an anger management course if you are aware that your behavior is negatively affecting your relationships at work or in your personal life.

4 | I think it is important to let people know how I feel/ I want to be honest

Rethink

You can be frank and direct with others about how you feel, but you will lose your audience if your emotions are louder than your words. Staying composed does not mean you care or feel less strongly about an issue. In fact, your ability to stay composed despite strong feelings and deliver an honest message without insulting others shows that you are willing to set aside your own convictions to address an issue that is important to you.

React

(a) Be respectful of whom you are talking to. It may be important for you to be expressive and painfully honest at home or with a co-worker, but more than likely you will want to edit what you say when speaking to clients or a superior.

(b) Before speaking, ask yourself how the other person would want to hear what you have to say. Some people need others to be direct and to the point; others require more concern about their feelings and a more diplomatic style of expression.

(c) Defend what you believe in with well-considered discussion, evidence to support your point of view and personal example, not through emotion.

Overdeveloped

Research has shown that strengths can become weaknesses because you can, in fact, do too much of a good thing. You cannot become less good at a competency in which you excel, but you can balance the behavior by developing a few Stabilizers to tone down an excessive strength.

Stabilizer	Overdeveloped
44 Networked	Is seen as unemotional and cold, or unable to relate to emotional decisions or excitable situations
27 Experimental	
24 Empathetic	
32 Informs Others	
4 Approachable	
45 Open	
43 Motivates People	
59 Unifies People	
2 Adaptable	
9 Communicates Well (Verbal)	

Instructions

Read the definition. If it applies to you, choose a few Stabilizers and develop them by selecting the relevant chapter and following the Strategies for Action.

For more instructions see the How To Use This Book section.

12. Confident

> "Nothing can make you feel inferior without your consent"
>
> Eleanor Roosevelt

Well Developed

Is confident when interacting with others, even those with greater authority

Underdeveloped

Lacks confidence and becomes insecure in the presence of others

Overdeveloped

Is seen as arrogant or overly confident

Instructions

Read the definitions on the left. If the Underdeveloped definition applies, go to the Strategies for Action section.

If the Overdeveloped definition applies, go to the end of the chapter.

Test Yourself

True	I am comfortable expressing myself in front of others
True	I set realistic standards for myself
True	I stick to my decisions once I have made them
True	I do not assume things are always my fault
True	I believe I am competent in what I do
True	Mostly, I have a "can do" attitude
True	I am not embarrassed easily

Note

Are you sure you need to develop this competency?

If the answer is "True" to most of the statements on the left, you probably do not need to develop this competency.

12 Confident

Strategies for Action

Most ineffective behaviors have an underlying thought or emotional pattern. By identifying these patterns, you can understand the impact they have and design strategies to counteract them.

① I do not have the right experience/Others know more than I do

② I am concerned about making a mistake/I want things to be perfect

③ I get overly anxious around specific people or in certain situations

④ I get embarrassed easily/I worry about looking foolish

Instructions

1. Read and select one or more of the ineffective ways of thinking/feeling to the left.

2. Find the corresponding number below that will help you to rethink this pattern and identify specific and practical actions that you can take.

---

1 | I do not have the right experience/Others know more than I do

Rethink

There is a saying that experience is something you gain one minute after you needed it. Nobody takes up a new position or embarks on a new assignment knowing everything about it.

Getting comfortable with managing a learning curve is important to preserve your confidence and sanity. There is always a bottom in the learning curve, before you master a new subject, where you will feel overwhelmed and possibly even lost. It happens to all learners. But the next time you find yourself at that point, you will have greater confidence.

Become used to being surrounded by others who know more than you. If you know more than everyone else, it limits your opportunities to grow.

Expect to be a student eager and willing to learn and tackle the learning curve throughout your career.

React

(a) Others may know more than you in some areas, but every person brings both strengths and weaknesses to their jobs. Promote your strengths by identifying the parts of a project to which you can add most value. If you are a good problem solver, for example, but are not familiar with the subject, you can still help the team to organize their ideas logically and add value by asking questions from an outsider's perspective. Which strengths do you add, regardless of your assignment?

80

(b) Roll up your sleeves and jump in. Nothing will give you more confidence than mastering what you did not know. Become involved in projects and assignments that will help you to gain knowledge in the areas in which you are least confident. Many companies have rotation opportunities for employees to work in different areas of the organization. Ask for assignments that are different from what you have mastered.

(c) Engage with people who know more than you or are experts in a particular field. Instead of comparing yourself to them, choose to learn from them.

(d) Do not pretend to know what you do not. It is perfectly acceptable that you are not an expert in everything. Defer questions you cannot answer to someone who can, or do your research and get back to the person. People appreciate honesty and will have more respect for you if you do not mislead them.

(e) Be a student. Accept the role of asking many questions.

(f) Do not give up at the moment things get particularly difficult or confusing. It is part of the learning process and the stage in which most people lose confidence.

(g) Ask to be included in meetings and conference calls even when you are not going to participate. The exposure is invaluable in getting comfortable with different settings and building confidence.

2 | I am concerned about making a mistake/I want things to be perfect

Rethink

Every mistake provides an opportunity to learn and develop. If they are being honest, most successful people will admit that they did not achieve their position without making mistakes.

A mistake is just a consequence of a choice or series of decisions — it does not define who you are and certainly should not end an otherwise successful career.

Worrying about what could possible go wrong is psychologically exhausting. A study in *Clinical Psychology & Psychotherapy* found that 85% of the things we worry about never occur!

It is important to set high standards for your work, but perfect is not a standard. It is a frame of mind that sets impossible goals and places unnecessary pressure on you. If everything you do has to be perfect, it can be too daunting to start anything at all. Perfectionism often paralyzes people and robs them of the confidence they need to tackle a project or task. Reframe you thinking. Getting things done in the best way you can is healthier and still sets high standards.

React

(a) Positive affirmation can help you to rewire your thinking. Be vigilant about negative thoughts and practice to replace them with positive thinking.

(b) Identify someone you admire for their self-confidence and discuss how they view the world. Note the differences in their views and yours.

(c) Do not place more importance on mistakes than they deserve. Write down the worst-case scenario. Unless someone's life is threatened, the consequences are really not as bad as you think.

(d) Read about the many famous people in history who were undeterred by their mistakes and went on to change the world. For example, Thomas Edison experienced 10 000 failures before perfecting the light bulb. It is a good thing that he had the confidence to continue after the first few hundred mistakes!

(e) You cannot predict anything100% correctly or control things fully. Make a list of the things over which you do have control versus the things you do not. Make peace with a balance between the two and focus only on the things you can control. For example, do your home work on the topic, rehearse your speech, become familiar with the setting in which you will be presenting it, get to know individuals in the meeting before the big day, and so forth. You have then done your part and the rest is beyond your control.

(f) Stop thinking too much about how things will be done and focus on getting started instead. Trust that the process will resolve itself. Choose something you have been putting off and tackle it today.

(g) Team up with someone who is action-oriented to help you get started and give you support.

(h) Remember that most projects have strict deadlines and always take longer to complete than you expected, so consider that when framing timelines.

(i) Prioritize your time. Some things require a great deal of attention and detail and others do not. For example, spending time to perfect an e-mail to a peer is unnecessary, but doing it to examine a contract carefully is time well spent.

3 | I get overly anxious around specific people or in certain situations

Rethink

Are you generally a confident person, except when exposed to specific people, groups or situations? Some people may be adept at conducting meetings, but presenting to large audiences terrify them. Others are comfortable interacting with peers but become self-conscious or nervous in the company of management.

A lack of confidence is often specific to situations or a certain context. If you are not constantly subjected to a situation that creates anxiety, it may appear to be manageable. But why wait until that situation appears to deal with it?

A sudden promotion or reassignment can change your context and suddenly create anxiety.

React

a) Exposing yourself to the situations or people that make you fearful is the best way to address your anxiety and gain confidence. The more exposure you have to these situations, the more you will raise your comfort level. Find ways to participate, if only minimally at first, in these kind of settings.

(b) Share your anxiety. Find someone who can give you support in times when you are most anxious. For example, if you do not like being in large groups but need to attend a networking function, find a co-worker who enjoys socializing to accompany you.

(c) If you are uncomfortable around those with greater authority, make a conscious effort to try to get to know them on a more personal level. It will help to challenge your assumptions about them and see them as individuals instead of authority figures. Talk to individuals while you are waiting for meetings to start; attend social gatherings that allow you to interact in a relaxed manner; gain insight into people by asking others what they think of them.

(d) Ask a professional counselor for techniques to relax and reduce anxiety. Breathing exercises, bio-feedback, visualization and hypnosis are just a few of the tools available to you.

---

4 | I get embarrassed easily/I worry about looking foolish

Rethink

Getting noticed despite a few mistakes is preferable to not being noticed at all. Do not allow a fear of looking foolish to stop you from participating. Often, we are our own harshest critics and we worry about things which most people in the audience would not even consider.

React

(a) Positive affirmation can help you to rewire your thinking. Be vigilant about negative thoughts and practice to replace them with positive thinking.

(b) Consider how you would react if someone else slipped up in front of you. You would not crucify them. We tend to be hardest on ourselves. When you look around the room, remind yourself that people leave room for mistakes and are more empathetic than you think.

(c) Get feedback about how your presentation went or how well your work turned out. Because you are your own worst critic, others can provide a more realistic perspective.

(d) Use your sense of humor and practice poking fun at yourself, even in public. It is an easy way to connect with others and take pressure off you. How many times have you looked at situations and found their funny sides in hindsight? Try using that perspective in the present.

(e) Focus on the issues or problem instead of yourself.

Overdeveloped

Research has shown that strengths can become weaknesses because you can, in fact, do too much of a good thing. You cannot become less good at a competency in which you excel, but you can balance the behavior by developing a few Stabilizers to tone down an excessive strength.

Stabilizer	Overdeveloped
41 Modest	Is seen as arrogant or overly confident
4 Approachable	
7 Collaborative	
2 Adaptable	
43 Motivates People	
52 Self-Aware	
46 Open-Minded	
22 Diplomatic	
47 Patient	
24 Empathetic	

Instructions

Read the definition. If it applies to you, choose a few Stabilizers and develop them by selecting the relevant chapter and following the Strategies for Action.

For more instructions see the How To Use This Book section.

13. Courageous

"I must stand up in search of the truth. If I don't, I only roll with the flow of the lie and make it stronger"

Anonymous

Well Developed
Challenges the status quo and is willing to speak out, even at great personal risk

Underdeveloped
Avoids communicating certain information, fearing the consequences

Overdeveloped
Is seen as aggressive and uncooperative or too critical

Instructions

Read the definitions on the left. If the Underdeveloped definition applies, go to the Strategies for Action section.

If the Overdeveloped definition applies, go to the end of the chapter.

Test Yourself

True	I feel comfortable to offer a dissenting opinion
True	I speak up when something has to be said; I do not wait until the last minute
True	I do not take it personally when people disagree with me
True	I do not follow the crowd when I believe otherwise
True	I am honest with people even if they will not like what I have to say
True	I have stood up before for something in which I believed

Note

Are you sure you need to develop this competency?

If the answer is "True" to most of the statements on the left, you probably do not need to develop this competency.

85

Strategies for Action

Most ineffective behaviors have an underlying thought or emotional pattern. By identifying these patterns, you can understand the impact they have and design strategies to counteract them.

(1) I do not want to be seen as a troublemaker/It is more important to get along than to stand my ground

(2) My position or opinion may be wrong

(3) Speaking up will not make much of a difference/No one is really listening anyway

(4) I get anxious or fearful when I challenge superiors

(5) I get too emotional when I stand firm/I do not know how to be courageous without being contentious

Instructions

1. Read and select one or more of the ineffective ways of thinking/feeling to the left.

2. Find the corresponding number below that will help you to rethink this pattern and identify specific and practical actions that you can take.

---

1 | I do not want to be seen as a troublemaker/It is more important to get along than to stand my ground

Rethink

Challenging the status quo can cause conflict but you should not allow this to silence your voice, unless you are simply being argumentative.

Open and honest communication is the blood supply of any organization. It must be encouraged by the company's culture and practiced by its individuals.

The path of least resistance may be to follow the norm, but it is not always the appropriate course of action.

Perhaps you feel you would jeopardize your relationship with peers or a supervisor by taking an opposing stand, or be seen as uncooperative. However, if your motives are based on a genuine interest to improve the status quo, your efforts will be respected.

Can you afford the risk of not contributing new ideas or improving processes because it will generate debate?

Leaders attain greatness because they have stood up for what they believed in, even if it meant not pleasing everyone.

React

(a) Choose your battles wisely. As long as you are not a habitual challenger of every opinion, you will not be labeled a troublemaker.

(b) Are you being too diplomatic? Be sure not to sugarcoat things to the extent that no one gets your point. People need to see your conviction and passion.

(c) If debate or uncertainty persists, take a vote and be the arbitrator when necessary.

(d) If you must voice extremely sensitive information or have concerns about unethical behavior but do not feel comfortable doing so on your own, consult the human resources department for the best course of action.

2 | My position or opinion may be wrong

Rethink

You assume your input will have a negative outcome if you speak out or stand firm on a decision that may turn out to be wrong. But courage will inevitably involve standing up for something in which you believe — despite the consequences.

There is always the likelihood that your position will not be adopted, but it will play some role in shaping the final decision. It is important to let your voice be heard.

React

(a) Treat what you have to say as important and give people the opportunity to hear you out.

(b) Prepare yourself well and know your topic. People may not agree with you, but they will respect a knowledgeable opinion.

(c) Instead of focusing on whether you are going to look bad, consider the consequences of not speaking out.

(d) Share your thoughts with a trusted peer or mentor. It can help to gain you confidence in your opinions and decisions.

3 | Speaking up will not make much of a difference/ No one is really listening anyway

Rethink

Have you resigned yourself to not getting involved? You may feel frustrated about processes moving too slow; perhaps your input has not been considered seriously in the past; or you are not confident that available resources can bring about change.

Whatever the reason, adopting a "why bother" attitude makes you part of the problem instead of the solution. It is exactly this culture that could benefit most from persistent challenging of the status quo.

It may take a while before your influence results in change, but keeping silent will guarantee that things just stay the same. Acting as if a problem does not exist does not make it go away.

React

(a) Instead of trying to challenge everything that needs attention, choose what you believe needs improvement most. What would have the biggest impact? Focusing on these issues will give you greater resolve when you are met with disinterest or resistance.

(b) If the issue is too big to challenge at once, break it down into smaller parts and stay focused on challenging one aspect at a time.

(c) Is someone else struggling to challenge the status quo? Lend them your support and find strength in numbers. Try to motivate others to join you in voicing your objections.

(d) You may be wasting energy if you do not understand the politics of an issue. Become more politically astute. Knowing the right person to engage for help to facilitate change will get you much further with less effort. If your stance is not well received, who else is there to listen to your opinion? Have you engaged the key decision makers? Think strategically about the people with whom you raise objections or concerns.

4 | I get anxious or fearful when I challenge superiors

Rethink

It may be normal to challenge your peers and team members, but challenging those in authority makes most people uncomfortable. But despite their greater knowledge and experience, your superiors have the capacity to learn. Remember that a fresh perspective is typically welcomed and could be highly valued, even if resisted at first.

It helps to raise your visibility when you are unafraid to challenge people in authority. Those who speak up are remembered.

React

(a) Expect and prepare for resistance from people with more experience or authority. Write down responses to the objections you anticipate. Preparation will give you the confidence to manage opposition. Rehearse the debate with trusted peers — there may be positions you have not considered for which you should be prepared.

(b) Outline your reasons well. If the person becomes defensive about being challenged, keep on redirecting the conversation back to the goal you want to achieve.

(c) Get to know authority figures who make you feel anxious. Knowing people better helps to dispel anxieties. Attend company parties where you can interact with them or ask others who know them.

(d) After you have presented your case, you may need to approach the subject again. You have the right to follow up more than once if you feel you are not being heard or the issue remains unresolved.

(e) Time your challenge carefully. Typically, authority figures are extremely busy and the wrong timing may harm how your input is received. Try to find a time when the person is less busy and schedule a meeting, if possible, to ensure you receive undivided attention.

5 | I get too emotional when I stand firm/I do not know how to be courageous without being contentious

Rethink

A courageous stand can become arrogant or disrespectful when a person is emotionally charged. Remember that people may respond negatively to your attitude, not your opinion.

One can quickly develop a reputation for being contentious, which discourages others from including or even seeking your opinion.

React

(a) Diplomacy is the key to not offending others when you stand firm on your opinion. Be honest but tactful. Acknowledge the current situation and make reference to what is working well.

(b) Speak in a calm, non-confrontational tone. It will encourage your audience to be more receptive and open to considering your position. Apologize if you have raised your voice.

(c) It is good to be passionate about your beliefs, but it is more important that you are able to articulate them well. Ensure you are thoroughly prepared for logical argument when challenging others. Prepare a business case if appropriate and outline the reasons why your position makes sense.

(d) Offer solutions when you challenge the status quo. Offering alternatives adds real value to the discussion and demonstrates your problem-solving skills.

(e) Just like you, most people are likely to defend their turf. Expect others to be argumentative and realize they are just as passionate as you are about the issue. Remain patient and agreeable and hear people out. They will find it harder to be aggressive with someone who is composed.

Overdeveloped

Research has shown that strengths can become weaknesses because you can, in fact, do too much of a good thing. You cannot become less good at a competency in which you excel, but you can balance the behavior by developing a few Stabilizers to tone down an excessive strength.

Stabilizer	Overdeveloped
11 Composed	Is seen as aggressive and uncooperative or too critical
46 Open-Minded	
22 Diplomatic	
24 Empathetic	
34 Listens Well	
35 Manages Conflict	
4 Approachable	
43 Motivates People	
7 Collaborative	
41 Modest	

Instructions

Read the definition. If it applies to you, choose a few Stabilizers and develop them by selecting the relevant chapter and following the Strategies for Action.

For more instructions see the How To Use This Book section.

14. Creative

> "Creativity requires the courage to let go
> of certainties"
>
> Erich Fromm

Well Developed
Creates many new ideas by seeing new connections between different and sometimes unrelated concepts

Underdeveloped
Is unable to create new or novel ideas by thinking beyond the obvious

Overdeveloped
Ideas could be too outrageous to be useful. Wants to reinvent everything when tried-and-tested approaches are more appropriate

Instructions

Read the definitions on the left. If the Underdeveloped definition applies, go to the Strategies for Action section.

If the Overdeveloped definition applies, go to the end of the chapter.

Creative

14

Test Yourself

True	I enjoy brainstorming and have many ideas to share during sessions
True	I like thinking about novel ways of doing things
True	I routinely entertain "what if" scenarios in my mind
True	I look for multiple solutions to a problem
True	I like to speculate and reflect
True	People tend to approach me for new ideas

Note

Are you sure you need to develop this competency?

If the answer is "True" to most of the statements on the left, you probably do not need to develop this competency.

Strategies for Action

Most ineffective behaviors have an underlying thought or emotional pattern. By identifying these patterns, you can understand the impact they have and design strategies to counteract them.

① I am a practical person/I am not the creative type

② I tend to fall back on what is familiar to me or what I already know

③ I believe people are continuously trying to reinvent the wheel

④ My work environment is very process driven and discourages creativity

Instructions

1. Read and select one or more of the ineffective ways of thinking/feeling to the

2. Find the corresponding number below that will help you to rethink this pattern and identify specific and practical actions that you

---

1 | I am a practical person/I am not the creative type

Rethink

There is creativity in everyone, even the most practically inclined among us. Being more creative can be as simple as allowing yourself the freedom to contemplate all possibilities, even the impractical ones. Although a practical approach is typically the most efficient, it may steer you from opportunities to stand out and add value in ways previously untapped.

During periods of innovation and fast growth, for example, creativity may supercede efficiency.

Try to achieve a mentality that allows you to engage in both creative and practical solutions and ideas.

The capacity to entertain both perspectives will increase your value to the organization.

React

(a) If you get an impulse to act, do it without too much thought or judgment. Try to act spontaneously at least once every week. Forget about whether it is practical or not.

(b) Spark your creativity by routinely asking yourself "what if" questions.

(c) Challenge your practical nature by contemplating simple scenarios involving your personal life: "What if I took a vacation next week to that place I have always wanted to go?" Notice the kind of negative thoughts or objections that instantly appear. Which objections are impossible to overcome? Do the same when thinking about solutions at work. An idea may seem impractical at first, but look more closely at the validity of your objections to it.

(d) Collect new ideas; ask others what their approach would be.

(e) Use an incremental approach to creativity. Not everything has to be done radically different — perhaps you can concentrate on one or two areas first.

(f) Ensure there are creative people in your team.

(g) Become involved in hobbies that encourage the use of imagery and the creative side of your brain, such as art classes or photography.

(h) Spend more time with creative people.

2. I tend to fall back on what is familiar to me or what I already know

Rethink

Past experience provides a fine well from which to draw inspiration, but it can also be a damper that prevents new, creative ideas from being heard. Remaining open to new possibilities and better ways of doing things, even if your method or approach has worked well for you, is important.

The more experience you have, the more aware you must be that you may be caught up in old patterns and habits.

Remember there is always more than one way to solve a problem or address an issue — do not limit yourself to your most comfortably familiar ways.

React

(a) Allow yourself time to reconsider an idea that has not been realized in the past. If you are impatient, you do not give creative, novel ideas time to form.

(b) Make a pact with yourself to not take a decision until you have entertained at least three different approaches.

(c) Choose, on purpose, to use a different, unfamiliar technique or methodology every once in a while.

(d) Partner with someone who is creative and can encourage you to think outside the box.

(e) Let others give their ideas before you offer yours.

(f) Opt for quantity instead of quality. The more ideas generated the more likely something innovative is to emerge. You want to collect as many ideas as possible.

(g) Keep ahead of the pack. Seek training and attend conferences that showcase the latest technology or trends in your industry.

(h) Be sure to balance your team with creative, innovative thinkers.

Rethink

Are you feeling frustrated by the continuous push to reinvent, repackage and resell? Well, that is how organizations remain competitive. It is necessary to continually tinker with products and services to stay abreast of changing consumer needs and trends.

Internal processes and policies are subject to constant redesign and adjustments too. And although some people spend too much time trying to reinvent the wheel, tinkering should be encouraged. If not, the organization has grown stagnant.

Some industries allocate a sizeable portion of budgets to research and development, and the ability to be creative and treat the common in uncommon terms is critical. But be sure to differentiate between wasting time and a genuine opportunity to improve a process, product or service.

React

(a) Create a list that identifies possible improvements in the item or issue at hand. It will make you more receptive to the need for change.

(b) From your perspective things may be working fine, but ask other people — even outside your team — what they perceive as problematic and why something needs to be redesigned.

(c) Try to suspend judgment, not only of others' ideas but also your own. Refrain from using statements such as "It's a good idea but ..." or "I don't think it is realistic…" Instead, withhold commentary until you have digested the idea. It will give you time to properly consider the possibilities and implications before making a judgment.

(d) Let someone else practice pitching their idea to you. The stronger their argument the more likely you are to be receptive to it. This will benefit both of you. Remember to remain open-minded.

4 | My work environment is very process driven and discourages creativity

Rethink

It can be challenging to express and develop your creativity when the environment in which you operate does not actively encourage it. The organization may value tradition; perhaps the industry is process driven; or the boss may be a linear thinker. Still, every organization can benefit from creative thinking.

Even in the most receptive of settings, some resistance can be expected when new ideas are introduced. In this type of environment it may not be enough to have creative thoughts — you may need to be creative about introducing and selling them as well.

React

(a) Find alternative ways to communicate your ideas if a group setting prohibits your creativity. Discuss your ideas individually with your mentor or team leader instead. Sharing your thoughts is more productive than keeping them to yourself.

(b) Try to become comfortable selling or promoting your ideas. Practice with a peer or someone with whom you feel comfortable. Note their objections. Each time you talk to another person, your pitch will become stronger. You just have to convince the right person who can champion your ideas.

(c) Grow a habit to float ideas by people with whom you feel comfortable. Do not discount ideas before you have done so. You may not think they are worthwhile, but let others be your sounding board.

(d) Translate your creativity into the language of business. Put together a business scenario that details the idea as thoroughly as possible. Define the problem, what went wrong previously, your solution, the return on investment etcetera. Your ideas are more likely to be credible if they are well organized and presented in a way that clearly demonstrates their benefit.

(e) Even if it is not encouraged by other managers, promote and reward creativity in your team.

Overdeveloped

Research has shown that strengths can become weaknesses because you can, in fact, do too much of a good thing. You cannot become less good at a competency in which you excel, but you can balance the behavior by developing a few Stabilizers to tone down an excessive strength.

Stabilizer	Overdeveloped
1 Achiever	Ideas could be too outrageous to be useful. Wants to reinvent everything when tried-and-tested approaches are more appropriate
17 Demonstrates Good Judgment	
18 Detail-Orientated	
29 Focused on Priorities	
36 Manages Ideas	
40 Market Aware	
48 Plans Work	
50 Problem Solver	
56 Technically Competent	
6 Bright	

Instructions

Read the definition. If it applies to you, choose a few Stabilizers and develop them by selecting the relevant chapter and following the Strategies for Action.

For more instructions see the How To Use This Book section.

15. Customer-Centric

> "It is the customer that pays the wages"
> Henry Ford

Well Developed
Builds relationships with and delivers services to both internal and external customers, with a focus on their needs

Underdeveloped
Is unable to relate well to customers and recognize their needs, or appears unwilling to act as such

Overdeveloped
Wants to accommodate unreasonable or inappropriate customer needs without consideration for the broader business issues

Instructions
Read the definitions on the left. If the Underdeveloped definition applies, go to the Strategies for Action section.

If the Overdeveloped definition applies, go to the end of the chapter.

Test Yourself

True	I keep my customers in mind when making my decisions
True	I communicate frequently with my customers
True	Satisfying my customers is a priority
True	I solicit information from my customers to help me to improve my service
True	I try to keep my customers excited about our products and services

Note

Are you sure you need to develop this competency?

If the answer is "True" to most of the statements on the left, you probably do not need to develop this competency.

Strategies for Action

Most ineffective behaviors have an underlying thought or emotional pattern. By identifying these patterns, you can understand the impact they have and design strategies to counteract them.

① I dislike my customer/There is no pleasing the customer

② I already know what the customer needs

③ I do not deal directly with clients/It is not my job

④ I have too many other demands/I have more important concerns

⑤ Once I close the deal, I lose interest in the customer

Instructions

1. Read and select one or more of the ineffective ways of thinking/feeling to the left.

2. Find the corresponding number below that will help you to rethink this pattern and identify specific and practical actions that you can take.

1 | I dislike my customer/There is no pleasing the customer

Rethink

Usually, you only hear from customers when they are dissatisfied or experience a problem. It is difficult to listen to people's criticism, particularly if it is unfair and delivered rudely or in an unacceptable manner. Nonetheless, being customer-centric means listening to complaints as well as compliments.

It is ideal if you like your customers, but it is far more important that you remain attentive and understand your customers' needs at all times, provide acceptable solutions when problems arise, and remain pleasant and professional even when they are not.

You may very well find that customers are more appreciative and cooperative when you are patient and prepared to listen to their grievances.

React

(a) You may have to sift through emotions and irrelevant information before you can provide a desirable solution for your customer. Listen carefully and restate the customer's request to ensure you have understood the problem correctly. This could take a while because the customer might not even know what they need.

(b) Remain patient and composed, even beyond what you may deem reasonable. Your first response will set the tone for the rest of the conversation. Patience allows you to hear the customer properly and avoid incorrect conclusions.

98

(c) Put yourself in their shoes and try to empathize with the reasons why they are upset. Restate their request to let them know you have understood. You may be defensive at first, but if you can understand why the client is feeling a certain way it will help to manage your emotions more effectively.

(d) Be creative with your solutions. There may be strict policies and procedures for assisting the customer, but creative alternatives can often accommodate their needs. People appreciate and remember that you have gone the extra mile to accommodate them.

(e) Perhaps your processes or products need improvement and not your client's attitude. Track repeated requests from customers and use the information to improve where needed.

(f) If the relationship with your customer is costing more than the benefit it creates, consider the pros and cons of continuing the relationship. Sometimes it is not worth the resources to continue.

2 | I already know what the customer needs

Rethink

You may have worked with your customers for a while and share good, established relationships, but their needs can change quickly. Failing to recognize their dynamic needs opens the door to competitors. What may have been the best option previously may now be less suitable.

Customers' loyalty depends on your ability to anticipate and accommodate their position. Remember, there is rarely one best product or service for all clients, so generalizations about their needs can be dangerous.

Always test your assumptions because they may reflect your vision and not your client's. Finally, do not expect customers to adapt to your products or processes — it works the other way round.

React

(a) Be highly attentive to information that can help you to anticipate future needs. Routinely generate conversations with clients about changes they experience in their market that will have an impact on them. These conversations can lead to ideas for new products or services which you would not have thought of without listening to their needs.

(b) Schedule customer calls on your calendar as part of your responsibilities. Habitually engage with your customers.

(c) If appropriate, use formal feedback techniques such as questionnaires to collect information about your clients' needs.

(d) Utilize client focus groups and feedback to test ideas before investing too much time and resources.

(e) Ask your clients about their likes and dislikes regarding both your product or services and your processes.

3 | I do not deal directly with clients/It is not my job

Rethink

You do not have to have direct contact with a client to have an impact on customer service. For example, you may not be handling the customer service call itself, but you could be more client-centric by improving the processes and procedures your company uses to handle customer calls.

Every person in the organization ultimately has an impact on the client, and it is vital for an organization that all employees have a customer-focused mindset and continually relate their work to their customers.

React

(a) Become familiar with the company's client base and the changes in trends that will affect clients' profiles, as well as new clients the company may be pursuing in the future.

(b) Try to identify and improve any process that has an impact on the client.

(c) You have both external and internal clients. Examine the quality of your relationship with people in other departments that count on you for information or to get their work done.

4 | I have too many other demands/I have more important concerns

Rethink

You may feel there is barely enough time to get through your daily workload. Remember, however, that all your work demands are ultimately driven by customers willing to pay for your product or service.

If your customer goes away your job disappears too, so it makes sense to prioritize customer focus regardless of your daily grind.

React

(a) Investigate how your work can be reorganized to make time to attend to your customers.

(b) Ensure that customers can reach you. Provide enough avenues for them to get in touch with you at all times, and alternatives if you are out of the office often.

(c) Set a policy for acceptable response times and monitor how compliant you and your team are.

(d) If there is absolutely no time available for managing your client relationships, talk to the relevant person about helping you reset priorities and getting assistance with your workload.

Rethink

Some people maintain high standards of customer service during clients' courting stage, but once they have committed and the deal is closed the standards drop or are neglected. This is risky practice for any business. Why waste the hard work it took to get their commitment because you lack proper follow-through?

Many organizations are heavily dependent on growth through referrals or repeat business, so maintaining or increasing customer service quality after the deal is closed is vital.

Good relationships require attention and care as long as they exist.

Remember, a customer will remain loyal as long as you continue to take care of them and have their best interests at heart.

React

(a) Apply the same set of standards to new and existing clients.

(b) What are the company's values? Is your behavior compatible with them?

(c) Team up with other people who can help you to manage the client's ongoing needs if, for example, you must focus on enlarging the client base. Even if you are removed from follow-up responsibilities, occasionally check the client's status. If you closed the deal, your name and reputation will always be linked to that client.

(d) Weigh the consequences of enlarging versus simply providing the promised services to your existing and new client base. What kind of additional resources and investments will be necessary to support growth? Is customer satisfaction as much of a priority as profit? The two are interdependent.

(e) Try to take equal or greater interest and pride in not only landing the customer, but keeping them satisfied in the long term. The latter is arguably a bigger challenge.

Overdeveloped

Research has shown that strengths can become weaknesses because you can, in fact, do too much of a good thing. You cannot become less good at a competency in which you excel, but you can balance the behavior by developing a few Stabilizers to tone down an excessive strength.

Stabilizer	Overdeveloped
1 Achiever	Wants to accommodate unreasonable or inappropriate customer needs without consideration for the broader business issues
13 Courageous	
29 Focused On Priorities	
12 Confident	
35 Manages Conflict	
42 Monitors Work	
48 Plans Work	
50 Problem Solver	
30 Global Thinker	
39 Manages Time	

Instructions

Read the definition. If it applies to you, choose a few Stabilizers and develop them by selecting the relevant chapter and following the Strategies for Action.

For more instructions see the How To Use This Book section.

16. Decisive

"It's better to be boldly decisive and risk being wrong than to agonize at length and be right too late"

Mary Moats Kennedy

Well Developed

Makes decisions quickly, even in the absence of complete data

Underdeveloped

Takes too long to make decisions and procrastinates or delays taking action

Overdeveloped

Is seen as impulsive and jumps to conclusions with too little consideration of important data

Instructions

Read the definitions on the left. If the Underdeveloped definition applies, go to the Strategies for Action section.

If the Overdeveloped definition applies, go to the end of the chapter.

Test Yourself

True	I do not regret decisions once they are made
True	I do not need an extensive amount of information to make a decision
True	I do not put off unpleasant decisions
True	I regularly meet my deadlines
True	I do not need many people's involvement to make a decision
True	I do not worry excessively about the consequences of my decision

Note

Are you sure you need to develop this competency?

If the answer is "True" to most of the statements on the left, you probably do not need to develop this competency.

16 Decisive

Strategies for Action

Most ineffective behaviors have an underlying thought or emotional pattern. By identifying these patterns, you can understand the impact they have and design strategies to counteract them.

① I want all options researched before I make a decision/It is more important to be right than quick

② I do not want to make the wrong decision/I worry too much about the impact

③ I need to finish one thing at a time/I am not good at multitasking

④ Decisions should involve all stakeholders/I want collective buy-in before making a decision

Instructions

1. Read and select one or more of the ineffective ways of thinking/feeling to the left.

2. Find the corresponding number below that will help you to rethink this pattern and identify specific and practical actions that you can take.

---

1 | I want all options researched before I make a decision/It is more important to be right than quick

Rethink

To collect information prior to making a decision is definitely important, but it is not realistic to expect to gather all possible options. In fact, your intuition is often as important as analysis in making a decision. The more you practice making decisions, the better you will become at "sensing" the next step without having to research every angle. Also, spending too much time on collecting information can quickly spiral into a lack of productivity.

Most work environments today involve a substantial amount of change and ambiguity, so being able to make timely decisions while unknowns abound is a matter of career survival.

The key is to develop the ability to make the best decision possible given the time frame in which you are working. Do not base the quality of a decision on the time you spent making it.

Thinking too much can affect a decision adversely. Do the best with what you have got and think of it as an accomplishment to be able to make quality decisions in less time and based on less data, instead of perfect decisions based on unlimited time.

React

(a) Work smart. Prioritize the information that is absolutely necessary and would be good to have, and spend your valuable time collecting the former.

(b) Split a big decision into smaller ones. Instead of focusing on getting all the information before you start a project, concentrate on the information needed to make smaller decisions. Treat each small decision as another piece of information you have gathered.

(c) Give yourself a deadline for research and commit to making a decision by then, based on the facts you have available.

(d) Sharpen and trust your intuition. In his book *Blink*, Malcolm Gladwell makes a strong argument for the benefits and accuracy involved in making decisions that are based on intuition. Find a workshop that can help you to get in touch with your intuition.

(e) Ask a trusted peer about the last decision they made guided by their intuition. You will begin to see how often people in business successfully rely on their intuition when making decisions.

(f) Practice making quick decisions about small issues that have little consequence.

2 | I do not want to make the wrong decision/I worry too much about the impact

Rethink

People are required to make an astounding number of decisions on any given workday. Think how much more content you would be if less of your energy was spent on worrying about making the wrong decision.

Being overly concerned about messing up can be crippling. Every time you make a decision, you rid your mind of a concern. Not being able to make decisions means you are constantly burdened with a list of unresolved items on your agenda or your mind.

Part of managing your career involves accepting the consequences, be it good or bad, of your decisions. And through practice and possibly even failure you will improve your ability to make the right decisions and showcase your value in your organization.

React

(a) Share your decision with a trusted peer to gain assurance. Use the person as a sounding board or to support your decision.

(b) Draw a decision tree with all the pros and cons. This will help to map your options and engage in a logical and not emotional approach.

(c) If you are procrastinating about a decision, you are suffering unnecessarily. Sooner or later the decision will have to be made, so why not do it sooner? Get it over and done with. Commit to a time frame for making the decision and tell other people so that you feel accountable.

(d) By not making a decision, you are making one already (to not do anything). Sometimes, any decision is better than no decision. If you are completely stumped, trust your instinct and go with it.

(e) If you are deliberating unreasonably about a decision, ask yourself: "Is this decision going to have a long-lasting effect on my life, the lives of others or the world in general?" If the answer is no, you can live with the consequences of the decision.

(f) If your decision has great consequences, do not tackle it alone. Get other stakeholders involved in the decision-making process.

(g) The long-term effects of chronic worry have been well researched and proven to have negative effects on your health. Ask yourself whether deliberating so much about the decision is damaging your health.

3 | I need to finish one thing at a time/I am not good at multitasking

Rethink

Timely decision making often requires getting information on various angles or coordinating multiple information sources to come to a conclusion.

Be careful not to be inflexible and getting overly focused on the task at hand when other options should be explored congruently. Thinking too linearly can send you far down a specific path and leave you with little time to consider other options.

There are too many competing demands in the workplace to expect to be able to progress from start to finish in one go.

The workplace is one big juggling act and the quicker you learn to cope with multiple demands the more successful you will be. Leaders play multiple roles on any given day, so expect to wear many hats when making your decisions.

React

(a) If you can only focus on one specific area, take time beforehand to delegate work that others could be doing in the meantime. Delegation allows your project to move forward even if there are setbacks in one area.

(b) Become proficient at multitasking. Being well organized is the key. Do you have an orderly system that keeps all your responsibilities documented and accessible for daily viewing? Prioritize so that you know what needs your immediate attention and what can wait. Continue to reprioritize as new demands arise.

(c) Keep sight of the bigger picture. As long as the general direction is forward, it is to be expected that some items will have to be put on hold.

(d) Instead of rewarding yourself once you have completed a project, wait until you have tackled a series of assignments within a predefined time frame.

(e) Work as a team when possible.

4 | Decisions should involve all stakeholders/I want collective buy-in before making a decision

Rethink

Although multiple inputs are often necessary to improve the quality of a decision, it can also paralyze the decision-making process and dilute the effectiveness of the solution if consensus requires too much compromise.
A good leader is able to bring people together and facilitate teams but, ultimately, their role is to decide on the course of action.

React

(a) Be honest with yourself. Ask whether you want to involve others for reassurance or because it will add value to the decision.

(b) If you are trying to reach a consensus, make sure only the appropriate stakeholders are involved in discussions to reduce distracting "noise". Write down a list that specifies the value each person will add.

(c) Solicit input from others. Give specific deadlines for feedback and announce a final deadline for when your decision will be made. And, of course, stick to that deadline.

Overdeveloped

Research has shown that strengths can become weaknesses because you can, in fact, do too much of a good thing. You cannot become less good at a competency in which you excel, but you can balance the behavior by developing a few Stabilizers to tone down an excessive strength.

Stabilizer	Overdeveloped
17 Demonstrates Good Judgment	Is seen as impulsive and jumps to conclusions with too little consideration of important data
18 Detail-Orientated	
8 Comfortable With Uncertainty	
31 Improves Processes	
34 Listens Well	
47 Patient	
48 Plans Work	
50 Problem Solver	
53 Strategic	
56 Technically Competent	

Instructions

Read the definition. If it applies to you, choose a few Stabilizers and develop them by selecting the relevant chapter and following the Strategies for Action.

For more instructions see the How To Use This Book section.

17. Demonstrates Good Judgment

"A wise man can see more from the bottom of a well than a fool can from a mountain top"

Author unknown

Well Developed

Exercises good judgment when making decisions and takes into account both facts and personal experience

Underdeveloped

Shows poor judgment and does not anticipate the consequences of decisions, or has taken wrong decisions previously

Overdeveloped

Is seen as stubborn or relies too much on own view of a situation. Is unwilling to consider other opinions

Instructions

Read the definitions on the left. If the Underdeveloped definition applies, go to the Strategies for Action section.

If the Overdeveloped definition applies, go to the end of the chapter.

Test Yourself

True	People consult me about challenges and problems
True	I do not believe I have all the answers
True	I analyze mistakes I have made in order to gain insight
True	I trust my intuition
True	I remain aware and observant of the world around me
True	I am not unduly influenced by what others think
True	I consider consequences carefully when making a decision

Note

Are you sure you need to develop this competency?

If the answer is "True" to most of the statements on the left, you probably do not need to develop this competency.

Demonstrateds Good Judgment

Strategies for Action

Most ineffective behaviors have an underlying thought or emotional pattern. By identifying these patterns, you can understand the impact they have and design strategies to counteract them.

① I am impulsive/I tend not to think things through

② I consider things but I tend to overlook important information/I focus on the wrong things

③ I am easily swayed by others' opinions

④ I allow personal motives to influence my judgment

Instructions

1. Read and select one or more of the ineffective ways of thinking/feeling to the left.

2. Find the corresponding number below that will help you to rethink this pattern and identify specific and practical actions that you can take.

---

1 | I am impulsive/I tend not to think things through

Rethink

Do you allow yourself ample time to consider the options and consequences of your decision?

Being decisive and taking quick action can be appropriate, but every decision should be made only after careful consideration of the consequences.

Haste can harm your decision. Some decisions are obviously extremely complex and demand ample time and proper analysis, and even seemingly simple issues can be deceptively complex in nature.

Unwise decisions typically result in more work and time invested for everyone involved.

React

(a) Do not go with your first impulse. It is wise to get out for a break, take a walk or sleep on it. Do whatever makes sense to give you time to make a good judgment call.

(b) Consider multiple potential scenarios and not just the obvious ones. Entertain several "what if" questions.

(c) Consider carefully what the consequences of your decision will be for all the stakeholders involved — yourself, the client, team members and your organization.

(d) What are the consequences of your decision in the short term and long term?

(e) Assemble a team of people to provide alternative perspectives and help you approach the problem thoroughly and from different angles. Brainstorming can help you flesh out the complexities of the problem.

(f) Look for case samples of similar issues and grasp the parallels and differences with your issue.

(g) Display the options visually, using tools such as a flow chart or software such as MindJet's Mind Manager.

② I consider things but I tend to overlook important information/I focus on the wrong things

Rethink

Carefully considering an issue is time wasted if it is based on irrelevant or incorrect information. Focus less on the quantity of the information and more on the quality and try to gather only opinions and points of view that are relevant.

Use your wisdom. Individuals with plenty experience or complex technical knowledge may have a lot of information to draw on, but that is not enough.

Knowledge does not guarantee good judgment. Other factors such as intuition, common sense and ethics are equally important in good judgment.

Countless examples exist of highly experienced business leaders and even presidents of countries who have made unwise, destructive decisions because they focused on profit or immediate gain instead of the wider impact of their policies.

React

(a) Consider the immediate and potential gains or losses when making a choice.

(b) Understand the impact on your stakeholders.

(c) Pay attention to warnings or red flags raised by others. Log these if you cannot investigate immediately but be sure to go back to give them careful consideration.

(d) Ask a trusted colleague to help you regain focus if you feel you are concentrating on irrelevant information or issues.

(e) Learn from other people's experience. Ask peers or experts to share the regrets they may have over a similar situation and how they would have changed their decisions.

(f) Weigh the opinions of trusted peers. Ultimately, it is your decision, but multiple perspectives could shed light on issues you have not even considered.

(g) Do not focus on just one aspect of a situation, for example, technical matters. Gather your information from as many diverse sources as possible.

(h) Learn from your experiences by taking time to reflect on them before, during and after your assignments. Keep a journal. What did you learn that you had not realized before? What surprised you? Which good decisions were made and which were ineffective?

(i) Apply common sense in your judgment. Getting caught up in too many details or investing time going in one direction only can cloud your perspective and make you lose sight of an obvious, simple solution.

Rethink

Good judgment means you should consider others' opinions, but not be governed by them.

It is particularly difficult to hold one's own when in the company of influential people or those with greater experience and knowledge than you. But, ultimately, you are accountable and should trust your own good judgment, not just other people's.

React

(a) Trust your intuition. If you have completed due diligence and a strong gut feeling is guiding you, your judgment is as valid as the other person's.

(b) Limit the number of people you ask for opinions to a trusted few.

(c) Try to anticipate people's resistance and prepare answers to defend your judgment. Having carefully examined possible objections enables you to defend your decision with confidence.

(d) When making a decision, take a step back and ask yourself whether it makes sense. It is easy to get swayed by classic textbook solutions, but they may be irrelevant in the context of your situation.

(e) Do not overlook the ethics of your judgment. If you feel your values are compromised, you must explore the issue further until you are comfortable.

(f) Be aware of other people's motives. You may be supporting their personal agendas without realizing it.

(g) Once you have considered all the information and made a decision, do not ask other people's opinions again. You did that before making your decision.

Rethink

Personal motives can harm good judgment. If your decision is not going to make sense to anybody but you, it is a good indication that you are allowing a personal agenda to govern your judgment.

Of course, everyone has a personal agenda, but it should be balanced with the goals of the team or organization. If not, the quality of your decisions will be affected and colleagues will stop trusting you and your judgment.

React

(a) Be honest with others and yourself about your personal motives. It gives them the opportunity to creatively find a mutual solution with you.

(b) Weigh carefully the value of getting your needs met versus the consequences of your decision.

(c) Base your judgment of a situation on logic instead of emotion. Regardless of how strong your personal motives are, is your decision a sound one?

(d) Ask a mentor or someone who knows you well whether they think your decision is unduly influenced by your personal motives.

(e) Ask yourself if your decision will make sense to everyone else too. If it does not, you need to look more closely at how you have arrived at your decision.

Overdeveloped

Research has shown that strengths can become weaknesses because you can, in fact, do too much of a good thing. You cannot become less good at a competency in which you excel, but you can balance the behavior by developing a few Stabilizers to tone down an excessive strength.

Stabilizer	Overdeveloped
46 Open-Minded	Is seen as stubborn or relies too much on own view of a situation. Is unwilling to consider other opinions
2 Adaptable	
27 Experimental	
31 Improves Processes	
34 Listens Well	
35 Manages Conflict	
37 Manages Negotiations	
40 Market Aware	
7 Collaborative	
41 Modest	

Instructions

Read the definition. If it applies to you, choose a few Stabilizers and develop them by selecting the relevant chapter and following the Strategies for Action.

For more instructions see the How To Use This Book section.

18. Detail-Oriented

"Everything is vague to a degree you do not realize
until you have tried to make it precise"

Bertrand Russel

Well Developed

Is well organized and methodical, and
pays attention to detail

Underdeveloped

Appears disorganized and lacks
attention to detail

Overdeveloped

Spends too much time on details and
loses perspective. Could be a
perfectionist

Instructions

Read the definitions on the
left. If the Underdeveloped
definition applies, go to
the Strategies for Action
section.

If the Overdeveloped
definition applies, go to
the end of the chapter.

Test Yourself

True	I can multitask and get several things accomplished at once
True	I have a system in place that keep me organized
True	I consider things carefully before rushing in
True	I take good notes and record things which I need to follow up
True	I can quickly access information I have stored without spending unnecessary time looking for it
True	I seldom make mistakes because I overlooked important details
True	I understand the issues or processes that will have critical negative consequences should I not be exact

Note

**Are you sure you need to
develop this competency?**

If the answer is "True" to
most of the statements on
the left, you probably do
not need to develop this
competency.

18 Detailed-Oriented

115

Strategies for Action

Most ineffective behaviors have an underlying thought or emotional pattern. By identifying these patterns, you can understand the impact they have and design strategies to counteract them.

① I am best at focusing on the big picture; it is the way I think

② I want quick results/I prefer instant gratification

③ I cannot manage everything on my plate/I feel disorganized at the best of times

④ I can always get someone else to deal with the details

Instructions

1. Read and select one or more of the ineffective ways of thinking/feeling to the left.

2. Find the corresponding number below that will help you to rethink this pattern and identify specific and practical actions that you can take.

1 | I am best at focusing on the big picture; it is the way I think

Rethink

How well do you pay attention to instructions? How aware are you of the so-called little things? Many people seem to stumble over details because their minds are preoccupied with the bigger picture.

If you are a big-picture person, spending time focusing on details will require extra effort. You have to work particularly hard to motivate yourself to do something you know, intellectually, will contribute to your productivity but which you find uninteresting.

However, it must be done. Focusing only on the big picture is like seeing only half of what is there. It is the details that allow you to be precise and knowledgeable about the direction you are going or in which you are leading your organization.

The ability to routinely step in and out of the big picture will give you the necessary balance.

People are counting on your directives to be based on careful consideration of the details, in addition to the big-picture vision.

React

(a) Train yourself to focus on the here and now, if only for short periods at a time. Set aside a specific amount of time every day to go over the details of a plan, whether you want to or not. Consider this the "construction time" any project requires.

(b) Try a baby-steps approach. Start with being methodical about smaller things, such as your Rolodex or filing system, that do not take up too much time, and then move on to bigger challenges. This will help you to see the benefits that a small investment of your time can create.

(c) Cultivate an active interest in what you do. When there is something you do not want to but simply must do, find a way to make it interesting or recognize it as a necessary step between where you are and where you want to be — and do it.

(d) Set up a system that reminds you to focus on details. Write a note on the back of your hand, put a colorful reminder on your computer screen, get a peer to remind you or add it to your electronic calendar so that it reminds you once a day.

(e) Partner with other people who have opposite strengths, for example, if you get the management position appoint a detail-oriented person as your assistant.

(f) Ask a trusted peer who is methodical to help you consider some of the details you are likely to overlook. Compare your list of details with the other person's. Which angles did you omit?

2 | I want quick results/I prefer instant gratification

Rethink

Remember the saying "Measure twice, cut once"? Being methodical means taking the time to consider, in an orderly fashion, the options and details involved in your project or assignment.

When you want instant results or immediate action, it is tempting to forego the time it takes to get things done properly. But what value are you placing on the quality of your work or decisions?

There may well be external factors such as time constraints that force us to balance quality with output, but careless or sloppy work should not be accepted simply because impatience trumped due diligence.

As a manager or leader, you set the example for the quality of work your company represents. It is your responsibility to ensure your employees value the importance of conscientious work and that you do not create extra work for yourself and others because you did not invest in appropriate time to address the details.

React

(a) Stop looking for the easiest way out. Most goals take hard work and dedication to accomplish. It is important to work smartly and quickly, but be careful not to make excuses about details because they require extra work. Identify the shortcuts you may be taking, including making assumptions about instructions, people etcetera.

(b) Break down your goal into smaller, detailed tasks — each small task that is completed brings a reward.

(c) Do a detailed project timeline that sets realistic points at which you can expect milestones to be reached. Do not try to rush the process unduly.

(d) Recognize whether a team approach would be better and assign ample resources to work on the details of a plan.

(e) Put quality-assurance practices in place to guard against any major flaws or oversights in your processes.

(f) Meditation is an effective way to bring calm and stillness to the mind. Incorporate it in your daily routine.

3 | I cannot manage everything on my plate/I feel disorganized at the best of times

Rethink

Are you always searching for things in the wrong places, yet you are sure you had put them exactly there?

As your workload increases, do you feel more disorganized and become inefficient? Being organized requires functional systems in place that keep you on track, which you have incorporated as part of your work routine. People will question the reliability of your work if you appear to be approaching it carelessly.

Being well organized helps you to work more productively and prepares you to handle the increased demands as your career advances.

React

(a) Keep relevant people informed of your workload if it starts to affect the accuracy of your work. It is that person's responsibility to delegate appropriately.

(b) Store all information for different projects or tasks separately in an organized manner, either electronically or in paper files, and ensure you can access it easily.

(c) Switching gears constantly consumes time. To increase your efficiency, bundle similar activities together. For example, do all your calls to different clients at one time, and send all your e-mails at another.

(d) Do you have systems in place that help to keep you organized? If yes, ensure you actually put them into practice. Can you list and describe your systems to others? They do not have to be complex — jotting notes in a designated notepad is a system.

(e) Ask meticulous co-workers about the systems they use to keep themselves organized. Maybe one will work for you.

(f) Take advantage of all of the organizing technology on your desktop, such as calendars, scheduling tools and project management software. You will be surprised to find many tools at your disposal; now you just have to use them.

(g) Keep things neat. Organize your desk and your surroundings as much as you can.

(h) Resist the temptation to put off doing something that would help you to be organized just because you can do it "later". This is what contributes to piles of papers, missing notes, unanswered calls and e-mails, or files lost in your computer.

(i) Are you constantly creating lists, spending more time trying to organize yourself than actually being organized? Do not set up systems you cannot follow or incorporate in a daily routine.

(j) Habits and routines help you to keep track of the details, because they are dependable.

4 | I can always get someone else to deal with the details

Rethink

Do you get away with not confronting details? Perhaps you are in a position in which others can rescue you from sifting through those pesky points.

Perhaps you have the authority to pass the minutiae to others. But perhaps they must always do parts of your work because they lack confidence in your ability to pay attention to details. Whatever the circumstances, remember that when details are your responsibility, you cannot take advantage of colleagues.

Be aware not to do it. Working through details makes you more knowledgeable and informed.

You will gain respect as someone willing to roll up your sleeves and tackle tough details and who does not shy away from unenviable tasks.

React

(a) To ensure accountability, announce to others your commitment to approach an issue methodically.

(b) Ensure you know your company's culture and the so-called lay of the land. You may have to adapt to higher expectations or a new culture. If necessary and expected, you will have to step it up a notch.

(c) Remember that some clients will expect more attention to detail than others. Assume they do.

(d) Partner with someone who will hold you accountable and demand careful consideration of details in your processes and decisions.

Overdeveloped

Research has shown that strengths can become weaknesses because you can, in fact, do too much of a good thing. You cannot become less good at a competency in which you excel, but you can balance the behavior by developing a few Stabilizers to tone down an excessive strength.

Stabilizer	Overdeveloped
27 Experimental	Spends too much time on details and loses perspective. Could be a perfectionist
30 Global Thinker	
1 Achiever	
16 Decisive	
29 Focused on Priorities	
8 Comfortable with Uncertainty	
46 Open-Minded	
2 Adaptable	
53 Strategic	
55 Takes Initiative	

Instructions

Read the definition. If it applies to you, choose a few Stabilizers and develop them by selecting the relevant chapter and following the Strategies for Action.

For more instructions see the How To Use This Book section.

19. Determined

"Get up one more time than you're knocked down"

Tom Peters

Well Developed
Sticks to a course of action despite obstacles and sees things through to the end

Underdeveloped
Appears to give up too early and lacks the ability to see things through to their conclusion

Overdeveloped
Sticks with a course of action beyond reason and is reluctant to try a different tack, despite supporting information

Instructions

Read the definitions on the left. If the Underdeveloped definition applies, go to the Strategies for Action section.

If the Overdeveloped definition applies, go to the end of the chapter.

Test Yourself

True	I rarely quit before I have completed a task or project
True	I recover quickly from emotional setbacks during a project
True	I have completed long-term projects successfully
True	I look for alternatives when I hit stumbling blocks
True	I do not like leaving anything incomplete
True	Once I start something I have been assigned, I know it is my responsibility to finish it

Note

Are you sure you need to develop this competency?

If the answer is "True" to most of the statements on the left, you probably do not need to develop this competency.

Determined

⑲ Determined

Strategies for Action

Most ineffective behaviors have an underlying thought or emotional pattern. By identifying these patterns, you can understand the impact they have and design strategies to counteract them.

① I lose interest once I have started projects/ I get bored

② I tend to make things too complicated/ I become overwhelmed

③ I lose confidence when things get difficult/ I am easily swayed

④ I get impatient about completing things

Instructions

1. Read and select one or more of the ineffective ways of thinking/feeling to the left.

2. Find the corresponding number below that will help you to rethink this pattern and identify specific and practical actions that you can take.

---

1 | I lose interest once I have started projects/I get bored

Rethink

You will have heard the saying that genius is 10% inspiration and 90% perspiration. The excitement of a new project can quickly wear off, but you must be prepared to remain engaged and focused on the ultimate goal. The biggest reward comes from completing work successfully, so do not deny yourself that accomplishment. Perhaps you find the details boring, but great ideas are only possibilities until the details are tracked, sorted and understood.

Think how much further a product or service can evolve beyond its origins if support and resources are available to allow it to mature in the long term.

Losing interest quickly is a challenge for highly creative and visionary leaders. Realize that any initiative you set in motion has an impact on your team and organization, and abandoning ideas midstream to pursue the latest impulse will influence your company's culture. There will be less commitment to support existing ideas and less confidence in new ones. It is better to have seen one great idea soar than to have hatched a dozen and never given them an opportunity to leave the nest.

React

(a) Ensure that new initiatives are introduced in a manner that creates buy-in from all stakeholders and that the infrastructure and resources exist to facilitate the appropriate follow-through.

(b) Celebrate small goals or milestones along the way. It may take a while to realize the project completely, and acknowledging the steps needed to get there will keep you motivated.

(c) Make progress, not inspiration, your primary goal. It means you must focus on the steps necessary to mature an existing product or service instead of trying to generate new ones. Make a detailed plan of the steps necessary to translate the idea into practice. Once you have identified these steps in your plan, you can apply the same framework for future ideas.

(d) Be sure to monitor your work processes. Once distracted by new initiatives, it is easy to abandon the monitoring of existing projects' progress. Why compromise the hard work and resources that have been invested because of a lack of oversight?

(e) Find a trusted peer that can cheer you on when you are struggling. An external perspective to remind you how close you are to your goal, or simply someone to listen to your feelings can be just the life vest you need when you are least inspired.

(f) Have you lost sight of your vision? Occasionally, reflect on the bigger picture and what it was that excited you about the work in the first place.

(g) First complete the things you least like doing and get them out of the way while your motivation is highest. It will be easier to tackle the less complex tasks when you have less energy.

(h) If you simply cannot get excited about working on a particular assignment or task, you may need some time to recharge by focusing on something else. Taking a break from the task at hand will give you a chance to recharge. Can you ask for assistance?

(i) If you are not a detail-oriented person, you are likely to lose interest quickly and prefer to move on to something new. Make sure there are people on your team who are more analytical or concerned with detail and can drive that aspect of the project.

(j) Certainly, some aspects of everyone's jobs are less interesting than others, but if nothing holds your interest or you are chronically bored, you should consider whether your position is right for you.

2 | I tend to make things too complicated/ I become overwhelmed

Rethink

Overly complicating a task can bring a quick end to your perseverance. Often great ideas do not get off the ground because they get lost in all the possibilities. Think simplicity.

React

(a) Keep things as simple as possible by narrowing your focus to one or two core drivers of the problem. Articulate what those drivers are.

(b) Focus on the starting point and not the finishing line. What is most important as a first course of action? List all the possibilities and choose only a few avenues on which to focus for now. There is never a perfect place from which to start. Once you have accomplished the initial steps, begin again.

(c) Assemble a strong team that has multiple skills and can tackle all the various angles of the project. You do not have to be an expert in every aspect.

(d) Do not linger on a problem too long before addressing it. The longer you leave an issue unaddressed the more overwhelming it becomes.

3 | I lose confidence when things get difficult/ I am easily swayed

Rethink

Prove to yourself what you are capable of by finishing what you started. Overcoming obstacles sharpens your mind and increases your self-confidence. Obstacles give rise to alternatives and create new paths, just like water in a stream that continually has to flow over and around rocks to reach its final destination.

React

(a) Often, once you gain a better perspective or have more information, obstacles are not as difficult to overcome as they first appeared. Ask a trusted colleague or expert to provide a different perspective. Someone else might be able to see an obvious solution that you cannot just then.

(b) Use obstacles as opportunities to have fun while being creative. There are always multiple ways to approach an issue. Do you need to start over again or simply change your course of action? Many plans have failed not because they were not good, but because they were inflexible.

(c) Your biggest obstacle may be your emotions or attitude. Examine the real reasons why you are contemplating giving up and make sure the reasons are based on logic, not emotion.

(d) Reflect on your original purpose for embarking on this route and become motivated again. Sometimes a shot of energy is all you need to get you over the hurdle.

4 | I get impatient about completing things

Rethink

Sometimes, our wish or need to complete a project leads us to give up when it does not happen within our desired timeframe. Understand how to pace yourself. What is worse, waiting a bit longer for the result or not having results at all?

ReAct

(a) Always add to your timelines to allow for contingencies. You want to start with a realistic timeframe for completion and mitigate unnecessary frustration.

(b) Do you have other things on your plate? There is no reason not to move on to another project if you are simply not able to focus on a specific task at the moment, but be sure to return at a later stage to address what you had left behind.

(c) Rather than give up altogether because things are not moving fast enough, find ways to improve the process so that it can be completed more quickly. This might involve recruiting additional resources to help.

(d) Does the whole task have to be done from beginning to end at once? Divide it into smaller tasks on which you can work progressively.

Overdeveloped

Research has shown that strengths can become weaknesses because you can, in fact, do too much of a good thing. You cannot become less good at a competency in which you excel, but you can balance the behavior by developing a few Stabilizers to tone down an excessive strength.

Stabilizer	Overdeveloped
14 Creative	Sticks with a course of action beyond reason and is reluctant to try a different tack, despite supporting information
2 Adaptable	
27 Experimental	
29 Focused on Priorities	
30 Global Thinker	
34 Listens Well	
1 Achiever	
53 Strategic	
50 Problem Solver	
46 Open-Minded	

Instructions

Read the definition. If it applies to you, choose a few Stabilizers and develop them by selecting the relevant chapter and following the Strategies for Action.

For more instructions see the How To Use This Book section.

20. Develops People

"A good boss makes his men realize they have more ability
than they think they have so that they consistently do better
work than they thought they could"

Charles Erwin Wilson

Well Developed
Develops others and provides an
opportunity for them to practice new
skills or improve existing ones

Underdeveloped
Is unwilling or lacks interest in
developing others

Overdeveloped
Throws people in at the deep end
without the necessary support or
resources

Instructions
Read the definitions on the
left. If the Underdeveloped
definition applies, go to
the Strategies for Action
section.

If the Overdeveloped
definition applies, go to
the end of the chapter.

Test Yourself

True	I have regular development discussions with my staff
True	I include staff in relevant meetings and projects to expose them to development opportunities
True	I regularly ask my subordinates what they would be interested to work on
True	I actively consider development opportunities for my staff
True	I use performance reviews and evaluation tools to identify development needs
True	I have a development plan in place for each of my staff
True	I have established a system to follow up on development actions
True	I understand the preferred learning styles of my staff

Note

Are you sure you need to develop this competency?

If the answer is "True" to
most of the statements on
the left, you probably do
not need to develop this
competency.

127

Strategies for Action

Most ineffective behaviors have an underlying thought or emotional pattern. By identifying these patterns, you can understand the impact they have and design strategies to counteract them.

① People should develop themselves/It is not my job to develop others

② I am under too much pressure at work to develop others/I rather do things myself/ I am impatient

③ Discussing people's developmental needs, especially behavioral aspects, makes me feel uncomfortable/I do not like to be critical

④ I do not know how to develop people or exactly what they are supposed to develop

⑤ The risk and consequences of failure are too high for me to develop others

⑥ If I develop others, they may be recruited by the competition

Instructions

1. Read and select one or more of the ineffective ways of thinking/feeling to the left.

2. Find the corresponding number below that will help you to rethink this pattern and identify specific and practical actions that you can take.

---

① | People should develop themselves/It is not my job to develop others

Rethink

Remember that, as a manager, staff development is one of your key responsibilities. You are in charge of people to maximize their efforts and improve the talent in your company now and in the future. It is accomplished by ensuring that those who work for you have a development path and stay motivated to stick to it.

Helping others to develop does not require excessive effort on your part — there are daily opportunities that require little effort, but you need to consider and use them. Your subordinates are also juggling competing demands and may not prioritize self-development unless it is expected of them. There will always be other demands on your time but playing an active role in the development of your staff is not a choice; it is an obligation you must fulfill to both your employees and organization.

React

(a) Do you encourage a culture of self-development? Discuss it openly and offer people opportunities to develop. Let them know it is one of your priorities and that you encourage them to be proactive about suggesting opportunities.

(b) Consider all requests for development. Ensure you do not demoralize people by turning down suggestions for events they would like to attend or projects for which they show enthusiasm. Give people the benefit of the doubt and reward them for having shown initiative. They will learn to gauge the types of activities that pay off.

(c) Praise people openly when they complete a development item. Praise is infectious and will help to motivate other team members. It will also send the message that self-development is valued.

(d) Do not keep your knowledge to yourself. It takes little effort to motivate others to develop themselves by reading articles, business journals or books that you have found particularly enlightening and recommend. Formalize the process by regularly sending a compilation of suggestions to which people can look forward.

> ## 2 | I am under too much pressure at work to develop others/I rather do things myself/I am impatient

Rethink

Somewhere between managing people and processes you are supposed to find the time to manage others' development? Yes. Too many managers neglect this requirement of their position because it never seems as pressing as other priorities.

Developing people requires a trade-off: you must give others the opportunity to practice a new skill or take on a responsibility whether you can do it better or not. And it will place pressure on your already busy schedule. Managers who are impatient with the process of teaching suppress the opportunities people have to gain self-confidence, mature and expand their skills set; they also risk demoralizing their staff.

It is short-sighted not to set aside any time to develop employees.

When the pressure is really high, you may have no one to delegate to if you have not made the appropriate investment in staff's development.

React

(a) Expose people to development by including them in meetings with groups they do not typically encounter: clients, higher management and other departments etcetera. They do not have to play an active role but could learn from the experience, and it does not impose on your time.

(b) Identify tasks you can delegate to subordinates to help them to improve weak skills.

(c) Set appropriate performance expectations which consider the person's experience, skills set and the position's context.

(d) Give staff adequate space and time to work through problems and prove themselves.

(e) Encourage people to take initiative. Do not overreact when a mistake is made; instead, use it as an opportunity for reflection and development.

3 | Discussing people's developmental needs, especially behavioral aspects, makes me feel uncomfortable/I do not like to be critical

Rethink

The development of subordinates is often neglected because managers must discuss talent deficiencies, which can be hard to do. Associating discussions about development with criticism is the wrong mind-set to have, and could result in you delaying necessary conversations or skirting issues that ought to be addressed.

Guiding others is one of a manager's key roles. Inevitably, it means raising awareness about both strengths and weaknesses in a person.

Weaknesses that go unchallenged can hinder a person's advancement or derail a career altogether.

A healthy relationship with subordinates depends on open communication and feedback that go both ways. It means you must provide honest and constructive guidance about what a person needs to improve.

As you progress in an organization, you will likely be required to manage an increasing number of people. Effective feedback and coaching skills will help you to maximize employees' productivity. You are in a privileged position to teach people and raise their self-awareness, but sometimes it means having difficult conversations.

React

(a) Ask a consultant or the human resources department to train you in coaching. It will build your coaching skills and allow you to provide feedback to staff more easily.

(b) Use tools such as 360° assessments to learn about a person's strengths and developmental needs. Collective evidence from various sources about the skills a person should improve is more weighty because it is harder to object to than if it came from one source only.

(c) Some subordinates will be better prepared to follow your guidance than others. Do not be defensive or take it personally. Most people dread feedback, and awareness is often preceded by denial. You may have to discuss the subject several times before a person can assimilate the feedback and is prepared to act.

(d) Ensure the employee understands the feedback's relevance to achieving success in a position. The person must fully grasp how a deficiency that has been identified affects their ability to perform well.

4 | I do not know how to develop people or exactly what they are supposed to develop

Rethink

Managers should always consider their employees to be "in development". But to figure out the best investment in development for different individuals at any given time is challenging. Resources are often tight and time constraints exist, so development choices need careful consideration.

130

Fortunately, there are many tools available to help managers shape the development paths of their staff.

Each person has different development needs, based on their interests, motivation level, potential and talent, that is, their behavioral competencies, work experiences and technical skills.

Some development needs will be obvious, for example, learning a new language for a long-term international assignment. But others will be less easy to define and could become problematic before they are identified. For example, someone's independence early in their career can lead to poor delegation or team work later.

Understanding early on that such independence could become an issue in future allows prompt intervention: you can ensure the person is assigned to team-based projects to learn to collaborate, for example. Development needs should not only be considered in the context of a person's current position, although it is a critical consideration and a good starting point. They should be seen against a broader canvass that paints various future career paths.

React

(a) Take advantage of assessment tools such as PeopleTree Group's 360° feedback, which informs you about a person's strengths and development opportunities.

(b) Prioritize the improvement of "knockout factors" and "derailers" that have been identified in a person's profile. Knockout factors are certain behavioral attributes that will cause a problem in every context regardless of a person's job, such as having poor relationships with bosses. Derailers result from a special combination of strengths and weaknesses. It may begin as a strength, but can create problems over the evolution of a career, such as when someone becomes a too independent loner. These factors need attention early on.

(c) Identify the development items that will have the greatest impact on an employee's current position.

(d) Consider the context of someone's current position or the future job the person is aiming for. For example, if someone is being groomed for a turnaround position, ensure their behavioral competencies are a good match for that type of position.

(e) Contact your human resources department, or a PeopleTree Group consultant at www.peopletreesuite.com, about the 9-Cell Matrix. It is used to identify people with high potential in the company and examine the best developmental strategies for people based on performance and learning agility predictors.

(f) Expose people to a variety of assignments. It is a practical way to uncover their strengths and weaknesses.

(g) Interest should play a key role in someone's development path. Ask people which assignments they find fulfilling and which challenges they would like to tackle.

(h) Peers can learn a lot from each other. Encourage discussion groups or informal lunch meetings during which they can share information or insights about their projects.

(i) Take into account that people learn differently. Some learn better on their own, others enjoy group learning; some learn from books and other require practical experience.

5

The risk and consequences of failure are too high for me to develop others

Rethink

An organization's gravest risk is not having a well-developed talent pipeline and adequate successors, especially for critical positions. It should concern you deeply if you are ready to advance to a new position but cannot because no one has been developed to step into your role.

To develop others indeed requires taking a chance on them and the outcome of their performance, but the perceived risk is often exaggerated, fueled by perfectionism and the high standards to which you adhere. Development does not happen overnight, so start today and slowly build the necessary talent while mitigating the risk involved.

React

(a) Identify successors for critical positions in your business and ensure a succession plan is in place. The PeopleTree Talent Manager system is a comprehensive succession management tool.

(b) Adopt a long-term development philosophy that allows you to build the necessary talent in others step by step.

(c) Take people along to key meetings and engagements where they can learn by observing you with little risk to you or the organization.

(d) Identify which of your responsibilities you can delegate to others as part of their development. Discuss and okay it with your supervisor — their support will make it easier for you to take the risk.

(e) Assign mentors to people so they can gain valuable knowledge and perspectives from someone other than you.

(f) Write down the consequences should someone you are developing take a misstep. Are these consequences as grave as you imagine them to be?

If I develop others, they may be recruited by the competition

6

Rethink

Strong talent being poached by a competitor, internal or external, is always a risk. But not maximizing people's development opportunities will ensure they become demoralized or bored and start looking for better opportunities elsewhere.

If good talent choose to take a different path, ensure that it is not because you limited their potential but because your guidance helped them to rise to it. If you are skilled at developing people, you will be able to repeat your performance with other candidates. Chances are, though, that people will want to remain under your wing. Managers who value and prioritize the development of others are scarce, and their staff is usually extremely loyal.

React

(a) Ensure you understand what motivates employees and offer incentives that acknowledge their talent and secure their loyalty.

(b) Ask individuals about the opportunities they would find interesting and ensure they have assignments that tap into those interests.

(c) Assign an individual you are developing to be a mentor to others. It will reinforce your confidence in the person and reward their skill.

(d) Raise individuals' visibility among higher management by communicating and promoting their successes and hard work.

Overdeveloped

Research has shown that strengths can become weaknesses because you can, in fact, do too much of a good thing. You cannot become less good at a competency in which you excel, but you can balance the behavior by developing a few Stabilizers to tone down an excessive strength.

Stabilizer	Overdeveloped
17 Demonstrates Good Judgment	Throws people in at the deep end without the necessary support or resources
23 Directs People	
24 Empathetic	
25 Empowers People	
28 Fair	
38 Manages Underperformance	
42 Monitors Work	
43 Motivates People	
48 Plans Work	
51 Recognizes Talent and Potential	

Instructions

Read the definition. If it applies to you, choose a few Stabilizers and develop them by selecting the relevant chapter and following the Strategies for Action.

For more instructions see the How To Use This Book section.

21. Develops Self

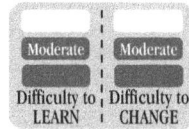

"Income seldom exceeds personal development"
Jim Rohn

Well Developed
Continuously develops new skills and enhances existing capabilities

Underdeveloped
Lacks the interest or motivation to develop new skills or improve existing capabilities

Overdeveloped
Is too preoccupied with own development and works on areas which add no value

Instructions

Read the definitions on the left. If the Underdeveloped definition applies, go to the Strategies for Action section.

If the Overdeveloped definition applies, go to the end of the chapter.

Test Yourself

True	I am currently working on developing one skill or competency
True	I actively research topics on which I am working
True	I volunteer for assignments that I know will challenge me
True	I routinely ask my boss and peers for feedback to help identify areas for development
True	I am keenly aware of my strengths and weaknesses
True	I read publications and literature related to my field
True	I have a personal development plan which I follow
True	I am eager for opportunities to learn and develop

Note

Are you sure you need to develop this competency?

If the answer is "True" to most of the statements on the left, you probably do not need to develop this competency.

135

Strategies for Action

Most ineffective behaviors have an underlying thought or emotional pattern. By identifying these patterns, you can understand the impact they have and design strategies to counteract them.

① I am too busy just getting my job done to work on personal development

② I do not know which areas to develop

③ I am very good at what I do/I do not really have weaknesses which can cause a problem

④ I do not want to focus attention on my weaker areas/Acknowledging your weaknesses puts your career at risk

⑤ I think it is more valuable to be a specialist than a generalist

⑥ You should stick to what you are good at/ You should play to your strengths

Instructions

1. Read and select one or more of the ineffective ways of thinking/feeling to the left.

2. Find the corresponding number below that will help you to rethink this pattern and identify specific and practical actions that you can take.

---

① I am too busy just getting my job done to work on personal development

Rethink

Performing your current duties well is not enough. Given the changing demands of work and the different career moves you may want to make, your talents must be developed continuously.

Unless you have no plans for promotion, you will want to actively invest time to prepare yourself for your next career step. Even if you plan to remain in your current position for some time, there are many changes, be it in technology, information or the nature of the market that will render your skills or experiences obsolete if you are not constantly improving them. And although your technical skills may be up to date, research shows that behavioral competencies contribute to approximately 50% of career success.

Different competencies will be required at progressive levels in your career, so there is always room for self-development. From a personal perspective, you will be a more interesting person when you pursue self-development opportunities. You will be prepared and able to share ideas and information and connect with a greater number of people.

React

(a) Reprioritize your self-development. If you consider it an item that you will get to later when you have time, it will not get done. Enter into a personal contract with yourself to act on self-development items weekly.

(b) Consider ways to improve your time management and organize yourself better to make room for self-development. Try to list all the activities that tend to waste your time, both at work and in your private life. Which of these can be replaced with self-development activities?

(c) Add self-development endeavors to your everyday schedule. For example, carry a trade magazine or newspaper with you to read while you are queuing or at lunch. Get CD books to listen to during your commute, or invite an expert to dinner and discuss issues of interest.

(d) It is difficult to set aside large chunks of time for self-development, so commit to short periods instead. Just half an hour a day, every weekday, gives you two and a half hours to pursue your development goal.

(e) We tend to make time for the things we consider fun or interesting. Self-development can be fun! For example, if you need to read more, go do it somewhere you enjoy, such as a park or coffee shop. If you have to improve your network, invite people you must get to know better to a restaurant you have always wanted to try. Sign up for a course with a friend or peer with whom you do not get to spend enough time.

2 | I do not know which areas to develop

Rethink

Individuals are seldom completely accurate about the areas in which their development focus should fall. In fact, as far as behavioral competencies are concerned, studies have shown that self-assessment is the least accurate method to judge personal strengths and weaknesses.

Understanding the importance of self-development is your first step, followed by being proactive about your own development. This is of paramount importance, because self-development is often not considered a priority and not actively integrated into an organization's culture.

You may find that your supervisor is supportive in helping to identify opportunities for your development, but not your manager. In the end, it is your responsibility to ensure that you have a development path that is aligned with your personal career goals.

React

(a) The more you know your strengths and weaknesses, the more targeted your development focus will be. Investigate the assessment methodologies available, such as a 360° evaluation that could provide objective feedback from colleagues who know you well. Utilize interest and career tests or computer programs that analyze skills and interests. Get help from a coach or your human resources department to administer the tests and aid their interpretation.

(b) Ensure you have a development plan for your current position. Identify the development items that would have the greatest impact on improvement in your skills.

(c) Be sure to consider multiple development angles and not just technical skills. For example, how well does your leadership style fit in with your team? What must you do to be better aligned with the company strategy? Does your relationship with your boss need improvement? Are you prepared for the cultural differences and demands of an imminent international assignment?

(d) Ensure that your development supports your long-term goals. Write down a personal mission or vision statement which helps to define where you want to take your career in the future. It will help you to focus on the right development choices.

(e) Read professional journals and trade magazines to remain up to date on the latest developments in your field.

(f) Find a mentor who can give you support, advice and assistance in directing your career.

(g) Let a coach help you with an individual development plan that outlines your learning needs and goals. A plan will help you to stick to your goals. Ensure that the plan has specific actions you must complete and measurable goals. Discuss a plan for follow-up — who will track your progress and how? Most development plans fail because they lacked follow-up.

3 | I am very good at what I do/I do not really have weaknesses which can cause a problem

Rethink

Even top performers have strengths and weaknesses. Tiger Woods, for example, is at the pinnacle of his game, yet he does not stop trying to improve. He may be relatively stronger at his long game than his short game, and recognizing it allows him to focus on improving an area that could elevate his level of performance even further.

A person may be highly skilled in one area, but would struggle if the context of the job changed. For example, you could suddenly face an international assignment or working with large groups. Your company might be on the verge of expanding into emerging markets, and learning a new language may suddenly become a key skill to develop. Reaching beyond your existing skills makes you better prepared for various assignments. And note that weaknesses in behavioral competencies can derail a person's career. They are always the least obvious to an individual, yet they should be as highly valued as technical skills and experience.

React

(a) Concentrate on the things you do less well. We all have strengths and weaknesses, so aim for experience and assignments in areas in which you are less proficient than others.

(b) Go from good to great. A top athlete does not stop trying to improve, even if they have broken a world record. If you are already very good at something, find an expert skills coach to help you use your strengths to achieve excellence.

(c) The more you know about yourself the better. Investigate the assessment methodologies available, such as a 360° evaluation that could provide objective feedback from colleagues who know you well. Get help from a coach or your human resources department to help interpret the assessment.

(d) Watch for overuses, blind spots, knock-out factors and so-called derailers. These are the four horsemen of self-awareness, yet people are typically ignorant about them. To find out more about these concepts, visit www.peopletreesuite.com to contact a PeopleTree Group consultant. Identify whether you match any of these profiles.

(e) Become involved in professional organizations where you can learn from others and network with peers. It is always an eye opener to see how much there is to learn when you expose yourself to other experts' knowledge.

4 | I do not want to focus attention on my weaker areas/ Acknowledging your weaknesses puts your career at risk

Rethink

Trying to brush weaknesses under the carpet means your energy is spent on hiding instead of strengthening your skills. Some people refrain from exposing themselves to new situations or broadening their knowledge because they have a reputation or image as an authority to uphold.

All individuals are relatively strong or weak in certain areas, and it is critical for your career development that you are honest about what those areas may be.

Most organizations invest substantially in employee training and development from entry to executive level. You deny yourself key training opportunities if you do not acknowledge areas for development. Chances are that your co-workers and supervisor are already aware of your weaknesses and would support your interest to improve them.

React

(a) Partner with someone who is strong in the area you need to develop for the duration of a project or task. You can learn from that person and have great support along the way, instead of forging ahead on your own.

(b) Think of learning something new as a form of play or exploration. This mindset promotes creativity and enthusiasm.

(c) Spend more time with people who are naturally curious, who try new things with abandon and without fears of looking silly or foolish. What is different about their approach to situations?

(d) Offer to help someone with tasks in which you are skilled or are comfortable doing. Do it in exchange for their support with tasks you have not mastered.

(e) Draw from your experience of learning a hobby, sport or doing a project at home. How satisfied did you feel when you were able to complete it? Were there times when you thought you were not up to the task? Why did you persevere?

(f) Engage a coach for added support and encouragement, especially when you are being too hard on yourself.

(g) There is no shame in letting people know you are actively trying to improve, but you do not have to publicize everything. If you are uncomfortable with people knowing, continue to work privately on certain items with the approval of your manager and the assistance of a coach.

Rethink

If you only value the prestige and position of being an expert in your niche, you may have limited interest in topics outside your field. Experts certainly have remained, and always will remain, invaluable contributors to an organization. Employees with extensive knowledge of a particular area can deal with its details and subtleties, which can make or break a project. Typically, they are the "go to" person who people consult when they need answers to detailed questions. But specialized knowledge and experience become less important the further you progress.

Senior-level managers need exposure to and knowledge about a vast range of topics. Generalists are extremely valuable, because their wide-ranging experience allows them to see issues and details from various perspectives, bringing a broad view to any project, as well as an understanding of how businesses intersect. The generalist may be a jack of all trades who is master of none, but it positions the person uniquely for executive-level management. Although you may favor the prestige associated with being an expert, do not discount the value of those who chose a less specialized path and the opportunities available to them.

React

(a) Read trade journals unrelated to your specific discipline.

(b) Gain a general understanding of how other divisions in your company operate. Go to lunch with people from other departments and ask questions about their work.

(c) Develop a network of contacts in a wide variety of disciplines.

(d) Familiarize yourself with tools that can help you to gather information. Tools such as news aggregators, Topix, Google News etcetera can all help to keep your finger on the pulse of different subjects.

(e) Take note and do further research when someone makes reference to a topic or book with which you are unfamiliar.

(f) Take continuing education courses in general business areas. Your company may sponsor some of them.

(g) Get involved in as many cross-departmental meetings as possible or assignments that involve multiple disciplines.

(h) Listen to business webcasts available through work.

(i) Find a mentor with extensive business acumen. Arrange to meet periodically to discuss various subjects.

6 | You should stick to what you are good at/You should play to your strengths

Rethink

Many people have a passion for a particular discipline or a natural ability to master a certain skill. People tend to gravitate towards their strengths and end up investing their energy solely in bettering those areas. Although it is smart to build on your strengths and go from good to excellent, investing time to get from bad to good can have an even greater impact on your career. Do not be overly concerned about your weaker areas, but if a clear weakness exist, it is critical to improve it for both your current position and promotion.

You make yourself vulnerable by not developing areas in which you are less comfortable. When your value is tied to a narrow skills set, your role in an organization is limited.

React

a) Have an open discussion with your manager and peers about what they think your weaknesses are. Be sure to include some of these items as part of your development plan.

(b) Be aware of the competencies, technical skills and experiences critical to your current position and any future promotion.

(c) Investigate the opportunities available in the organization to undertake rotational assignments.

(d) Sign up for courses available through your company that will broaden your skills set.

(e) Ask to be included in interdisciplinary meetings to increase your general knowledge about all business units.

(f) Be aware of what is happening outside your field. Read news magazines or articles from other business fields at least once a week.

(g) Test and extend your strengths. For example, if you have been working in accounting, grab opportunities to work in financial forecasting. Both draw on your analytical skills and require working with numbers, but they involve different types of application. If you are skilled at technical writing, try penning a feature article for a magazine. You will draw on your natural ability in written communication but will broaden your skills.

(h) Try to begin a new hobby completely unrelated to your work or your perceived talents. You may be surprised by how much you enjoy it and it will make it easier to pursue activities that do not necessarily draw on your strengths.

Overdeveloped

Research has shown that strengths can become weaknesses because you can, in fact, do too much of a good thing. You cannot become less good at a competency in which you excel, but you can balance the behavior by developing a few Stabilizers to tone down an excessive strength.

Stabilizer	Overdeveloped
1 Achiever	Is too preoccupied with own development and works on areas which add no value
19 Determined	
29 Focused on Priorities	
34 Listens Well	
31 Improves Processes	
39 Manages Time	
52 Self-Aware	
54 Takes Accountablity	
55 Takes Initiative	
56 Technically Competent	

Instructions

Read the definition. If it applies to you, choose a few Stabilizers and develop them by selecting the relevant chapter and following the Strategies for Action.

For more instructions see the How To Use This Book section.

22. Diplomatic

"Diplomacy: The business of handling a porcupine without disturbing the quills"

Author unknown

Well Developed
Is tactful and can communicate in a non-confrontational and polite manner

Underdeveloped
Is too direct or blunt. Upsets others by being too direct and tactless

Overdeveloped
Is too polite and struggles to be direct

Instructions

Read the definitions on the left. If the Underdeveloped definition applies, go to the Strategies for Action section.

If the Overdeveloped definition applies, go to the end of the chapter.

Test Yourself

True	I see disagreement as an opportunity for understanding
True	I am able to defuse tense situations
True	I relate well to people even if they are different from me
True	I communicate delicate information in a tactful manner
True	I am able to be honest without being disrespectful

Note

Are you sure you need to develop this competency?

If the answer is "True" to most of the statements on the left, you probably do not need to develop this competency.

143

Strategies for Action

Most ineffective behaviors have an underlying thought or emotional pattern. By identifying these patterns, you can understand the impact they have and design strategies to counteract them.

① I do not know how to be diplomatic

② I think it is important to be direct with people or speak exactly what is on my mind

③ I value facts more than emotions/If you are right, it does not matter how you say it

④ I feel unsure of myself/I have not had much practice in being diplomatic or interacting with people quite different from me

Instructions

1. Read and select one or more of the ineffective ways of thinking/feeling to the left.

2. Find the corresponding number below that will help you to rethink this pattern and identify specific and practical actions that you can take.

1 | I do not know how to be diplomatic

Rethink

Most often, getting tasks done requires others' help and cooperation. Knowing how to build and maintain relationships with people is vital if you hope to be effective. It is especially important to build relationships with those who do not agree with you, are angry with you or who have issues with your organization.

React

(a) Depersonalize the interaction. Think of yourself as acting in a role, for example, as a manager dealing with staff, a customer service representative dealing with a customer etcetera. You are not being attacked by the other person or people; they are interacting with your role.

(b) Think before you speak. Once you have said something, you cannot take it back. People will remember utterances that provoked a strong emotional response. Saying something that offends, humiliates or criticizes will damage a relationship.

(c) Manage your emotions. Being aware of your own emotional triggers will help to prevent emotional outbursts that can damage a relationship. Think of it as identifying your "red buttons", for example, someone making a racist comment or implying you lack intelligence may provoke a stronger than usual reaction from you.

(d) Listen more than you talk. Diplomacy requires an understanding of people, their agendas, belief systems and values. These things can be identified if you listen to what is not being said, too. Most of the time you get important information not just from the message, but from its delivery. Be aware of timing and tone.

2 | I think it is important to be direct with people or speak exactly what is on my mind

Rethink

You can be sure that your honesty and directness will not always be appreciated, particularly if you do not edit what you say. You may feel it is only honest to speak what is on your mind, but tactlessness risks damaging your relationships. And if people are not receptive to what you have to say, you greatly decrease the chance of being heard and the information leading to a productive outcome.

Being diplomatic is less about censoring your message and more about using your intelligence — it is about how the message is delivered, and why.

React

(a) Consider the reasons why you want to communicate certain information to someone. Is the message critical to the parties involved, or are you satisfying a personal and emotional need by sharing it?

(b) Good timing is essential. You may be more successful in sharing your thoughts later, so be patient and hold off if you believe people will be more receptive at a later stage.

(c) Put yourself in the other person's shoes. There are probably some things about which you are sensitive that would offend you if someone shared them with you. Make the effort to understand the impact of what you have to say on the person. Weigh whether it is important enough to say at all. If it is, how would you have liked to hear it?

(d) Remain composed throughout. It puts you in a better position to handle conflict or tense situations. Do not take things personally. In tense circumstances, you can expect emotions to run high and people will be more prone to launching unfair attacks. If you are feeling too emotional, refrain from responding and take time to collect your thoughts. You can ask for time to think things through, if necessary. Keep your tone of voice consistent and calm, because raising it will only encourage others to do the same.

(e) Get a good reading on your audience and adjust your strategy accordingly. Invariably, some people will need more delicate handling than others.

3 | I value facts more than emotions/If you are right, it does not matter how you say it

Rethink

You may have strong opinions, but being diplomatic requires that you create an environment in which others feel safe to express opposing points of view. It is tempting to tell people how misguided they are. Concentrate on listening, rather than telling people what you think, and you will find it becomes easier to build strong relationships.

React

(a) It is difficult to establish a mutually respectful relationship if you do not genuinely listen to what people have to say. Whether you agree or not, acknowledge the other person's point of view. Focus on being attentive instead of telling people "the way it is".

(b) Ask people's opinions and do not make quick judgments or speak dismissively, indicating you already have all the answers.

(c) Guard against aggressive body language or behaviors that others could perceive as overly authoritarian or arrogant, for example, raising your voice, interrupting people or cutting them off, crossing your arms in front of your body, or tapping your foot impatiently.

4 | I feel unsure of myself/I have not had much practice in being diplomatic or interacting with people quite different from me

Rethink

Getting along with people we like or with whom we have much in common is easy. The challenge lies in knowing how to do this successfully with diverse groups. We must learn to build strong relationships and manage tension despite our obvious differences. We cannot expect to comprehend fully all the people with whom we interact, but we can hold ourselves accountable for treating everyone with respect and an open mind.

React

(a) Guard against hidden biases. You may be quite diplomatic with most people, except those from a particular group. Consider taking the implicit association test which is available at www.understandingprejudice.org/iat/. It will help to identify subconscious biases.

(b) If you struggle to understand another person's perspective, focus on your commonalities. They tend to be universal, for example, an appreciation of good service, desire to advance a career, recognition of the importance of quality family time — anything that binds you and the person together.

146

(c) Read biographies or watch documentaries about great politicians. Note how they interact with different interest groups, get their message across or state their opinion without offending or alienating people who hold different views.

Overdeveloped

Research has shown that strengths can become weaknesses because you can, in fact, do too much of a good thing. You cannot become less good at a competency in which you excel, but you can balance the behavior by developing a few Stabilizers to tone down an excessive strength.

Stabilizer	Overdeveloped
1 Achiever	Is too polite and struggles to be direct
13 Courageous	
16 Decisive	
17 Demonstrates Good Judgment	
23 Directs People	
35 Manages Conflict	
37 Manages Negotiations	
38 Manages Underperformance	
54 Takes Accountablity	
9 Communicates Well (Verbal)	

Instructions

Read the definition. If it applies to you, choose a few Stabilizers and develop them by selecting the relevant chapter and following the Strategies for Action.

For more instructions see the How To Use This Book section.

23. Directs People

"The orchestra plays mechanically, using mechanical energy; the conductor moves his hands, and his movements have an effect on the music artistry"

Leon Theremin

Well Developed
Provides clear objectives and instructions to others

Underdeveloped
Expects people to work too independently and does not provide clear objectives or instructions

Overdeveloped
Micro-manages people by providing too much detail and limits opportunities for others to take initiative

Instructions

Read the definitions on the left. If the Underdeveloped definition applies, go to the Strategies for Action section.

If the Overdeveloped definition applies, go to the end of the chapter.

Test Yourself

True	People are able to follow my instructions
True	People rarely misunderstand what I want or need from them
True	I am aware that people learn in different ways and may need things explained accordingly
True	When I give instructions, I ask questions to ensure they have been understood
True	I am comfortable stepping in to provide direction
True	I ask whether people are clear about our objectives or deadlines
True	I check in with people periodically to see if they need direction
True	I do not wait until people are struggling before I provide direction

Note

Are you sure you need to develop this competency?

If the answer is "True" to most of the statements on the left, you probably do not need to develop this competency.

Strategies for Action

Most ineffective behaviors have an underlying thought or emotional pattern. By identifying these patterns, you can understand the impact they have and design strategies to counteract them.

① I am uncomfortable telling people what to do

② It is important for people to take the initiative or work independently

③ Instructing others takes time away from my work/I prefer to do things myself

④ People misinterpret my directions/ My instructions are often misunderstood

Instructions

1. Read and select one or more of the ineffective ways of thinking/feeling to the left.

2. Find the corresponding number below that will help you to rethink this pattern and identify specific and practical actions that you can take.

① | I am uncomfortable telling people what to do

Rethink

Do not assume that people will be offended or resentful if you step in to provide direction. Directions or instructions are not the same as orders. Most people appreciate direction if it helps them to sort out problems. When people understand what is expected of them, they are able to work more effectively.

Unclear instructions or ambiguous objectives generate unnecessary work and make people resentful. Instead of worrying about stepping on someone's toes, learn to recognize when direction is needed and how to communicate instructions.

By providing direction to others, you are increasing their understanding and improving their ability to focus. You are also helping them understand how to achieve their goals.

ReAct

(a) Try to motivate people while instructing them. Give direction enthusiastically and point out the advantage of doing things a certain way.

(b) Be as inclusive as possible when providing direction, especially when resistant individuals are involved. Welcome their suggestions and let them know their feedback is valuable.

(c) Watch your tone of voice and mannerisms to ensure you do not seem bossy. This is particularly important if you are uncomfortable or tense. A person under stress often sends the wrong message inadvertently.

(d) By their very nature, some people are intimidating. If you have to provide them with direction, get to know them on an individual level. It will help you to make a connection with them and is likely to dispel some of your preconceived ideas.

(e) If people get defensive while getting instructions, remain composed and do not take things personally. The goal is to get them to move forward in a productive manner and with an appropriate mindset. Try to find out what makes them defensive by talking privately to each person. Ignoring their attitude will not make it go away, and it will become increasingly difficult for you to provide direction without meeting resistance. Show people that you care about the fact that something is bothering them.

2 | It is important for people to take the initiative or work independently

Rethink

Clear directives do not stop people from working independently — they actually empower people to do so.
Without adequate direction, people typically require clarification and an unnecessary dependency on a manager or supervisor develops as the project progresses.

If you want your subordinates to work as independently as possible, take enough time to provide them with clear direction and instructions. Be aware that not everyone is able or willing to ask for the direction they need. Unless you have created an environment in which questions are encouraged, you could find yourself picking up tasks that could have been done independently or fixing work that would have been done correctly with the right support.

React

(a) Schedule time to check in with each individual periodically, even if not for assistance.

(b) Never assume everyone works well independently. Some people simply require more direction than others, and when they get it they perform well.

(c) Get to know your team. People have different styles and needs, and the more you get to know them the better you will understand their position.

(d) Be realistic about those you supervise. Take into account not only personalities but people's experience, skills and level of maturity. For example, someone new to a position is likely to require more direction than a seasoned employee.

(e) Pair more experienced individuals with new employees to maximize the amount of direction they get.

(f) Take advantage of assessment instruments such as 360° feedback or the Birkman personality assessment for a better understanding of the people you work with or manage.

(g) Be accessible. When people ask for assistance, ensure you give them the appropriate time and are patient with their questions.

3 | Instructing others takes time away from my work/ I prefer to do things myself

Rethink

Would you just as soon do it yourself instead of wasting time on instructions to others? This could be a sound choice if it was a one-off task, but typically jobs will come round again and require your intervention once more.

At first, giving people adequate instructions and guidance to learn may take more time than you think you can afford, but eventually your involvement will be minimal, if needed at all.

Make room for your development and growth rather than busy work and, in the process, contribute to the development of others.

React

(a) First delegate those items that need the least instruction and support from you. Rate the tasks according to a scale from least to most direction required on your part and clear them first.

(b) Avoid spending time on repeating instructions. Confirm that your instructions have been understood — ask the person to summarize what they have to do.

(c) Create written instructions, where appropriate, which can be used as reference by colleagues in doubt before asking you. It will allow you to focus your time on addressing specific queries.

(d) Provide direction and preserve time simultaneously, for example, let a subordinate shadow you and give instructions to others as you perform the task.

(e) Be prepared for questions and feedback and do not become defensive or abrupt. People will refrain from asking questions that could clarify confusion.

(f) Include directing others as one of your performance measures. It will help you to prioritize time to do it.

4 | People misinterpret my directions/My instructions are often misunderstood

Rethink

Do you end up having to reshape people's focus all the time? Perhaps, throughout a project, you are often asked to repeat your instructions. Yet you cannot see why people find it so hard to get what you want. The problem may lie in your lack of appropriate direction from the start.

Managers often expect their colleagues to be able to read their minds or fill in the gaps, but those gaps are simply too wide. Ensure you are realistic about the amount of context or direction a person needs to fill in the picture. It frustrates people and wastes their time when they struggle to decipher your instructions.

React

(a) Never assume your directions are perfectly clear. Ask whether people have understood you. Get feedback about the quality of your instructions.

(b) Ensure you highlight and emphasize key points.

(c) Adapt your style of direction to the individual or audience. "One size fits all" is not an appropriate approach. Consider people's work styles, level of experience and skills. People grasp concepts differently, so consider how you explain them. A discussion may be best for an eloquent person, but a spreadsheet may work better for someone methodical. An experienced engineer, for example, may only have to understand the overall objective, while a new hireling would need detailed instructions. Also, consider people's competencies. Some people are more comfortable with ambiguity or more resourceful than others and require less direction.

(d) Communicate the big plan — lay it out. Map a project plan with tasks and deadlines to provide direction for the team. It allows you to frame discussions about progress and you can direct colleagues in a structured way.

(e) Understand the problem or task and its objectives. Take time to organize your thoughts and instructions.

(f) Ensure you stick to the point and do not digress. Too much information and many tangents will confuse people and muddle the waters.

(g) Check where your attention goes. If you are preoccupied with multiple things at once, the direction you are providing may be compromised. Repeat what the person has asked you. Turn off your cellphone and use a private space, if possible, to minimize distractions. You must be focused to give relevant, meaningful instructions.

(h) Communicate instructions both verbally and in writing. Hard-copy instructions ensure people know what you want and limit neglected items. If possible, write your instructions to people in an e-mail or memo, or ask them to take notes.

Overdeveloped

Research has shown that strengths can become weaknesses because you can, in fact, do too much of a good thing. You cannot become less good at a competency in which you excel, but you can balance the behavior by developing a few Stabilizers to tone down an excessive strength.

Stabilizer	Overdeveloped
20 Develops People	Micro-manages people by providing too much detail and limits opportunities for others to take initiative
22 Diplomatic	
25 Empowers People	
28 Fair	
34 Listens Well	
36 Manages Ideas	
4 Approachable	
43 Motivates People	
51 Recognizes Talent And Potential	
59 Unifies People	

Instructions

Read the definition. If it applies to you, choose a few Stabilizers and develop them by selecting the relevant chapter and following the Strategies for Action.

For more instructions see the How To Use This Book section.

24. Empathetic

"People will forget what you said, people will forget what you did, but people will never forget how you made them feel"

Bonnie Jean Wasmund

Well Developed
Demonstrates a genuine concern for and interest in others

Underdeveloped
Appears uncaring and cold. Is unable to respond appropriately to emotional issues

Overdeveloped
Gets too involved in personal issues, loses objectivity and is seen as easy to manipulate

Instructions
Read the definitions on the left. If the Underdeveloped definition applies, go to the Strategies for Action section.

If the Overdeveloped definition applies, go to the end of the chapter.

Test Yourself

True	I understand that people experience situations differently
True	I care about people's feelings
True	I am available to someone who needs to talk
True	I can imagine how someone might be feeling in certain circumstances
True	I think it makes me a better manager to care about others' feelings

Note

Are you sure you need to develop this competency?

If the answer is "True" to most of the statements on the left, you probably do not need to develop this competency.

Strategies for Action

Most ineffective behaviors have an underlying thought or emotional pattern. By identifying these patterns, you can understand the impact they have and design strategies to counteract them.

① I am too busy to listen to others' problems

② Emotions have no place in the workplace/People should leave their feelings at home

③ I am not good with emotional issues; they make me uncomfortable

④ I cannot be empathetic if I cannot relate to a person

Instructions

1. Read and select one or more of the ineffective ways of thinking/feeling to the left.

2. Find the corresponding number below that will help you to rethink this pattern and identify specific and practical actions that you can take.

1 | I am too busy to listen to others' problems

Rethink

Being interested only in your work and not in the people with whom you share it robs you of the opportunity to stay in touch with sentiments felt within your team and the organization. Do you know how people feel about different policies or the direction the company is taking? How effectively your staff is working with each other? How motivated your key talent is feeling? This information is easily available if you are willing to invest some time in listening to colleagues' concerns.

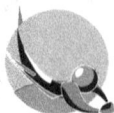

React

(a) How well do you know your peers? Or the people who work for you? Are most of them strangers because you do not give them the time of day? Schedule a lunch or take brief breaks during the day to interact and get the scoop on colleagues' lives.

(b) Be available to listen, but set polite time limits. Tell the speaker that although you only have a short time, you really want to hear what is bothering them.

(c) Sometimes it really is impossible to make time to talk during a particularly busy day. Suggest meeting with the person after hours or in lunchtime.

(d) If you sincerely feel someone is monopolizing your time, diplomatically point out that you cannot give the person the adequate time they deserve and suggest they talk to someone who assists employees.

2 | Emotions have no place in the workplace/People should leave their feelings at home

Rethink

Hoping to remove emotions completely from the workplace is unrealistic. People are emotional beings by nature and their feelings will have an impact on their work.

A Chinese metaphor translates empathy in an enlightening manner — it calls it "the reasoning heart". That is because empathy requires you to consider carefully what someone is experiencing in order to care enough about their feelings. Ensure your reasoning heart is beating for those at work.

React

(a) Create an environment in which people are encouraged to talk about their feelings. Set an example by being frank. Always ask people how they feel about situations or assignments.

(b) How good are you at reading people? Someone may be upset but reluctant to say so. If you pay close attention and use your intuition, you will be able to sense when someone is battling with emotions. If you believe someone is upset, do not ignore it — ask the person about it, if appropriate.

(c) If time is an issue, tell the person that although you can only talk for a short time, you really want to hear about their problem.

(d) Use statements that convey your understanding and empathy, such as "I am sorry for what you are going through" or "I understand how you would feel that way".

(e) Ask yourself how you would feel if the tables were turned. How would you want someone to respond to you?

3 | I am not good with emotional issues; they make me uncomfortable

Rethink

Some people feel too uncomfortable to deal with others' feelings. People's tolerance and comfort levels vary and depend on personality, socialization, cultural practice, gender, family dynamics and so forth. The reasons are numerous and complex, but the point is some people actively avoid emotional situations.

There are many ways to remain empathetic and help others to feel understood without assuming the role of therapist or counselor. Being empathetic is often as simple as listening, and that should not make you feel uncomfortable. With practice, you will get more comfortable in dealing with people's feelings.

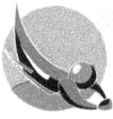

React

(a) It is not necessary to provide answers or solutions when people share their feelings with you. You can give advice if it is solicited or, if you do not have an opinion, you can admit that you cannot comment although you certainly understand why the person feels the way they do.

(b) Practice effective listening skills. Be available when someone needs to talk. Restate what the person has said so that they know you have listened. Try to understand the triggers that have led the person to their current emotional condition.

(c) Become more comfortable by opening up somewhat to a trusted peer. The worst that can happen is that the person does not care. Avoid being that type of person.

4 | I cannot be empathetic if I cannot relate to a person

Rethink

Empathy means you can put yourself in someone else's shoes, regardless of their size or shape. The ability to be empathetic towards those who are different from you, or even in conflict with you, sets you apart from the rest. Many situations one encounters at work are universal.

If you are male, there will be female things you cannot relate to and vice versa. But you can understand the feelings of any colleague who has been passed up for promotion or is dealing with a lot of stress. Feelings are universal and transcend race, gender, religion, age and culture. All people are capable of feeling the wide spectrum of emotions that encompasses the human experience.

To be empathetic, focus less on trying to identify with the person, and more on the feelings they are experiencing and being able to show that you genuinely care.

React

(a) Consider hidden biases or stereotypes you may harbor and which may prevent you from caring about people from a particular group. You cannot pick and choose your peers or clients, so selective empathy is not productive.

(b) Do not try to agree or disagree with the person, just be open to what is being said. Imagine the person as a close friend or family member who shares an experience with you. How sensitively would you act?

(c) Spend time in the company of people with whom you have difficulty to relate. Ask them to explain their experience to you. You will be surprised to learn about things other people have to endure, which you may not have to face.

Overdeveloped

Research has shown that strengths can become weaknesses because you can, in fact, do too much of a good thing. You cannot become less good at a competency in which you excel, but you can balance the behavior by developing a few Stabilizers to tone down an excessive strength.

Stabilizer	Overdeveloped
1 Achiever	Gets too involved in personal issues, loses objectivity and is seen as easy to manipulate
13 Courageous	
17 Demonstrates Good Judgment	
23 Directs People	
29 Focused on Priorities	
35 Manages Conflict	
38 Manages Underperformance	
39 Manages Time	
42 Monitors Work	
54 Takes Accountablity	

Instructions

Read the definition. If it applies to you, choose a few Stabilizers and develop them by selecting the relevant chapter and following the Strategies for Action.

For more instructions see the How To Use This Book section.

25. Empowers People

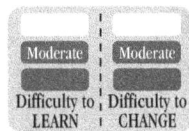

"Few things help an individual more than to place responsibility upon him and to let him know that you trust him"

Booker T. Washington

Well Developed
Assigns meaningful and important tasks and responsibilities to others and gives them authority to act

Underdeveloped
Is unwilling to allow others to take responsibility or assigns only trivial tasks and responsibilities to them

Overdeveloped
Abdicates too much work to others who lack the authority to complete it

Instructions
Read the definitions on the left. If the Underdeveloped definition applies, go to the Strategies for Action section.

If the Overdeveloped definition applies, go to the end of the chapter.

Test Yourself

True	I give people the authority to make decisions without my approval
True	I assign progressively greater responsibilities to my subordinates
True	I support other people's decisions once they have made them
True	I remain composed and reassure people when they make mistakes
True	I consider carefully the type of resources and support a person may need to complete an assignment successfully
True	I delegate meaningful responsibilities to others, not tasks just to keep them busy

Note

Are you sure you need to develop this competency?

If the answer is "True" to most of the statements on the left, you probably do not need to develop this competency.

Strategies for Action

Most ineffective behaviors have an underlying thought or emotional pattern. By identifying these patterns, you can understand the impact they have and design strategies to counteract them.

① I do not know how to delegate effectively

② I do not trust that others will get things done well enough/I like to control things myself

③ I do not have the opportunity to delegate/I do not have direct authority to delegate to others

Instructions

1. Read and select one or more of the ineffective ways of thinking/feeling to the left.

2. Find the corresponding number below that will help you to rethink this pattern and identify specific and practical actions that you can take.

1 | I do not know how to delegate effectively

Rethink

Assigning work to others may seem an easy task but, in fact, delegating responsibility is one of managers' biggest challenges. Skillful delegation is a critical opportunity managers have to empower their subordinates. Delegation requires that time is set aside to consider the talents in others and how these can be utilized to most effectively and efficiently meet organizational goals.

React

(a) Focus on the process and not only the people. Set your controls by planning work processes well. Invest time beforehand to lay out clear timeframes, goals and instructions. Once you have provided directives, allow people to follow them and test your controls.

(b) Give people tasks that are meaningful, not just stuff to keep them busy. Be sure to also give individuals the sort of responsibility that would make a difference in their careers.

(c) Use assessment tools to better understand the talent and strengths of individuals in your team, and delegate accordingly. For example, someone with strong persuasion skills can be assigned to lead the negotiation phase of an assignment.

(d) Ask people what they would like to do and give them opportunities to explore that interest.

162

(e) Delegate equitably. Examine to whom it is you usually delegate and why. Managers have a tendency to delegate to those who have performed well previously, at the expense of others who may do just as well with a little more guidance.

(f) Consider experience level, timeframes and resources available when delegating an assignment. Ensure your expectations are realistic, based on all of the above, so that you do not set someone up for failure. Impossible tasks do not empower people.

2 | I do not trust that others will get things done well enough/I like to control things myself

Rethink

Micromanagers establish an unhealthy dependency between them and their subordinates. At worst, they demoralize those who report to them. The savvy manager empowers the team so that it can function in a self-sufficient and effective manner, even in the manager's absence.

The way people go about meeting their goals is less important than the support and guidance you provide in helping them to reach those goals. Remember that, at different points in your career, someone trusted you enough that you could prove yourself and achieve your current position.

Likely, your subordinates will make mistakes, but these are the most valuable lessons people learn, and how well they handle their mistakes gives you insight into their character. At first, when you hand over responsibility, tasks may not be completed as expertly as you hoped. Some adjustments will have to be made, including setting back a deadline, perhaps. A short-term risk is associated with handing over responsibility, but demoralizing and losing talent is a bigger risk, which no manager should be taking.

React

(a) Verbalize clearly to subordinates that you give them authority to make decisions on their own. Having responsibilities is not empowering if one has to run every decision by one's manager. By nature, people are cautious about making wrong decisions, so if in doubt they will probably ask for approval.

(b) Establish a culture of trust. Make it clear that people are expected to manage their own work and that you are available when they need assistance.

(c) Agree to checkpoints in the process where you will review a person's work. In between these points, refrain from crowding the person.

(d) Regardless of how much you would want a task to be done in a particular way, remind yourself that there are many approaches. You may learn something new if you give someone freedom.

(e) If you are uncomfortable giving a person responsibility, team them with a stronger performer. Help them to evaluate the experience once the project is finished.

(f) Assume that extra time will be needed when someone is new to an assignment or testing new skills. It gives the person room to succeed in their assignment and learn at the same time.

163

(g) Delegate meaningful responsibilities that have a substantial impact. Constantly getting menial tasks is demoralizing and does little to empower people.

(h) During delegation you may well discover someone who does not perform in a certain area. Use this as an opportunity to discover their strengths or find the necessary interventions. If someone continually underperforms, despite your best attempts, you can choose development, reassignment, or let the person go.

3 | I do not have the opportunity to delegate /I do not have direct authority to delegate to others

Rethink

If you do not have subordinates, you may not have had the opportunity to empower others by delegating to them. This may be the case, but empowering others can be accomplished in small ways such as the right attitude towards colleagues. Do not assume that, because you do not have subordinates, you are not responsible for empowering others. Effective teamwork often needs multiple people to take the lead and delegate to others. Your awareness of the parts they could play in a project and facilitating their participation send the signal that you value the empowerment of the team.

React

(a) Take the lead in your team when it is sensible to do so. It is not always necessary to wait for your supervisor to delegate. Coordinate with your peers which tasks each will do and encourage others to cultivate new skills.

(b) If you are particularly skilled in an area, invite other team members to work with you on that aspect.

(c) Readily share interesting and new information or insights you have recently acquired.

(d) Observe other managers who are good at empowering their team. Note what the person does well. Ask why people like working for that person.

(e) Tell your manager that you would like to gain experience in managing others and discuss the opportunities for you to do so. You may be assigned as team leader on a particular project, or perhaps serve in a special committee. Ask for increased authority in decision making and delegation.

(f) There are many opportunities to empower others outside of work. Practice your empowerment skills with your family members and through any groups or associations in which you are involved.

Overdeveloped

Research has shown that strengths can become weaknesses because you can, in fact, do too much of a good thing. You cannot become less good at a competency in which you excel, but you can balance the behavior by developing a few Stabilizers to tone down an excessive strength.

Stabilizer	Overdeveloped
20 Develops People	Abdicates too much work to others who lack the authority to complete it
1 Achiever	
23 Directs People	
24 Empathetic	
28 Fair	
51 Recognizes Talent and Potential	
32 Informs Others	
42 Monitors Work	
43 Motivates People	
54 Takes Accountablity	

Instructions

Read the definition. If it applies to you, choose a few Stabilizers and develop them by selecting the relevant chapter and following the Strategies for Action.

For more instructions see the How To Use This Book section.

26. Ethical

"Live one day at a time, emphasizing ethics rather than rules"

Wayne Dyer

Well Developed
Acts in line with the dominant values of the organization

Underdeveloped
Makes the wrong call when faced with ambiguous decisions or acts contrary to the values of the organization

Overdeveloped
Is seen as contentious and applies values too rigidly, without consideration of alternative views

Instructions
Read the definitions on the left. If the Underdeveloped definition applies, go to the Strategies for Action section.

If the Overdeveloped definition applies, go to the end of the chapter.

Test Yourself

True	I am aware of the company's values
True	How I act at work reflects the organization's values
True	I make amends if I have behaved inappropriately
True	I think about the company's values when faced with an ambiguous decision
True	My values stay consistent regardless of the situation
True	I think the company values are important

Note

Are you sure you need to develop this competency?

If the answer is "True" to most of the statements on the left, you probably do not need to develop this competency.

26 Ethical

Strategies for Action

Most ineffective behaviors have an underlying thought or emotional pattern. By identifying these patterns, you can understand the impact they have and design strategies to counteract them.

① I do not think a company's values are that important

② My ethics tend to change based on the situation or people with whom I am intracting

③ I follow my own values/I apply my own values when making decisions

④ I do not agree with the company's values

⑤ There are incentives to act unethically in my organization

Instructions

1. Read and select one or more of the ineffective ways of thinking/feeling to the left.

2. Find the corresponding number below that will help you to rethink this pattern and identify specific and practical actions that you can take.

---

① I do not think a company's values are that important

Rethink

It is not uncommon for people to think the company's values do not relate to their work, or even to be unaware of them altogether. Values provide a company and its employees with a framework for desired behavior.

Values can be translated in many ways during the day's work. You, for example, may personally rate productivity highest, but one of your company's top values is customer service. You may think you are wasting your time having to make calls to clients when you need to complete an assignment for your manager. But the company values dictate that keeping the customer content should be the number one priority.

Organizational values create cohesion and ensure that all employees work from the same template and share the same culture.

React

(a) Familiarize yourself with your company's values.

(b) Initiate a discussion among your colleagues and team mates to examine how well your group is doing at abiding by the company's values.

(c) Try the following exercise: List the company values on paper. Then, for each value, list the things you do that promote the value and the things that contradict it. Write down what you can do differently to bridge any shortcomings.

(d) Let the company values guide you during difficult and ambiguous decision-making times.

2 | My ethics tend to change based on the situation or people with whom I am interacting

Rethink

It is important to know how to maneuver through complex and ambiguous situations in the workplace, but using unethical behavior to do so is wrong.

As an individual representative of your organization, you will have to make tough decisions that require you to stick to the company's principles regardless of the situation, the people with whom you are interacting or what you stand to gain.

Acting in a consistent manner sets predictable expectations for others and lets people know you can be trusted to make the right decision. As a leader, all your actions are under scrutiny and they will set the example for what is or is not acceptable in your company.

React

(a) Think of someone who is considered to act unethically. Write down what it is about them that makes you consider their behavior unethical. Would you make the same decisions the person made under the same circumstances?

(b) When facing a tough decision, think of someone who is respected for their ethical behavior. What would that person do in your shoes? Ask them, if possible.

(c) Ask yourself before taking action: "Even if everyone involved does not get what they want, will their dignity and rights be respected through my decision?"

(d) Reflect on any ambiguous decision afterwards. How did it turn out for all concerned? If you had to do it over again, what would you do differently?

(e) Do the "publicity test": If you had to explain your decision on national television, would you be comfortable doing so?

3 | I follow my own values/I apply my own values when making decisions

Rethink

Some people have strong values and will act accordingly, regardless of the expectations of them at work or in their personal lives. It may seem inconsequential for people to act as they wish, but organizations depend on their employees' commitment to a shared culture and expect them to abide by those values. This is an implicit contract between employer and employee.

When a person behaves in a way that solely accommodates their own values, it has negative consequences on their team members and, ultimately, can result in the person being fired.

React

(a) Weigh the consequences of your behavior. Is it worth risking your position?

(b) Is there any work situation in which your values are unrealistic? Will you have difficulties to accept the culture in a similar organization?

(c) Can you concede that there are some values not important enough to risk your position for?

(d) If you cannot adhere to anyone else's values, including those of your company, then perhaps you should consider working independently. If you do so, keep in mind that you may nonetheless need to take your client's values into consideration.

4 | I do not agree with the company's values

Rethink

This is an important observation and you need to act on it. It is difficult to promote your career and personal happiness in an environment that is not aligned with your values.

React

(a) Talk to a respected colleague or your superior about how you could reconcile gaps.

(b) Realize that your work will not necessarily fulfill all your values. You can also satisfy your personal values through your life outside of work. Get involved in activities that promote the values you are not able to address through work.

(c) Consider whether it is really the values of the organization with which you have an issue, or the behavior of particular individuals or your team. If necessary or possible, find a reassignment.

(d) If you cannot reconcile your values and those of the company, you should consider moving to another organization.

5 | There are incentives to act unethically in my organization

Rethink

Individuals with power in an organization may openly or overtly create inappropriate incentives for others. It happens for a variety of reasons — pressure to meet targets, personal gain, and to exert power and control.
Whatever the reason, you may feel caught between a rock and a hard place. Sometimes, the pressure just to keep up can be overwhelming enough to create incentives to act unethically.

You do not have to search far to see the damaging results of such collective behavior — just think of the scandals and consequences created by Enron, WorldCom, Arthur Andersen and Tyco, for example. Entire industries can implode because of unregulated behavior fueled by unethical incentives — just recently it happened to the mortgage and loan industry in the US.

No doubt there may be much at stake personally when an individual chooses to take a stand against unethical behavior, but there is more to lose by following this path: your peace of mind, mental health, sense of values and self-respect. Remember, it becomes easier to justify your actions or accept the status quo the longer you fail to act. A leader has many responsibilities and none are as great as protecting your stakeholders from unethical practices.

React

(a) Do not assume that everyone is aware of the situation or feels differently about it. If your superior is not receptive, identify who in the chain of command will be open to your concerns so that you will have an alternative listener.

(b) Collect as much documentation as possible to support your position and provide evidence.

(c) There is safety in numbers. Are you the only one with objections? Identify others that have raised concerns and present your objections collectively.

(d) Know your legal rights. There are laws to protect whistle-blowers. Talk to a human resources representative in confidence about your concerns and advise them if the matter has great implications and cannot be resolved at your level.

(e) If the unethical behavior is pervasive in your industry or organization's culture, you will be better off leaving. You may be leaving your job, but you will be taking a huge step towards a career of which you can be proud.

Overdeveloped

Research has shown that strengths can become weaknesses because you can, in fact, do too much of a good thing. You cannot become less good at a competency in which you excel, but you can balance the behavior by developing a few Stabilizers to tone down an excessive strength.

Stabilizer	Overdeveloped
17 Demonstrates Good Judgment	Is seen as contentious and applies values too rigidly, without consideration of alternative views
2 Adaptable	
22 Diplomatic	
27 Experimental	
24 Empathetic	
28 Fair	
30 Global Thinker	
46 Open-Minded	
34 Listens Well	
49 Politically Astute	

Instructions

Read the definition. If it applies to you, choose a few Stabilizers and develop them by selecting the relevant chapter and following the Strategies for Action.

For more instructions see the How To Use This Book section.

27. Experimental

	Hard
Moderate	
Difficulty to LEARN	Difficulty to CHANGE

> "All progress is experimental"
> John Jay Chapman

Well Developed
Enjoys trying new things and is willing to experiment and take calculated risks

Underdeveloped
Avoids the unknown and is too fearful of the risk of failure

Overdeveloped
Takes unnecessary risks to try something new

Instructions

Read the definitions on the left. If the Underdeveloped definition applies, go to the Strategies for Action section.

If the Overdeveloped definition applies, go to the end of the chapter.

Test Yourself

True	I am not afraid to try new things to gain valuable experiences
True	I am open to exploring new ways of doing things
True	I often test new ideas, products or services to find the best solutions
True	I am a proponent of innovation and I like to invent creative ideas to improve processes and work in general
True	I think time spent experimenting is time well spent

Note

Are you sure you need to develop this competency?

If the answer is "True" to most of the statements on the left, you probably do not need to develop this competency.

Strategies for Action

Most ineffective behaviors have an underlying thought or emotional pattern. By identifying these patterns, you can understand the impact they have and design strategies to counteract them.

① I am not comfortable taking risks/I have had negative experiences with experimenting

② I value what is tried and tested/I prefer sticking to what I know

③ Experimenting is not actively encouraged in my environment/I may be perceived as wasting time

Instructions

1. Read and select one or more of the ineffective ways of thinking/feeling to the left.

2. Find the corresponding number below that will help you to rethink this pattern and identify specific and practical actions that you can take.

---

1 | I am not comfortable taking risks/I have had negative experiences with experimenting

Rethink

People who take risks and experiment with new approaches get burnt every once in a while, which may have happened to you. Do not let previous setbacks keep you from being experimental. It would not be a risk if success was guaranteed, and every setback provides a learning opportunity that increases your odds of success in the next endeavor. Of course, the upside to risk taking is that when you do succeed your contribution to the organization will be well recognized.

Remember, with most investments, the bigger the risk the greater the reward.

React

(a) Start with low-impact, least-consequence experimentation and see how even small risks can pay off.

(b) Document the benefits of doing things differently. What is currently not working and what does it cost the organization? Use this as motivation to experiment.

(c) Find a mentor who is used to taking risks. Ask them to help you evaluate the consequences and potential reward. Ask them how they deal with the occasional failure, how much they have gained in the long run from taking chances, and what their experience have taught them.

2 | I value what is tried and tested/I prefer sticking to what I know

Rethink

Most people prefer to operate within their comfort zone and rarely step outside of it. If you often find yourself thinking "Why are we always reinventing the wheel around here?", or typically saying to others "We have done this before, why not continue to do what has worked in the past?", you may be relying on your comfort zone too much. In the process you could be setting up stumbling blocks for yourself and others that prevent experimentation.

Although it is necessary to draw on experience and proven solutions, do not allow that to limit your creativity. Ironically, systems that are most durable and survive the longest are those open to change.

Think about experimenting as a way of adding more value to that which has already been achieved.

React

(a) Be receptive to challenging the status quo and encourage others to do the same.

(b) Consider the conditions and context of the problem you are trying to resolve and determine whether they have changed in any way. If they have, it may be time to consider that a different approach is in order.

(c) Change your work groups or teams so that new ideas can be introduced.

(d) Try experimenting with small changes instead of revamping or overhauling an entire system, policy or design.

(e) Studies have shown that people work harder when they have a choice in how they try new and different things. Experiment in a manner that fits your personality and makes sense to you — but be sure to do it.

(f) Be aware of your general attitude towards doing things differently, and try to stay positive about others' ideas. Always shooting down requests to try a new approach is a surefire way of discouraging a culture of experimentation.

3 | Experimenting is not actively encouraged in my environment/I may be perceived as wasting time

Rethink

You may be willing to experiment more than you already are but believe it is not encouraged or valued in your team or organization. Being willing to experiment takes extra effort and time and can be an added burden or drain your energy, especially if you are fighting political battles to gain support at the same time. But some things are worth fighting for.

If you are able to demonstrate the potential reward, you can be an agent of change even in the most resistant environment.

175

React

(a) Effectively communicate how your time and effort could positively affect the bottom line.

(b) Anticipate objections and be prepared for the rejection or rebuttal of your ideas.

(c) Support experimentation within your team or unit by publicly acknowledging and praising colleagues' efforts, regardless of their success or failure.

(d) Include experimentation as part of your subordinate's performance measures.

(e) Assign teams to work solely on experimental projects and innovative approaches.

(f) Be politically savvy. Try to gain support from key decision makers.

(g) Choose your battles. People may be more receptive to experimentation in one area than another. Start where the least resistance exists.

Overdeveloped

Research has shown that strengths can become weaknesses because you can, in fact, do too much of a good thing. You cannot become less good at a competency in which you excel, but you can balance the behavior by developing a few Stabilizers to tone down an excessive strength.

Stabilizer	Overdeveloped
18 Detail-Orientated	Takes unnecessary risks to try something new
19 Determined	
32 Informs Others	
34 Listens Well	
47 Patient	
48 Plans Work	
50 Problem Solver	
17 Demonstrates Good Judgment	
29 Focused on Priorities	
40 Market Aware	

Instructions

Read the definition. If it applies to you, choose a few Stabilizers and develop them by selecting the relevant chapter and following the Strategies for Action.

For more instructions see the How To Use This Book section.

28. Fair

"Win or lose, do it fairly"
Knute Rockne

Well Developed
Treats people fairly regardless of race, gender, cultural differences or personal styles

Underdeveloped
Treats people unfairly as a result of differences in race, gender, culture or personal style

Overdeveloped
Tries to treat all people the same, without consideration for differences in race, gender, culture or personal style

Instructions

Read the definitions on the left. If the Underdeveloped definition applies, go to the Strategies for Action section.

If the Overdeveloped definition applies, go to the end of the chapter.

28 Fair

Test Yourself

True	I give everyone appropriate opportunities
True	I consider whether I am being fair before I act
True	I do not let my personal feelings about someone dictate how I behave towards them. I consider everybody's interests, not only mine
True	I am comfortable around people who are different to me

Note

Are you sure you need to develop this competency?

If the answer is "True" to most of the statements on the left, you probably do not need to develop this competency.

Strategies for Action

Most ineffective behaviors have an underlying thought or emotional pattern. By identifying these patterns, you can understand the impact they have and design strategies to counteract them.

(1) My personal feelings play a large role in the way I treat people/I tend to have favorites

(2) I treat everyone equally

(3) I identify better with certain groups/I feel uncomfortable around people different to me

(4) Certain types of diversity make me uncomfortable (race/gender/ethnicity)/I have strong negative opinions about certain groups

(5) I am looking out for my best interests/I need to stay competitive

(6) I do not have much experience in interacting with people different to me

Instructions

1. Read and select one or more of the ineffective ways of thinking/feeling to the left.

2. Find the corresponding number below that will help you to rethink this pattern and identify specific and practical actions that you can take.

---

1 | **My personal feelings play a large role in the way I treat people/I tend to have favorites**

Rethink

If you have established a good relationship with someone because of their personality or work style, or because they perform consistently well, you may give that person preferential treatment. Conversely, feelings of resentment may reflect in your treatment of an employee.

People can detect even subtle differences in your behavior towards others, which can make them feel they do not get equal treatment. This can cause resentment and mistrust among your peers or subordinates.

Circumstances can change quickly and so can feelings, but the repercussions of unfair treatment last much longer.

React

(a) Subtle behavior says just as much as overt action. Examine closely whether you recognize yourself doing any of the following on a regular basis: directing most of your questions to one particular person, being less attentive to certain people and cutting them off more often, making yourself more available to some than others, being more judgmental or negative about a particular person's ideas, inviting some people to lunch and not others, and giving unequal praise or recognition. If you answer yes to one or any of the above, you should try to act more fairly.

(b) Hand out assignments fairly to avoid sending a message that you have favorites. Giving one or two people the most desired projects all the time lessens your ability to develop your team's talents and denies people the opportunity to prove themselves. Consider creative ways to engage a person who is not performing well, instead of alienating them. For example, pair a strong and less strong performer together on a team assignment.

(c) Ensure you do not compare employees, publicly or privately, or constantly use one person as an example of excellence. You may foster a loss of respect or resentment for the person among team members.

(d) In discussions and meetings, encourage input from everyone and give everyone a chance to be heard.

(e) Be aware of adverse body language when the person is talking to you, such as rolling your eyes, keeping your arms tightly crossed or not smiling when appropriate.

(f) If you harbor resentment towards a particular person, talk to them in private. Strong negative feelings that go unaddressed will become disruptive and can lead to passive-aggressive behavior.

(g) Let a mediator facilitate the discussion if the issues cannot be resolved among yourselves.

2 | I treat everyone equally

Rethink

This sounds just and reasonable at first, but think about the consequences of treating everybody equally. If two people must complete a race of 100m and one is handicapped and in a wheelchair, do you let them start from the same position?

Treating them equally does not take into account their differences, but treating them fairly will. Another example is golf with its setting of handicaps for players, which gives golfers of different levels of skill an equal opportunity to play — and win.

React

(a) Identify unavoidable differences that will have a negative impact on people and take these into account when interacting with them. For example, if someone has just joined your team, they will need time to form relationships and may require more effort than members who have worked with each other for some time.

(b) Some differences are temporary, for example, technical skills can be acquired. But if a team member takes beyond a reasonable time to acquire these skills and you continue to compensate for them, it will be seen as unfair by the others.

(c) Not everyone dislikes being treated unfairly, especially the person who benefits. And not everyone makes a fuss when unfairness is at play, but everyone reacts to it. People may withdraw, be less cooperative or even sabotage others. Remain aware of how people perceive their environment.

(d) Use a so-called cloak of ignorance, a philosophy which first removes all characteristics from the people involved. Then it asks you to make a decision about them based on a characteristic, provided you are prepared to be put in that situation and assume that characteristic. For example, there are 10 people in a lifeboat and you have to decide which one to throw off. If you decide to throw the oldest person overboard, you must be prepared to be put in the boat as the oldest person.

3 | I identify better with certain groups/I feel uncomfortable around people different to me

Rethink

Most of us feel a greater sense of affiliation with certain groups than others. We relate to them better and they provide a sense of tribe or identity, which helps to define who we are or how we act.

Work groups are characterized by common beliefs or values. They may be quite diverse in terms of race, gender, culture or ethnicity, but they will usually have a shared view of other groups. For example, unions and management tend to see each other as socialists and capitalists, which shapes how they treat each other.

Getting to know and understand how other people see the world can help to build productive relationships.

React

(a) It is vital to be aware of any bias you may have towards one particular group or more. It may seem obvious, but many people do not recognize their prejudices. Get feedback from others, too. Give some thought to the groups which make you most uncomfortable. Once you are honest with yourself, you can begin to address your issues.

(b) Get to know a few individuals from groups that are different to you. Working with people closely on a project or spending social time with them could change your assumptions.

(c) Examine your behavior around people from the groups against which you are biased. Do you avoid asking them questions? Do you limit the time and attention you give them? Are you less approachable, more judgmental or spend little or no time socially with people from different cultures?

Rethink

Stereotypes you may harbor will have an impact on how well you can adapt in different work settings, as well as your ability to manage a diverse group of people fairly. You cannot assess people effectively if you make judgments based on your biases. As companies have continued to expand globally, international boundaries have become less pronounced.

Diversity in the workplace is now more common than uniformity. New groups have been entering the workforce in record numbers, especially women and certain ethnic groups, and the labor pool is more diverse than ever. It is key to accept this and capitalize on these differences.

Focus on maximizing performance and productivity through the diversity at your disposal. Also examine the reason why differences between you and others make you uncomfortable.

Your criticism of others could shed light on personal insecurities or a fear of losing your turf to outsiders. Do you harbor resentment towards people who you believe have been given an unfair advantage because of their minority status? You might not agree with them, but companies have adopted policies to provide equal opportunities for all. One's expectation is not that a particular group gets favorable treatment, but that everyone has an equal opportunity from the start. But the reality is that, without such policies in place, the playing field is not level.

If you are biased against a person because of their race, do they stand the same chance to be hired as the candidate against whom you are not biased, even if the two perform exactly the same?

React

(a) Stereotype yourself. With which group would other people lump you? List the stereotypes you will face based on how you may be categorized. Do they accurately describe who you are and how you perform?

(b) Learn to link things you like with diversity. For example, increase your exposure to diverse groups through hobbies you enjoy. If you like reading, read about other religions; if you enjoy travel, visit foreign places with unfamiliar cultures; if you enjoy eating, tour the ethnic restaurants in your city.

(c) Attend a diversity awareness course through your company, if available.

(d) At work, maximize your exposure to talented people from diverse groups. Invite people from other groups to your meetings or to work on your projects. Find a well-respected person in the company who falls into a group against which you may feel biased and ask them for advice or expert opinion.

(e) List the things you may have in common with the person that makes you feel uncomfortable. Challenge yourself to define at least 10 things, big or small.

5 | I am looking out for my best interests/I need to stay competitive

Rethink

Looking out for number one — you — works well if you do not plan on working collaboratively. Otherwise, looking out for number one and everyone is the best practice.

Success does not have to come at others' expense. In fact, your ability to manage your relationships with all people is critical to career success and required for effective leadership. And remember, when you consider others' best interests they will consider yours as well.

React

(a) Give credit to others for their hard work and promote the entire group's accomplishments whenever possible, even if you played the largest part in them. Promoting the team's work is the same as promoting yourself, but adds a small dose of humility.

(b) Do not withhold information that others need to do their jobs. It is not only unfair, but creates a highly inefficient work environment.

(c) Consider what other people stand to lose because of your comments or decisions. Would you want to be in their shoes?

6 | I do not have much experience in interacting with people different to me

Rethink

Although you may not actively seek interaction with diverse groups, you are always surrounded with opportunities to do so, both at work and in your private life. Take advantage of each opportunity to open your world and perceptions. Being exposed to a variety of people and cultures helps to keep you grounded and promotes fair behavior. It can be as easy as initiating a conversation with someone who would not normally attract your interest.

React

(a) Attend cultural events such as foreign films and exhibitions in your city.

(b) Take advantage of international assignments whenever possible.

(c) You do not have to cross oceans to be exposed to diverse groups. Ask for assignments that involve global teams.

(d) Mentor people in your company who have diverse cultural backgrounds or are from a different gender or race, or seek a mentor from a different background.

(e) Observe people. Which differences based on the group they belong to do you see in their behavior?

184

Overdeveloped

Research has shown that strengths can become weaknesses because you can, in fact, do too much of a good thing. You cannot become less good at a competency in which you excel, but you can balance the behavior by developing a few Stabilizers to tone down an excessive strength.

Stabilizer	Overdeveloped
13 Courageous	Tries to treat all people the same, without consideration for differences in race, gender, culture or personal style
2 Adaptable	
23 Directs People	
32 Informs Others	
17 Demonstrates Good Judgment	
35 Manages Conflict	
37 Manages Negotiations	
38 Manages Underperformance	
43 Motivates People	
51 Recognizes Talent and Potential	

Instructions

Read the definition. If it applies to you, choose a few Stabilizers and develop them by selecting the relevant chapter and following the Strategies for Action.

For more instructions see the How To Use This Book section.

29. Focused on Priorities

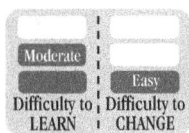

"A major part of successful living lies in the ability to put first things first. Indeed, the reason most major goals are not achieved is that we spend our time doing second things first"

Robert McKain

Well Developed
Differentiates between critical and less important priorities

Underdeveloped
Has no sense of what is really important, or focuses too much on irrelevant issues

Overdeveloped
Is so focused on a few priorities that non-critical but urgent tasks or activities are ignored

Instructions

Read the definitions on the left. If the Underdeveloped definition applies, go to the Strategies for Action section.

If the Overdeveloped definition applies, go to the end of the chapter.

Test Yourself

True	I have a clear picture every day of what I need to accomplish
True	I prioritize mission-critical activities and organize my time accordingly
True	I am not easily distracted from my priorities
True	If I am distracted, I can refocus quickly on my work
True	I can sort through information quickly to get to the point

Note

Are you sure you need to develop this competency?

If the answer is "True" to most of the statements on the left, you probably do not need to develop this competency.

Strategies for Action

Most ineffective behaviors have an underlying thought or emotional pattern. By identifying these patterns, you can understand the impact they have and design strategies to counteract them.

① I get distracted easily

② I tend to follow what others think is important/ I have difficulty saying no

③ I have difficulty changing my course of action once I have started

④ I lose sight of what I am working towards/ My goals are unclear

⑤ I tend to be controlling/I want to do things myself

Instructions

1. Read and select one or more of the ineffective ways of thinking/feeling to the left.

2. Find the corresponding number below that will help you to rethink this pattern and identify specific and practical actions that you can take.

1 | I get distracted easily

Rethink

One of the biggest challenges in the workplace is to manage all the little things that happen during the course of the day and still get the important work done. It is easy to get distracted by any number of things, for example, doing what we like to do instead of what we have to do; having tangential conversations; doing other people's work instead of ours; and even simple noises in the office.

We are often our own worst enemy. Even tasks that may seem urgent can distract from real priorities. Not everything that needs to be done immediately is important, and you could spend your day putting out fires and chasing tasks instead of goals.

Focused people are able to meet their goals by recognizing and navigating through multiple distractions. Ultimately, managing distractions is every person's responsibility, but one must first recognize what those distractions are.

React

(a) Do an end-of-day evaluation for a week. Write down the things on which you spent your time. How many of these were actually related to your goals? Which distractions prevented you from being more focused? Adopt a solution for your top distractions. For example, many people get sidetracked by checking e-mails. If this is your Achilles' heel, allow yourself to check e-mails twice a day only and respond to them only once you have dedicated proper time to your critical goals.

(b) Get creative about ensuring that you have some uninterrupted time every day to think through complex issues and reflect on what has been discussed. For example, make your schedule flexible and go to work early or leave late, keep your door shut to discourage interruptions and, if possible, work outside of the office for a few hours.

(e) Politely excuse yourself from lengthy conversations that are going nowhere and are not directly related to your goal. Your time and priorities are just as important as the other person's.

(c) Make sure you are not allotting most of your time to activities you find enjoyable or easy. Try to first do the things that you find hard to do.

(d) Discern what is really urgent. Is the task important to accomplishing your goal or must it be done to accomplish someone else's? Delegate the tasks that must be completed immediately but can be done by someone else.

2 | I tend to follow what others think is important/I have difficulty saying no

Rethink

Are you prone to "group think"? This term was coined by psychologist Irving Janis in 1972 and describes a type of thought exhibited by group members who try to minimize conflict and reach consensus without critically testing, analyzing and evaluating ideas.

Although your conclusions or opinions may differ from those of the group, you lose the opportunity to give input that could help to focus your team if you are not comfortable championing them. Priorities should make sense to you, even if they do not represent the group consensus.

Do you have trouble telling others that you cannot help, even if your plate is full? Being overly eager to please and help others can quickly distract you from your priorities.

Not setting boundaries will create unnecessary work for you. Remember that it is not your responsibility to take on other people's work, and most people will not know that you cannot take on more responsibility unless you communicate it to them.

React

(a) When examining an issue, always ask your own questions first and try to derive at your own conclusions independently of others. Once you have done this, you can contribute to and remain open-minded about the opinions of a larger group.

(b) If you feel strongly about a course of action but anticipate resistance, be sure to build appropriate support for your case. Get feedback from experts on the subject that will support your findings or suggestions and present a well-documented business case with as much detail as possible.

(c) Speak out if necessary, even if it makes you or others uncomfortable. Not offering input means you cannot fault the results if the group takes the wrong course of action.

(d) Assume the role of devil's advocate. This gives you the opportunity to consider and provide dissenting opinion and, in so doing, serves a key function in helping the group to consider alternatives.

(e) Agree to assist someone only if you can realistically add it to your workload.

(f) Practice saying no politely. The more you do so the more comfortable you will get with establishing boundaries.

3 | I have difficulty changing my course of action once I have started

Rethink

It is productive to remain on a course of action, but only if you have selected the right course.

Adjusting your direction is difficult once you have committed resources and time to a particular path. However, an important element of being focused is the ability to sift through new information continually and understand how changes can necessitate an adjustment in your focus.

Being focused requires directing our efforts at the best course of action at any given point in time, and that means being open to doing things differently at any given point in the process.

React

(a) Revisit your strategy several times throughout a project to assess if there are any changes in assumptions, resources or circumstances that require you to adjust your focus. Be open to feedback.

(b) An important role of the person providing you with oversight is to help guide that on which you need to focus. Periodically, get feedback on whether you should adjust your priorities.

(c) Do not spend all your time on one project or assignment. Take a break from it and work on another assignment for a while. Getting away from the details helps to give you perspective on what is really important.

4 | I lose sight of what I am working towards/ My goals are unclear

Rethink

A clear understanding of the end goal is necessary to keep a person focused on priorities. There may be multiple ways of reaching your destination, but there is only one destination.

Do not risk spending unnecessary energy and resources because of a lack of clarity.

React

(a) Seek clarity and direction before getting into the details of any project. Do you and your team really know what you are supposed to do? Do you have ample instructions to proceed on your own? Define your goal.

(b) If you do not already have a yearly work plan, meet with your superior to develop one with specific goals and targets. Agree to revisit your work plan on occasion to adopt any necessary changes.

(c) If you are confused about your progress, ask for assistance in time. It is more productive to be honest about needing help than to spin your wheels and waste time and resources going in the wrong direction.

(d) Keep your boss and team members informed and up to date with your progress. Without feedback, you may not realize you are going in the wrong direction. You could do this with a weekly e-mail, for example.

(e) Resist the temptation to finish the assignment completely before discussing your progress with someone. You may waste much energy perfecting something that has to be redone.

(5) I tend to be controlling/I want to do things myself

Rethink

No single person can control all aspects of a project, and trying to do so dilutes your ability to stay focused on the activities that are true priorities. You may be impatient with the pace of the project and think you are better served by doing everything yourself. But your energy and time are finite and you will yield greater returns from investing both in activities which will have a greater impact and which only you are skilled to do. You will also have more time to manage others when your day is not cluttered with activities that can be delegated. In the end, you may not be able to get to a task as soon as someone else and may inadvertently be causing a bottleneck in progress by trying to do it all yourself.

React

(a) Practice your delegation skills. Be selective about what really needs your attention and delegate the rest to others. Assess how important a task is. You may not be able to delegate presenting to the board but you can certainly delegate researching data for the presentation.

(b) Stay well informed about your subordinates' workload. You should not be in a position in which you are overwhelmed and team members or subordinates are idle.

(c) Assess and be realistic about whether you can get the task done quicker with your current workload or should assign it to someone else.

(d) Work as a team player instead of an independent achiever. You can always get more work done by managing or being part of a collaborative team.

Overdeveloped

Research has shown that strengths can become weaknesses because you can, in fact, do too much of a good thing. You cannot become less good at a competency in which you excel, but you can balance the behavior by developing a few Stabilizers to tone down an excessive strength.

Stabilizer	Overdeveloped
15 Customer-Centric	Is so focused on a few priorities that non-critical but urgent tasks or activities are ignored
17 Demonstrates Good Judgment	
30 Global Thinker	
31 Improves Processes	
2 Adaptable	
34 Listens Well	
55 Takes Initiative	
8 Comfortable with Uncertainty	
6 Bright	
53 Strategic	

Instructions

Read the definition. If it applies to you, choose a few Stabilizers and develop them by selecting the relevant chapter and following the Strategies for Action.

For more instructions see the How To Use This Book section.

30. Global Thinker

> "What we see depends mainly on what we look for"
>
> John Lubbock

Well Developed
Can shift focus away from the details and gain a broader perspective

Underdeveloped
Is too focused on the details and cannot see the whole picture

Overdeveloped
Loses sight of the importance or impact of relevant details

Instructions

Read the definitions on the left. If the Underdeveloped definition applies, go to the Strategies for Action section.

If the Overdeveloped definition applies, go to the end of the chapter.

Test Yourself

True	I am knowledgeable about current and potential future trends
True	I have perspective on many aspects of the business
True	I am good at forecasting consequences or results
True	I think about the future of the business when making decisions
True	I can decide and act without having the whole picture

Note

Are you sure you need to develop this competency?

If the answer is "True" to most of the statements on the left, you probably do not need to develop this competency.

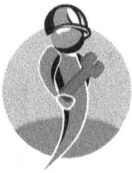

Strategies for Action

Most ineffective behaviors have an underlying thought or emotional pattern. By identifying these patterns, you can understand the impact they have and design strategies to counteract them.

① I am not much interested in things outside my technical area or my field of expertise

② My work environment is focused on detail/ I prioritize detail, rather than the big picture

③ I have had little exposure to other social norms or cultures/My experiences are rather one-sided

④ I do not grasp how things are interconnected/ I tend to be a linear thinker

Instructions

1. Read and select one or more of the ineffective ways of thinking/feeling to the left.

2. Find the corresponding number below that will help you to rethink this pattern and identify specific and practical actions that you can take.

---

1 | I am not much interested in things outside my technical area or my field of expertise

Rethink

Increasingly, as you become highly specialized and your interests focused on a single field of expertise, it could be difficult to think globally. The latter involves being able to consider the many moving and static parts that comprise a business. Be cautious to not only deepen your knowledge, but to broaden it as well. The global picture provides the context which governs how technical expertise is applied.

React

(a) Investigate other opportunities available in your organization that are related to your discipline but less technical. Your company perhaps offers courses or certificates in management-related fields that could help to create a balance with your technical skills.

(b) Ask to be included in interdisciplinary meetings to raise your exposure to other business areas.

(c) Be aware of what happens in the rest of the world. Read news magazines and articles about trades other than yours.

(d) Ask to mentor new recruits in exchange for being mentored by someone in an area outside your discipline.

(e) Start a "futurist club". Establish a group drawn from peers and friends in your field of expertise, who meets regularly to discuss ways in which your discipline or technology could affect the future of your organization and, in effect, the world.

(f) Read literature about how your discipline has evolved. Which external factors have influenced the way you do business today?

2 | My work environment is focused on detail/I prioritize detail, rather than the big picture

Rethink

Many people operate more comfortably in the world of absolutes and find it difficult to juggle the complexities and details of the bigger picture that, typically, includes a lot of unknowns. Consider the details as the muscle-building exercises a healthy organization needs, and global thinking as its stretching and flexing exercises. Both types are equally necessary to maintain a healthy business and drive quality decisions, and each needs attention.

React

(a) Include future scenarios and how they may have an impact on your work when planning your assignments or projects.

(b) Assemble teams in which both global thinkers and detail-oriented people are well represented. You will be exposed to the way global thinkers approach problems and achieve more balanced output.

(c) Allow yourself time to explore creative options and brainstorming. Do not accept your first idea. Create at least three options before you take action. Consider how to get the same results through different means.

(d) Switch between projects often so that you do not get buried too deep in the details of one only. Come up for air.

(e) Delegate some of the detailed work to others to give yourself time to discuss and contemplate big-picture issues.

3 | I have had little exposure to other social norms or cultures/My experiences are rather one-sided

Rethink

Limited experience of or exposure to a variety of cultures, countries, people or activities is a disadvantage to a global thinker. Such exposure provides a rich well of perspectives from which to draw and allows one to gain a broader view of reality, of how things are or could be.

One's bias and assumptions are tested when exposed to unfamiliar norms and situations.

195

React

(a) Attend diverse cultural events in your city, such as foreign films or exhibitions.

(b) Take advantage of international assignments when possible.

(c) Request opportunities to work with global teams. It will help to broaden your exposure to different management styles, problem-solving techniques etcetera.

(d) Mentor people in your company from diverse cultural backgrounds, race and different gender, or seek a mentor who comes from a different background to you.

(e) Expose your brain to new forms of stimulus regularly, for example, a different genre of books, art or music. Learn a foreign language. Visit museums.

(f) Start a hobby that will introduce you to new people and skills you have not sampled, such as dancing, woodworking, cooking or pottery. Volunteer to work for groups with whom you cannot necessarily identify, such as the elderly or the poor. Choose hobbies that encourage the use of imagery and the creative side of your brain, such as art class or photography.

4 | I do not grasp how things are interconnected/I tend to be a linear thinker

Rethink

Each decision made, policy generated or path followed has an impact on something else. Global thinkers are uniquely sensitive to the complex interactions that exist between systems, and use this insight to improve their decision-making skills.

React

(a) Write down the pros and cons of your various options and pay close attention to the global impact of each option — the potential influence on people, money, time and existing processes.

(b) Assume there is always more than one way to solve a problem. Do not limit yourself to comfortable or familiar solutions. As a rule, ensure you have considered at least three different approaches.

(c) Get input that challenges your linear thinking. Consult peers and co-workers to find scenarios you may have overlooked.

(d) Check in with others. You will stay in touch with the issues that concern them.

(e) Try to find value in the things that others overlook.

Overdeveloped

Research has shown that strengths can become weaknesses because you can, in fact, do too much of a good thing. You cannot become less good at a competency in which you excel, but you can balance the behavior by developing a few Stabilizers to tone down an excessive strength.

Stabilizer	Overdeveloped
1 Achiever	Loses sight of the importance or impact of relevant details
16 Decisive	
17 Demonstrates Good Judgment	
29 Focused on Priorities	
31 Improves Processes	
39 Manages Time	
42 Monitors Work	
18 Detail-Orientated	
48 Plans Work	
56 Technically Competent	

Instructions

Read the definition. If it applies to you, choose a few Stabilizers and develop them by selecting the relevant chapter and following the Strategies for Action.

For more instructions see the How To Use This Book section.

31. Improves Processes

> "We can't solve problems by using the same kind of thinking we used when we created them"
>
> Albert Einstein

Well Developed
Continuously looks for ways to improve or re-engineer processes

Underdeveloped
Overlooks or appears to be disinterested in opportunities to improve work processes

Overdeveloped
Reduces everything to a process and loses sight of bigger-picture issues because of a focus on marginal and incremental improvements

Instructions

Read the definitions on the left. If the Underdeveloped definition applies, go to the Strategies for Action section.

If the Overdeveloped definition applies, go to the end of the chapter.

Test Yourself

True	I identify, analyze and improve key processes in the organization
True	I continuously look for ways to increase the output, efficiency and effectiveness of processes
True	I identify weaknesses that can hamper processes in fulfilling their purpose
True	I ensure that relevant representatives from all the functional areas involved participate in improving processes
True	I try to find technological applications to improve work processes
True	I create an environment in which people are encouraged to openly and regularly discuss ideas for continuous improvement
True	I document and reflect on lessons learnt
True	I support collaborative initiatives to improve processes

Note

Are you sure you need to develop this competency?

If the answer is "True" to most of the statements on the left, you probably do not need to develop this competency.

199

Strategies for Action

Most ineffective behaviors have an underlying thought or emotional pattern. By identifying these patterns, you can understand the impact they have and design strategies to counteract them.

① I do not know how to go about improving processes/I have limited experience in process re-engineering

② If the process is not broken, why tinker with it?

③ Changing established processes creates anxiety and is disruptive/Change is not a predominant aspect of our company's culture

④ During process improvement I tend to focus on internal needs rather than external demands

Instructions

1. Read and select one or more of the ineffective ways of thinking/feeling to the left.

2. Find the corresponding number below that will help you to rethink this pattern and identify specific and practical actions that you can take.

1 | I do not know how to go about improving processes/ I have limited experience in process re-engineering

Rethink

Quality management used to focus on inspection of the final product to ensure it was in no way defective before it left the factory. This approach was fundamentally changed by Japanese car manufacturers who created a quality mindset or "kaizen", which required employees to consider quality throughout the manufacturing process. This process, known as total quality management or TQM, was greatly influenced by W. Edwards Deming, an American statistician, professor and quality consultant who is credited with aiding the Japanese post-war industrial revival.

A wide variety of literature now exists about practices such as TQM, international standardization organization and the Six Sigma business management strategy. They all assist companies in designing best processes. Process re-engineering can add great value in the form of efficiency and cost reductions.

React

(a) Do your research. Investigate quality management practices and processes on the Internet and become familiar with the various models and methodologies. Look for patterns and common practices, and find case studies that explain the whole process from initial identification of the problem through to implementation, the results achieved and the challenges faced.

(b) Pick an appropriate methodology. The Six Sigma strategy, for example, is a complex, time-intensive, detail-oriented process that requires proper training to implement effectively. It also gives a better return in a high-transaction environment in which small changes can have big consequences. There are many other approaches that are less intensive or easier to use, which may be better suited to a service- or experience-oriented environment.

(c) Find an expert in the company. You will benefit from their experience without having to make mistakes.

(d) Consider engaging an external quality-management consultant. Talk to them about the projects they have implemented to ensure their experience matches your needs. If cost is an issue, consider hiring a consultant to help you implement a small project and apply its principles independently to a larger-scale project.

(e) Ensure you get input from employees and customers when improving processes. The people in the trenches and those using the product are closest to the problem and in the best position to give you valuable feedback.

(f) Look at your competitors and other industries or businesses that operate under similar conditions. There is much to learn from studying what others have done to improve their processes. For example, if your business distributes products through a channel instead of directly to the consumer, look for related businesses in non-competing industries that are recognized as leaders and speak to them. Most companies are happy to share their successes and experiences, especially if you are not a competitor.

(g) Attend workshops or seminars that expose you to different ways of thinking in the area of process management.

(h) When improving processes, keep the customer in mind. Internally, the process might be highly efficient, but does it meet the customer's needs?

2 | If the process is not broken, why tinker with it?

Rethink

To remain ahead of competitors, it is best never to be satisfied with the status quo. A mindset that seeks continuous improvement and experimentation is the key in a competitive environment.

Companies survive by continually creating new and improved ways of delivering products and services, which requires innovation and risk. Assume that your competitors are doing the same.

Investing time in thinking of new ways to do business does not mean you will change what currently makes sense, but it prepares you for improvement when the opportunity does arise.

React

(a) Focus your attention on the significant difference between a good product or service and a great one. Think about the instances when you received excellent service or were fully satisfied with a product you bought. Then consider the instances when you received poor service or purchased an inferior product. Use these reflections to identify a process in your organization that works sufficiently but could benefit from improving parts of it. Write down your thoughts about how these changes could have a positive impact on customers both internal and external.

(b) Identify potential areas for improvement within your organization. Then organize a brainstorm meeting and invite people from all the relevant areas or functions to participate. Document the potentially beneficial elements identified. Determine the actions that should be taken next and who will be responsible for them.

(c) Stay on top of market trends regarding process improvement, for example, best practices, Six Sigma, lean thinking etcetera.

(d) Expose yourself as much as possible to what goes on in your industry. Attend trade shows, conferences and webinars that cover cutting-edge topics and highlight innovative products or services.

(e) Keep abreast of emerging trends globally and in your region. Read trade journals, leading magazines and newspapers, and any other progressive literature. Download podcasts or sign up for e-zines and e-alerts regarding the marketplace, industry trends, technological and scientific advancements, and breaking news.

(f) Develop a healthy skepticism about your processes. Ask yourself why you do things the way they are done. Question information presented to you.

---

3 | Changing established processes creates anxiety and is disruptive/Change is not a predominant aspect of our company's culture

Rethink

Changing the way employees conduct their business is often met with resistance. New technology, changing roles or a shift in resources can cause anxiety and create resistance. Often, the effort seems greater than the benefits. For example, think of the home renovation process.

To see improvements in your home, you will have to endure dust, disruption to your daily activities and even conflict with the contractor. But the end result is usually worth it.

Not changing an inefficient practice simply because it may be disruptive is quite risky for you and your company. Change is always disruptive and there will always be individuals who resist change. Consider your company and how it operated 10 years ago. If nothing has changed, you are the exception.

Most companies experience significant changes in technology, customers, people, markets, competitors etcetera. No matter how uncomfortable it is or how much resistance you encounter, continuous improvement is an essential business process and worth the effort if its result will yield opportunities.

Remember, the more people are exposed to change, the more they will learn to accept it as part of company culture. In the long term, you are likely to face less resistance to major process improvement efforts. It is essential that you promote an environment of continuous improvement throughout your organization. Foster a company culture in which people can share their ideas for improvement in a non-judgmental, supportive environment, without fear of embarrassment or penalty.

React

(a) Understand the process of change. It has been studied extensively and is much more predictable than you think. Learn to understand some models of change, the phases of change and how people respond to them, how to deal with resistance, and how to get commitment and support for the new and different.

(b) Consider the alternative to change. Project the consequences of changing versus not changing.

(c) People avoid change because of the initial pain, so focus on and promote the end result.

(d) Identify individuals who are energized by change. Openness to the new is a fundamental personality trait and you will always find people willing to champion the cause. They are likely to be passionate and enthusiastic about change, which can be infectious. Ensure they get the resources and support they need to be change agents and use them to lead project teams.

(e) Avoid complacency, that is, not asking tough questions. Establish a formal process whereby you specifically consider what you have done that has improved the business in some way, and do this at least twice a year. How significant was that improvement, which benefits did it have, what would have happened if you had not made the change? Such a process will create an opportunity for you to celebrate your success and reflect on missed opportunities, which will motivate and encourage more process improvement efforts in the future.

(f) Encourage employees to participate in the improvement of work design and processes to ensure you get input from many sources. Organize regular feedback and brainstorm sessions with your team as well as cross-functional peers to strengthen your improvement initiatives.

(g) Empower others to design their own work processes. Encourage your team to research best practices of industry leaders and within other areas of the organization. This practice increases employee support for the process and improves morale.

(h) Be careful not to establish a yes-man culture. Ask a trusted peer whether people feel this way about giving input. Ensure people know that all ideas are valuable, even if their ideas are contrary to yours.

Rethink

Focusing on customers is the key to a successful process design. If you please the customer and respond well to their needs, your process is successful.

Sam Walton, founder and former CEO of Wal-Mart, promoted a simple yet effective strategy: be customer-centric. He believed — and taught his employees — that the customer is the only boss, because the customer always has the choice to take his money somewhere else. Maximizing customer satisfaction is a moving target at which your processes should always be aimed.

React

(a) Keep abreast of what your internal and external customers expect now, and anticipate their future needs before they know what those are. You will have to perform a market analysis that includes changes in customer demographics, competition and technology. Establish various processes to get customer feedback regarding features, value, price, quality, convenience etcetera on a regular basis.

(b) Always design your processes with your customers in mind, including product design, materials used, manufacturing, distribution channels as well as customer service and support.

(c) Brainstorm ways to improve customer satisfaction with your team. Put yourself in your customers' shoes. What would please them? What would dissatisfy them? Use the answers to look for ways to improve your processes to build further customer support.

(d) Experience your own services and products. There is no better way to identify opportunities for improvement than to get first-hand experience of the products or services you sell. For example, a multinational manufacturer of adult diapers made their company's executives wear them for a day. It fundamentally shifted the way they thought about their customers and their products.

(e) Treat your suppliers as customers. They are a key aspect of your business, and improving processes to benefit both parties will improve your bottom line.

Overdeveloped

Research has shown that strengths can become weaknesses because you can, in fact, do too much of a good thing. You cannot become less good at a competency in which you excel, but you can balance the behavior by developing a few Stabilizers to tone down an excessive strength.

Stabilizer	Overdeveloped
27 Experimental	Reduces everything to a process and loses sight of bigger-picture issues because of a focus on marginal and incremental improvements
30 Global Thinker	
34 Listens Well	
46 Open-Minded	
53 Strategic	
29 Focused on Priorities	
15 Customer-Centric	
14 Creative	
40 Market Aware	
7 Collaborative	

Instructions

Read the definition. If it applies to you, choose a few Stabilizers and develop them by selecting the relevant chapter and following the Strategies for Action.

For more instructions see the How To Use This Book section.

32. Informs Others

Difficulty to LEARN: Easy | Difficulty to CHANGE: Moderate

"There must be a happy medium somewhere between being totally informed and blissfully unaware"

Doug Larson

Well Developed
Keeps people informed with relevant and well-timed information

Underdeveloped
Does not provide people with necessary information promptly, or seems to be uncommunicative

Overdeveloped
Confuses or overwhelms people with too much information that is irrelevant or inappropriate

Instructions

Read the definitions on the left. If the Underdeveloped definition applies, go to the Strategies for Action section.

If the Overdeveloped definition applies, go to the end of the chapter.

Test Yourself

True	I give feedback to others promply enough for them to take action, if necessary
True	I consider my audience before deciding how to inform them
True	I am willing to supply information that will not be well received
True	Even when I am upset with someone or disagree with them, I will share information freely
True	I regularly inform people about the goings-on in the organization to keep them in the loop and motivated
True	I ensure my supervisor or manager is informed about the status of my work

Note

Are you sure you need to develop this competency?

If the answer is "True" to most of the statements on the left, you probably do not need to develop this competency.

32 Informs Others

207

Strategies for Action

Most ineffective behaviors have an underlying thought or emotional pattern. By identifying these patterns, you can understand the impact they have and design strategies to counteract them.

① I am reluctant to share information which will disappoint or cause conflict

② I get caught up in my work/I do not take the time to share information

③ I sometimes keep information from others on purpose

④ I do not want to bother people/I provide information on a need-to-know basis

⑤ Our organizational structure is not conducive to sharing information

Instructions

1. Read and select one or more of the ineffective ways of thinking/feeling to the left.

2. Find the corresponding number below that will help you to rethink this pattern and identify specific and practical actions that you can take.

1 — I am reluctant to share information which will disappoint or cause conflict

Rethink

Do you delay informing relevant people about a setback, or shy away from sharing information because it may be received unfavorably? The longer you wait the more stress you create for yourself and possibly others, especially if action must be taken.

People are usually reluctant to talk when the information may have negative consequences or reflect poorly on their performance. But often we have unrealistic perceptions of consequences and hold on to information unnecessarily. Withholding necessary information will not improve the situation in any way and is likely to worsen it. It is your responsibility to ensure others are informed about good and not-so-good news.

React

(a) Get perspective. Ask a trusted peer who can treat the situation more objectively to give you their take on its gravity. The circumstances may not be as grave as they appear.

(b) Acknowledge the mistakes, but focus on the solution. If people are upset by the information, give them a chance to express themselves without trying to defend yourself. You have acknowledged the mistakes and it is unproductive to get caught up in defending them at this point.

208

(c) Do not make it worse by sugarcoating reality. Be truthful with the information you provide. Trying to make the outlook brighter to diminish a negative response means appropriate action cannot be taken, which can create further problems.

(d) Learn to confront people. Start by working on your conflict-management skills. Research the topic or engage a coach.

(e) Choose the most appropriate form of communication to ensure the information is received in the best way possible. Is it appropriate to inform people via e-mail, for example? It could be too impersonal for certain information.

(f) Speak up immediately. Every day you allow to pass will generate more stress for you, because it will become increasingly difficult to explain why you did not share the information sooner.

2 | I get caught up in my work/I do not take the time to share information

Rethink

Busy managers and organization leaders are often guilty of not taking the time to keep others informed. With the many demands they have, they easily overlook its importance. But a lack of timely information about changes in the company's strategy or its general direction, in particular, can have a demoralizing effect.

Whether the head of an organization or an individual contributor, relevant people depend on you to keep them informed about your progress and key issues.

React

(a) Agree when and how you will keep relevant people informed. It can be in staff meetings, via e-mail correspondence or with a status report. The key is to establish a system that forces you to treat informing others as the priority it deserves to be.

(b) Schedule a realistic amount of time to share information and transfer knowledge. Because of tight schedules, the temptation is to be sparing with time for informational meetings. But people need to know sharing information is a priority for you, not an inconvenience.

(c) In the interest of time you may summarize too much. Ensure you provide enough context and history to make your information easy to digest.

Rethink

People sometimes withhold or hoard information on purpose. Some specialists, for example, are tempted to get payment for their knowledge and keep it closely guarded. Older experts may be reluctant to mentor a younger generation. Whatever the reason, a mentality in an organization of "he who has information has power" can be pervasive and have disastrous effects. Not only does it stifle open information flow and ideas, but it punishes people by capping their development. It has its roots in an industrial-age world in which ownership meant control. But in the information age, the value of information increases when it is shared.

Withholding information as a way to improve your position or get back at others is not a good idea — such tactics are highly visible and can earn you a reputation of being difficult, unethical, untrustworthy and someone who does not play for the team. It sets the tone for how others will treat you. You may achieve a short-term goal, but your actions will contribute to a hostile work environment and create stress for everyone. Even withholding information because of a lack of trust is a short-term strategy that will not yield productive, long-term results.

React

(a) During meetings, listen to the type of information people may need to do their jobs and, if you have such material, share it with them.

(b) Establish informal, regular "learning reviews" during which people get together to share what they have learned.

(c) Create mentorship programs and reward people who transfer their knowledge to others.

(d) Developing others is highly valued in an organization. Add the skill to your development plan and engage a coach to help you.

(e) If you withhold information because of strong negative feelings towards a person or an unresolved issue with them, try to resolve it through conversation. A person you both respect can assist in mediating the conflict in a professional manner.

(f) Be aware when favoritism determines with whom you share information, and the kind of information you reveal. Make a list of the people from whom you typically withhold information and discuss your reasons with a coach.

(g) You may be the only one who does not trust a person. Talk to a peer or mentor about your beliefs. It is important to get perspective and, sometimes, simply a reality check.

(h) Ask yourself whether your primary motive for withholding information is personal gain. If so, let it go.

4 | I do not want to bother people/I provide information on a need-to-know basis

Rethink

When you provide information on a need-to-know basis, you make a judgment about what is important to others, which is not always accurate or fair. Information facilitates processes. Proper information allows managers to effectively monitor work and keep abreast of problems. But we often overlook the need to inform others when we are working hardest to prove ourselves, or racing to receive credit for success. Too much information will create fewer problems than too little information.

React

(a) As a rule, assume people want to know everything. It is better to curb what you say than to be seen as unresponsive or lacking in customer service.

(b) If you think you may inconvenience people, ask them to clarify how much information they need.

(c) Copying relevant people on e-mails is a quick and easy way to keep them informed without extra work on your part. They can choose to ignore or read the correspondence. Do it habitually.

(d) Be conscious of the information people simply have to know and brief them. Take particular care to inform others about controversial issues and matters that negatively affect a client.

(e) How well informed are your internal and external customers? Establish a system to ensure you communicate important information about new products or changes in procedures and delivery dates in a timely manner. It mitigates any risks involved and sends a message to clients that you care and are in control.

(f) Do not assume your responsibility stops once you have informed people. As much as you can, create and follow up on further reminders.

(g) Ensure you have someone else on the team who is informed enough to understand the status of your projects and can step in when you are unavailable.

(h) Do not be tempted to finish a project completely before discussing it with your superior. Send constant updates or divide the project into smaller milestones on which you can report. Agree beforehand what those milestones will be.

5 | Our organizational structure is not conducive to sharing information

Rethink

As a result of their hierarchy, reporting structures or strong silos, some organizations restrict the ease with which information is shared. Although organizational structures exist for a reason, they should allow and encourage the easy trading of information if the company were to be successful. Information of little value to one division can be critical to others. For example, information about shrinking product margins may have little value to someone in finance, but enormous value to someone in marketing.

Information needs to be transferable and accessible across organizational boundaries and considered a tradable resource regardless of the level, group, division or country you represent.

React

(a) Think about the knowledge you have that may be valuable to other groups and share it with them.

(b) Communicate the usefulness of sharing information across teams and find ways of rewarding and encouraging it.

(c) Create opportunities for cross-functional interaction to break down structural silos.

(d) Get to know people from different divisions. It will facilitate swapping information.

(e) Understand the company's politics: who supposedly owns which information, who you should include in correspondence, and so forth. It will allow you to access information without crossing political boundaries.

Overdeveloped

Research has shown that strengths can become weaknesses because you can, in fact, do too much of a good thing. You cannot become less good at a competency in which you excel, but you can balance the behavior by developing a few Stabilizers to tone down an excessive strength.

Stabilizer	Overdeveloped
22 Diplomatic	Confuses or overwhelms people with too much information that is irrelevant or inappropriate
26 Ethical	
29 Focused on Priorities	
34 Listens Well	
39 Manages Time	
10 Communicates Well (Written)	
48 Plans Work	
49 Politically Astute	
58 Trustworthy	
9 Communicates Well (Verbal)	

Instructions

Read the definition. If it applies to you, choose a few Stabilizers and develop them by selecting the relevant chapter and following the Strategies for Action.

For more instructions see the How To Use This Book section.

213

33. Inspires a Future

> "A leader has the vision and conviction that a dream can be achieved. He inspires the power and energy to get it done"
>
> Ralph Nader

Well Developed

Gets others to accept and trust a vision of the future and inspires them

Underdeveloped

Is unable to inspire others with a particular vision of the future and seems more focused on the here and now

Overdeveloped

Creates an unbelievable or intangible vision with which people cannot identify

Instructions

Read the definitions on the left. If the Underdeveloped definition applies, go to the Strategies for Action section.

If the Overdeveloped definition applies, go to the end of the chapter.

Test Yourself

True	Every now and then I remind people of the part their work plays in the bigger picture
True	I routinely talk about our common cause and build consensus centered on the company vision
True	I look for clues that people's energy levels are low and try to inspire them once more
True	I keep all stakeholders informed about the organization's progress
True	I am an effective motivational speaker

Note

Are you sure you need to develop this competency?

If the answer is "True" to most of the statements on the left, you probably do not need to develop this competency.

Strategies for Action

Most ineffective behaviors have an underlying thought or emotional pattern. By identifying these patterns, you can understand the impact they have and design strategies to counteract them.

① Our company has no distinct future and change is constant

② I am not fully committed to the mission or vision of the company

③ I do not consider myself an inspirational person/I do not understand what inspires others

④ I do not like to be the cheerleader or the one who must sell a vision

⑤ I do not like to create unrealistic expectations/ I believe it is better to promise less and deliver more

Instructions

1. Read and select one or more of the ineffective ways of thinking/feeling to the left.

2. Find the corresponding number below that will help you to rethink this pattern and identify specific and practical actions that you can take.

---

1 | Our company has no distinct future and change is constant

Rethink

It is challenging to inspire a future when an organization is rapidly changing or a new vision has marked a radical departure from the past. In times of ambiguity, it is vital to ensure that everyone remains confident about the company's future and direction.

As a leader and manager, it is your responsibility to curb people's apprehension and fears, and inspire them to handle the challenges change brings, with a common purpose in mind. Continual change in a company and constantly fluctuating directions are confusing. Nevertheless, employees must be able to change directions quickly and reconfigure processes to keep up with the changing demands, and your ability to inspire them will help to facilitate this.

React

(a) Review the company's mission and vision.

(b) If they are vague, discuss them with other leaders in the organization and clarify them. Ensure you understand why decisions were made to move in this direction. Understanding the reasons behind change helps you to make a convincing case to those you supervise.

(c) Expect people to be apprehensive and doubtful about change.

(d) Anticipate that there will be many questions and concerns, so prepare to respond. You can get a list of common questions by asking representatives of various divisions to supply their key concerns.

(e) Present the vision as a work in progress rather than something that is set in stone. It communicates to everyone that the road ahead will involve trial and error, as well as adjustments.

(f) Ensure you highlight what will remain the same, such as company values, commitment to excellence, core products etcetera. It will comfort employees.

(g) Talk to leaders who have successfully implemented turnaround strategies. Which challenges did they face in trying to inspire others?

(h) Remember humor when discussing the difficulties that might be encountered in steering the company on a different course. Humor is a bonding tool and humanizes you, which may help employees to see your side and approach change with less apprehension.

(i) Encourage a culture in which people tolerate and even thrive during times of ambiguity. Support experimentation and reward innovative approaches to nurture such a culture.

2 | I am not fully committed to the mission or vision of the company

Rethink

You cannot expect others to be inspired about the future if your attitude about it is negative, or if you lack commitment to the company's vision or mission. Perhaps you have made limited input in the current direction or are skeptical about its success. Whatever the reason, you as a manager are responsible for promoting the course the organization has taken and inspiring others to align with its vision, especially when change is imminent.

Your subordinates will want inspiration from you. Rectifying your attitude lets you act professionally and takes their needs into consideration, too.

React

(a) Do not voice your disagreement.

(b) If you feel tempted to share your personal opinions, ask yourself whether your comments will change things or whether you will just be venting.

c) Be aware of the impact your words may have on morale, especially should you openly express concerns about the decision-making process or leadership.

(d) Watch your body language, for example, do not roll your eyes or shake your head during discussions about the company's goals, or cross your arms tightly and speak disinterestedly in a monotone when talking about its future.

(e) No matter how you fake it, create some motivation to accept the company's vision or direction. It will make it easier for you to convey enthusiasm and motivate others. If you do not believe in it somehow, you will not be perceived as authentic. Write down the reasons for your skepticism to identify exactly what makes you uncomfortable.

(f) Challenge your logic — get a fresh perspective on the situation from a mentor or respected peers.

(g) If you are not sold on the company course that has been set, ensure you find ways to change that in the future by becoming more involved in the decision-making process. If appropriate, talk to those who made the decision to learn their rationale. Become involved in a committee or task force, or volunteer to be part of the project that generates the decisions being made. If you are really passionate about change, try to influence others by lobbying behind the scenes.

3 | I do not consider myself an inspirational person/ I do not understand what inspires others

Rethink

Some people are naturally good at motivating and inspiring others. They can move crowds to tears and rally people to support a common cause with remarkable ease. Do not worry if you do not fall in that category — you are not alone. Many great leaders have learned how to inspire others through years of observation and practice, and often do so through small actions instead of great public speeches.

Inborn talent or not, everyone has the ability to inspire others. Individuals do it every day in less publicized ways: the parent who encourages a child to dream of higher education, the coach who motivates the neighborhood baseball team; the volunteer who enthusiastically supports the local charity. The common ingredient in their inspiration is the belief that a common goal and purpose can be achieved. If you can believe that too, you will be able to inspire others.

React

(a) Schedule regular meetings with staff to engage them in the company's direction and create excitement among them.

(b) Ensure you are accessible to your subordinates. They should be able to openly discuss their ambitions for their future within the company.

(c) Up your energy level so that your enthusiasm shows. Leaders often make the mistake of delivering their message as if it were an unpleasant task. Be optimistic and impart excitement when talking about the company's future. Be animated. Raise people's interest by encouraging constructive questions.

(d) Ensure you can clearly articulate the benefits of the direction the company is taking.

(e) Do not be discouraged by detractors. Some people may be disinterested, others skeptical or even outright resistant. If you can isolate these individuals, talk to them privately about their negativity and try to address their concerns. Pretending that they do not matter risks having them influence the attitude of the entire group. Also, be prepared to answer the key questions from detractors. Do not respond defensively — find patience in the knowledge that your position is stronger when change is accepted, not forced.

(f) Your message will often have to be delivered through formal presentations. If resources permit, engage a professional speechwriter who can translate your ideas into motivational words. It takes a highly specialized writer, so get help if necessary. If you want to inspire an audience, the investment will pay off handsomely.

(g) Practice your speech in front of the mirror, your family or a peer. Would you be inspired? Were they? Ensure you trust your message, or your delivery will not be believable.

(h) The reasons behind people's inspiration is as diverse as people themselves. One size will not fit all while you try to instill a vision for the future. Be aware of the different audiences to whom you will have to present. Your message to the board will differ from your message to your line workers or members of the press.

(i) Add a down-to-earth touch to your message by using humor and metaphors or analogies to which your particular audience can relate.

(j) Learn to become an accomplished futurist. To inspire others, you have to know how to get them to use their imagination and believe in possibilities — things they are unable to see just then.

4 | I do not like to be the cheerleader or the one who must sell a vision

Rethink

Inspiring a future is similar to selling a product, but with one major difference — it is the company's vision that is being promoted. You are not just selling a commodity, but a future and purpose for everyone in the company. You have to get others to accept this future for the same reason that drives your performance. You have to help them to understand the long-term benefits they will gain in exchange for their commitment. As with any sales campaign, you cannot manipulate the consumer's level of buy-in completely; it requires effort and resources. Remember, though, without some amount of marketing and sales efforts even the best product will remain on the shelf.

React

(a) Selling an idea to others does not have to be a large production. Each individual you talk to is a customer, so use the opportunity to do your pitch informally and show your enthusiasm for the direction the company is taking.

(b) Use others to help you to spread the word. Ask other managers to make it a priority and encourage or reward them for inspiring a vision of the future in others.

(c) Spearhead a formal communication campaign, which is supported by the executive team. It could take many forms, for example, e-mails, webcasts or company-wide presentations, depending on resources. Consult your change management or communications team to devise an effective marketing plan.

(d) Ensure the company's vision and mission are clearly communicated in the annual report.

(e) Remember, action often has a greater impact than words as far as inspiring others is concerned. Ensure you act according to the mission and vision you are selling.

5 | I do not like to create unrealistic expectations/I believe it is better to promise less and deliver more

Rethink

It is hard to inspire people when you give bigger credence to the probability of failing than the possibility of success. It may seem more practical to focus on what can be achieved with certainty, but people are probably already aware of that.

Inspiring others is more about appealing to people's imagination and emotions, and getting their commitment despite uncertainties the future holds.

The Civil Rights movement in the US was based on a dream of equality which, at the time, seemed impossible. Leaders such as Martin Luther King did not inspire others to action by managing their expectations but by raising them far beyond that which people had ever imagined possible.

React

(a) Focus less on how you will get there and more on what your destination actually looks like.

(b) Do not shy away from setting ambitious goals and objectives for yourself and the team. If you are successful, you will have raised the bar beyond average. If the outcome falls short, you will likely have achieved what was expected anyway.

(c) Become inspired about greatness by learning about inspirational leaders. Read biographies or listen to famous inspirational speeches.

(d) If it makes you feel more comfortable, let people know you are aiming for the stars and that how you get there is a work in progress with all the trial and error it involves.

Overdeveloped

Research has shown that strengths can become weaknesses because you can, in fact, do too much of a good thing. You cannot become less good at a competency in which you excel, but you can balance the behavior by developing a few Stabilizers to tone down an excessive strength.

Stabilizer	Overdeveloped
2 Adaptable	Creates an unbelievable or intangible vision with which people cannot identify
40 Market Aware	
56 Technically Competent	
32 Informs Others	
53 Strategic	
9 Communicates Well (Verbal)	
43 Motivates People	
48 Plans Work	
22 Diplomatic	
58 Trustworthy	

Instructions

Read the definition. If it applies to you, choose a few Stabilizers and develop them by selecting the relevant chapter and following the Strategies for Action.

For more instructions see the How To Use This Book section.

34. Listens Well

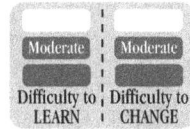

"A good listener is not only popular everywhere,
but after a while he gets to know something"

Wilson Mizner

Well Developed
Listens with the intention of genuinely understanding others' thoughts and feelings

Underdeveloped
Misunderstands what people try to communicate or seems disinterested in what they have to say

Overdeveloped
Places too much importance on listening and allows people too much time to make a point

Instructions
Read the definitions on the left. If the Underdeveloped definition applies, go to the Strategies for Action section.

If the Overdeveloped definition applies, go to the end of the chapter.

Test Yourself

True	I am interested in and sincerely open to others' suggestions
True	I believe that, at times, others will know more than me
True	I am able to repeat or summarize what people have told me
True	I let people finish before I suggest a solution or course of action
True	I can understand what people are trying to say even if they have difficulty expressing themselves
True	I show interest regardless what people are talking about
True	I am not easily distracted while people are talking to me

Note

Are you sure you need to develop this competency?

If the answer is "True" to most of the statements on the left, you probably do not need to develop this competency.

Strategies for Action

Most ineffective behaviors have an underlying thought or emotional pattern. By identifying these patterns, you can understand the impact they have and design strategies to counteract them.

① I do not have time to listen

② I feel like I know better than most/I tend to interrupt others

③ I have too much on my mind/I am easily distracted

④ I am impatient with people/I listen to some people but not to others

Instructions

1. Read and select one or more of the ineffective ways of thinking/feeling to the left.

2. Find the corresponding number below that will help you to rethink this pattern and identify specific and practical actions that you can take.

1 | I do not have time to listen

Rethink

At work, few people feel they have much time to listen to others. Indeed, this may be true, but you simply cannot work effectively with others or build strong relationships if you do not listen to what they have to say. Making the time to listen helps you to understand how to assist your team better and remain abreast of issues. It does not take nearly as much time to lend an ear as you may think and, as a manager, listening allows you to delegate work more efficiently. Whatever time you can give is better than no time at all. Investing just a small amount of time to listen will have a positive impact, so do the best you can.

React

(a) Prioritize carefully how much time you can give to others and to whom you give it.

(b) If time is really a constraint, try appointing or selecting a key person who represents the interests of the group.

(c) Ask people beforehand to summarize what they need to tell you in a few key points. Make it clear what your time constraints are and how much time you have available before you will have to leave.

(d) If possible, make use of lunchtime or travel time to catch up with others.

(e) Manage the time you do make available for others. If the topic requires a full hour of conversation but you have allotted only twenty minutes, it is likely you will get impatient and stop listening properly as time begins to run out.

2 | I feel like I know better than most/I tend to interrupt others

Rethink

To be attentive, it is necessary to be genuinely open to what others have to say. Having predetermined conclusions means you are going to be more concerned with what you know or want to say and less attentive to another person's input.

Not listening well will predispose you to making incorrect assumptions and can quickly be perceived as arrogance. People with seniority or those in positions of authority might find it particularly challenging to listen attentively to the opinions of juniors.

People, regardless of their level or skills, are always in a position to contribute new ideas and fresh perspectives and the organization benefits from a culture that encourages their contribution.

React

(a) Show interest and listen, even if you are already familiar with the topic or have a solution yourself. There may be a fresh perspective from which you can benefit or additional data that has not been considered. Even if nothing new emerges from the discussion, being attentive encourages people to get involved and makes them excited about thinking problems through.

(b) Remain silent on purpose and do not interrupt others to give your opinions before they have had ample time to express themselves. Interruptions are very frustrating for the person trying to talk and it means you are focusing on what you have to say instead of the other way round. Be aware of how often you routinely interrupt people.

(c) In some situations, being attentive requires you to step away from the situation to allow what has been said to sink in. If appropriate, give yourself time before making comments to people, but be sure to get back to them later.

(d) Be aware of dismissive behavior that indicates you are bored or disinterested, for example, looking around while someone is talking to you, checking your watch, going through work on your desk, avoiding eye contact etcetera.

(e) Stop whatever you are working on and show the person that you are willing to listen and think about what they have to say. If it really is not the best time to do so, schedule a time to meet soon.

(f) Choose to mentor someone. It is one of the best ways to share your knowledge and expertise and, at the same time, practice being attentive with someone at a different professional level than you.

Rethink

Have you ever started listening to someone only to realize you have not heard a thing they said? The stress of work and its competing demands occasionally make it seem impossible to focus on one thing or one person at a time.

Having a large number of responsibilities may make it particularly difficult to maintain a reasonable attention span. Moreover, our modern-day environment and its media technologies all contribute to a culture in which speed is revered, and we are always pressured to move on to the next trend just to stay in the game.

Attention deficit has increasingly become a challenge for individuals in our fast-paced world. Nevertheless, the need to stay connected and remain attentive in the presence of others is critical to the management of people and the understanding of client needs.

React

A meditation is one of the most effective ways to still the mind. The many techniques for meditation include chanting or exercises to control your breathing. Try meditation as a calming exercise you routinely do outside of work.

(b) It is better to be 100% present for 15 minutes than barely present for an hour. During a conversation, be aware when irrelevant thoughts creep into your mind. Keep reining in your thoughts to the situation at hand.

(c) Keep your mind focused and attentive by rephrasing or summarizing what the person has said. Ask if you have understood the person correctly. Use language and gestures that show concern and understanding during the conversation, for example, nod often and use phrases such as "I see", "I understand" and "That makes sense".

(d) If you are concerned about a pressing deadline, consider asking the person to wait a day or two until you can listen without distractions. Schedule that time on your calendar and be absolutely sure to honor it.

(e) Give yourself time to switch gears before starting a new conversation. You may find yourself far into a new meeting still thinking about the previous one. Take a quick walk, if possible, or grab a beverage. Spend a few minutes connecting at a personal level with the new person.

(f) Reduce the amount of distractions that compete with your attention. When lending your ear to someone, shut off the phone. You can always get your messages afterwards. Do not sit in front of the computer and continue using it when someone is talking to you.

4 | I am impatient with people/I listen to some people but not to others

Rethink

Do you need people to be extremely direct and to the point, but find that they are not? Perhaps someone has not prepared well and you feel your time is being wasted. It is easy to be attentive when the other person is articulate and presents the problem in a style similar to yours. The real challenge is remaining patient with those who are different from you and who do not seem to address your needs immediately.

At work, you will have to interact with a diverse number of personalities, work styles, skills and experience levels, and you can expect your patience to be tested often. Remember, too, that there are multiple levels of listening.

Being overly impatient predisposes you to listening at a highly superficial level. You may miss the emotional content or message behind someone's words if you are only concerned with them getting to the point.

React

(a) When someone is not doing well getting their point across or taking too long and you find yourself getting impatient, act as a facilitator instead of zoning out, getting frustrated or interrupting. Help the person to get their point across by asking simple questions or restating what they are trying to say. Steer them diplomatically through the conversation. If you teach a person how to articulate effectively, you do not have to work so hard at figuring out what they are trying to say.

(b) Put yourself in the other person's shoes. Imagine what they may be feeling. Perhaps the person is nervous or shy. Some extra patience may be required, depending on the circumstances.

(c) Teach those around you how you like to be briefed or which type of communication you prefer. Do not assume people can read you well.

(d) Are you attentive to some but not others? Unknowingly, you may be discriminating against certain people. Identify with whom you tend to be less attentive — younger people, women, minorities? Strive to be fair in listening. Write a list of the people with whom you are not attentive. Try to identify common patterns or themes among them.

(e) If you have a particular dislike for someone or they have upset you, take the person aside and discuss your differences professionally. You want to set an example for others, show that differences can be resolved and demonstrate that everyone in the organization will be heard.

Overdeveloped

Research has shown that strengths can become weaknesses because you can, in fact, do too much of a good thing. You cannot become less good at a competency in which you excel, but you can balance the behavior by developing a few Stabilizers to tone down an excessive strength.

Stabilizer	Overdeveloped
1 Achiever	Places too much importance on listening and allows people too much time to make a point
13 Courageous	
35 Manages Conflict	
38 Manages Underperformance	
16 Decisive	
39 Manages Time	
37 Manages Negotiations	
48 Plans Work	
29 Focused on Priorities	
54 Takes Accountablity	

Instructions

Read the definition. If it applies to you, choose a few Stabilizers and develop them by selecting the relevant chapter and following the Strategies for Action.

For more instructions see the How To Use This Book section.

35. Manages Conflict

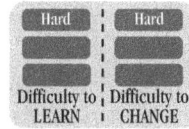

> "Peace is not the absence of conflict but the presence of creative alternatives for responding to conflict — alternatives to passive or aggressive responses, alternatives to violence"
>
> Dorothy Thompsonn

Well Developed
Recognizes, handles and resolves conflict promptly

Underdeveloped
Avoids conflict or is seen as overly aggressive

Overdeveloped
Sees conflict and tries to manage it when it is simply healthy disagreement

Instructions

Read the definitions on the left. If the Underdeveloped definition applies, go to the Strategies for Action section.

If the Overdeveloped definition applies, go to the end of the chapter.

Test Yourself

True	I do not delay addressing topics that will create conflict or make people uncomfortable
True	I can mediate successfully in a conflict situation
True	I remain composed during conflict
True	I can diplomatically discuss things that people might not want to hear
True	I see conflict's positive outcome after it has been resolved
True	I do not instigate conflict, even accidentally

Note

Are you sure you need to develop this competency?

If the answer is "True" to most of the statements on the left, you probably do not need to develop this competency.

Strategies for Action

Most ineffective behaviors have an underlying thought or emotional pattern. By identifying these patterns, you can understand the impact they have and design strategies to counteract them.

① I do not see the usefulness of conflict/I value getting along with others

② Being aggressive or forcing people to back off is my best way of dealing with conflict

③ I am not comfortable confronting people/I do not want to be the bad guy

④ I do not know conflict-management techniques/I have not had much experience in handling conflict

⑤ My organization frowns upon conflict/It discourages confrontation

Instructions

1. Read and select one or more of the ineffective ways of thinking/feeling to the left.

2. Find the corresponding number below that will help you to rethink this pattern and identify specific and practical actions that you can take.

---

1 | I do not see the usefulness of conflict/I value getting along with others

Rethink

In settings that involve many personalities and multiple agendas, such as the workplace, conflict is likely and needs to be managed. Up to 30% of a manager's time is typically spent dealing with conflict. But conflict is often necessary to achieve resolution.

If managed well, conflict situations give people the opportunity to voice concerns and protect their interests. Conflict addresses problems, allows people to be honest and helps them to learn how to recognize their differences and use them to their benefit.

Capitalizing on diversity often means having to manage contradictory opinions. Conflict only becomes a problem when it is mismanaged, because it affects productivity negatively, lowers morale and causes even greater conflict or inappropriate behaviors.

Do not avoid necessary conflict in an attempt to humor everybody. Firstly, it is unrealistic to expect that you can meet everyone's needs at all times, especially when competing needs are at play. Secondly, unaddressed conflict leads to even greater discord in the long run. Lastly, competitors take advantage of accommodators and chronic people-pleasers because they are easiest to manipulate.

React

(a) If you are asked to help others to resolve conflict among them, facilitate an honest discussion during which all parties have an opportunity to be heard.

Focus the conversation on facts and do not allow insults or a lack of respect to enter the discussion.

(b) Reaching consensus may be too lofty a goal at first. You can measure success by your ability to facilitate a respectful understanding among the parties.

(c) Conflict is often avoided, or at least better managed, by proactively explaining to employees why decisions were made, especially when they were uninvolved in the decision-making process. Providing clarity prevents people from reaching their own conclusions or trusting rumors more than management.

(d) If the conflict is about resources, for example, disagreement about who does what or stress about working with inadequate resources, clarify their allocation.

(e) Remember what will be addressed by managing the conflict — leadership problems, poor team performance, a lack of sharing information etcetera.

(f) Ensure you do not concede too quickly just for the sake of peace. When dealing with overly competitive and aggressive people, you will have to bring strong conviction to your position.

(g) If you are going along with others, examine your reasons. It is acceptable when in everyone's best interest to do so, including yours, or as a strategy to promote your interests in the future, for example, in situations that will enhance your negotiating powers later.

> **2** | Being aggressive or forcing people to back off is my best way of dealing with conflict

Rethink

Aggression and intimidation work well if you want people to leave you alone, but it is not a sound approach to resolving issues. Some people abuse their authority over others when handling conflict. One's personality, voice or even size can be misused to get one's way. If this sounds like bullying — it is.

It will definitely take more time and patience to address conflict in a democratic manner, but it will be more effective and fair. Remember that it may scare the bears when you make a lot of noise in the forest, but they will come back as soon as the noise dies down.

Understanding what employees want will yield a more productive strategy. Also, realize that people are less likely to voice their concerns if they are intimidated by you. A manager or leader who is seen as a bully will develop a reputation of being unfair and will be kept in the dark about colleagues' needs.

React

(a) Handle conflict with a particular individual by engaging in a rational, unemotional conversation. It is the best way to clarify the issues.

(b) Be patient and assign value to the process, not just the outcome.

(c) Instead of using intimidation to make gains, make it your goal to put the other person at ease.

(d) Keep your voice calm and use a normal tone to discuss the matter.

(e) Be aware of your body language — it often says more than your words. Leaning into people's space and pointing repeatedly in their faces, for example, are signs of aggression. Your body language should remain open and welcoming.

(f) Be aware of the role personal chemistry plays in conflict. The actual issue may be less strong than the confrontational chemistry between people. For example, two people with strongly opposing views on an issue are likely to butt heads. We often dislike in others what we dislike in ourselves. Which characteristics of your personality do you find least attractive?

(g) Write down five traits in others that trigger your aggression. These come in every shape and size: people who talk constantly and never listen, who must always have the last word, who never commit, who criticize anything they did not create themselves, who stab you in the back or gossip all the time. Be aware that these traits may bring out the worst in you while you manage conflict.

(h) Ask a trusted peer to alert you when you walk over others. It may be difficult for you to spot your behavior, especially because you are unlikely to think you are doing anything wrong.

(i) Take an aggression management course if your temper is an issue or you fly off the handle easily.

---

3 | **I am not comfortable confronting people/I do not want to be the bad guy**

Rethink

Do you cringe at the thought of having to confront people? It may involve telling your bosses their approach is not working, or reprimanding subordinates for work not done correctly. Perhaps there is a sensitive discussion to be had with a client. Dealing with disagreement is never pleasant, especially if you find conflict discomfiting.

Managers regularly struggle to confront others, but healthy confrontation is just a means to achieve a mutually beneficial end or an opportunity to collaborate that did not exist before. Effective teams generally go through a "form, storm, norm and perform" period and confrontation is part of the process. In the end, everyone involved stands to gain if you are comfortable to confront them through honest and constructive dialogue.

Ignoring issues to avoid discomfort is self-serving and will only prolong discord among people unnecessarily. Avoiding conflict is unproductive and should only be allowed if no positive outcome whatsoever exists.

React

(a) Deal with conflict immediately. Do not allow the situation to worsen or tensions to build unnecessarily. The longer matters remain unresolved, the more difficult it will be to defuse people's emotions, and the harder it will be to convince you to tackle them.

(b) Begin any discussion about the issue with a clear definition of its objectives and likely positive outcomes. Focusing on positive results validates the need for confrontation.

(c) There is strength in numbers. If appropriate, rally support from others to confront the other side.

(d) Remind yourself that you are working towards a positive goal, and that you or others feeling temporarily uncomfortable is worth the effort.

(e) Consider creative ways to resolve the conflict. Ask a trusted peer or mentor to provide suggestions. Practice with an issue about which you feel strongly.

(f) Keep practicing. Feeling confident to confront others may require doing it enough times to realize that your anxieties are unwarranted.

---

(4) | **I do not know conflict-management techniques/I have not had much experience in handling conflict**

Rethink

Conflict-management skills do not come naturally to most of us. They can be challenging to develop because conflict is fueled by competing opinions, values, personalities and needs, and confrontation is often emotionally charged. Developing an assortment of techniques to use in conflict management is a good investment of your time, because you will have to draw upon these skills throughout your career.

React

(a) Communicate and keep people informed. Often, a lack of communication is the root of conflict. People become upset when they continuously face surprises or are not informed about new decisions, programs etcetera.

(b) If tempers rise when confronting others, focus inward on your behavior, not theirs. Speaking to someone as if they are not upset is an effective strategy to remain composed.

(c) Be aware of using language that makes people defensive. For example, rather say "It appears there is a misunderstanding" than "You don't understand". Also avoid sweeping generalizations when making your argument, such as "You and your team always do what you want".

(d) Be aware of your non-verbal communication, for example, maintain eye contact and nod while you listen.

(e) Focus on facts, not the person involved.

(f) Listen actively. You want to reach a mutually beneficial outcome, and that cannot be done without understanding the other side's position. If you supposedly know all the answers before discussions begin, you will not manage conflict well. Allow the other person time to vent and let them explain without interrupting or judging what is said. Verify that you truly hear each other. Repeat and rephrase what you have heard the other person say and confirm accuracy. Let them confirm that you have listened properly.

(g) If possible, always have conflict-related discussions in private. There is no need to include unnecessary ears or solicit unwanted input.

(h) Most often, it is best to be open and honest about your feelings. People will appreciate your sincerity and be more sympathetic to your position.

(i) End your discussion with action items for which all parties involved are responsible. Ensure there is agreement and support from both sides regarding these items. If you cannot come to an agreement there and then, consider taking time to reflect and cool down, and reconvene later.

(j) Agree to disagree, or seek a third party to mediate when issues simply cannot be resolved.

(k) Many books are available to learn more about conflict management. These include *Interpersonal Conflict* by William W Willmot and *Conflict Resolution* by Daniel Dana.

(l) Enquire about possible conflict-management courses you could take through the company. The human resources department could help.

(m) Ask your boss about opportunities to attend meetings that could give you first-hand exposure to conflict-management practices.

(n) Take advantage of assessment tools to help you identify and mitigate the risk of conflict in your team. The PeopleTree Talent Management™ system lets you assess different team styles and how individuals will likely perceive each other based on these styles.

5 | My organization frowns upon conflict/It discourages confrontation

Rethink

Different cultures react differently to confrontation; so do different industries and organizations. An approach often depends on the leadership's style of management. But regardless of the organizational culture, conflict arises all the time, whether it is between individuals, groups, due to differing opinions or protection of turf. However, conflict does not need to play out in a manner that is overly aggressive or assertive.

To the extent that conflict creates healthy debate and opportunity rather than disruption, it will be more welcomed by individuals and the organization.

React

(a) Acknowledge tension openly instead of denying it — it is the first step towards action.

(b) Redefine your perspective on confrontation. Encourage honesty and promote creative, constructive debate within your team and throughout the organization.

(c) If you lead within the organization, you will set an example for everyone else. Ensure you are open to being challenged.

(d) If a situation cannot be resolved through discussion and the other party's behavior clashes with policies and procedures, seek support from the human resources department.

(e) If you are in conflict with your boss, you will have to learn how to get along despite their arrogant or controlling behavior. Try to learn as much as you can about your boss's personality and expectations. Talk to others who work well with your boss and ask their advice.

Overdeveloped

Research has shown that strengths can become weaknesses because you can, in fact, do too much of a good thing. You cannot become less good at a competency in which you excel, but you can balance the behavior by developing a few Stabilizers to tone down an excessive strength.

Stabilizer	Overdeveloped
8 Comfortable With Uncertainty	Sees conflict and tries to manage it when it is simply healthy disagreement
1 Achiever	
2 Adaptable	
34 Listens Well	
13 Courageous	
43 Motivates People	
37 Manages Negotiations	
46 Open-Minded	
17 Demonstrates Good Judgment	
59 Unifies People	

Instructions

Read the definition. If it applies to you, choose a few Stabilizers and develop them by selecting the relevant chapter and following the Strategies for Action.

For more instructions see the How To Use This Book section.

36. Manages Ideas

"An idea that is developed and put into action is more important than an idea that exists only as an idea"

Hindu Prince Gautama Siddharta

Well Developed

Takes new ideas from conception to fruition by managing the innovation process

Underdeveloped

Is seen as unsupportive of innovation or does not know how to manage the process of turning an idea into practice

Overdeveloped

Invests in innovation too much or misreads the market's readiness for new ideas

Instructions

Read the definitions on the left. If the Underdeveloped definition applies, go to the Strategies for Action section.

If the Overdeveloped definition applies, go to the end of the chapter.

Test Yourself

True	I give people the freedom to experiment and the necessary resources to do it
True	I encourage people to share new ideas
True	I value and support creativity
True	I listen to everybody's ideas, even if they are different from mine
True	I believe innovative ideas require a plan if they are to be executed

Note

Are you sure you need to develop this competency?

If the answer is "True" to most of the statements on the left, you probably do not need to develop this competency.

36 Manages Ideas

237

Strategies for Action

Most ineffective behaviors have an underlying thought or emotional pattern. By identifying these patterns, you can understand the impact they have and design strategies to counteract them.

① I do not know how to generate or solicit new ideas

② I encourage people to generate ideas but often do not act on them or there is little follow-up

③ If the idea is not mine, I tend to be less interested in making it happen/ Other people cannot add much value

④ I do not have the time or resources to bring new ideas to fruition

⑤ I prefer sticking with the tried and tested/The risk of failure is too high

Instructions

1. Read and select one or more of the ineffective ways of thinking/feeling to the left.

2. Find the corresponding number below that will help you to rethink this pattern and identify specific and practical actions that you can take.

---

1 | I do not know how to generate or solicit new ideas

Rethink

The first step in managing ideas is to support innovation and nurture an environment in which creativity is valued. One isolated meeting is unlikely to foster a revolutionary breakthrough, and creativity on demand is rare.

Regular opportunities for employees to share thoughts generate a greater pool of ideas because they are bounced off one another and give rise to spontaneous creativity.

You cannot force creativity, but you can champion its use in many ways that will yield many original ideas and establish a culture of innovation.

React

(a) Stimulate creativity by always encouraging employees to offer any thoughts on a new approach, product or service that can be implemented both now and in the future.

(b) Ensure your team includes a few highly creative people — they tend to force others to think about new ideas too.

(c) Start an ideas campaign to get everyone involved in generating ideas. Present a business problem to employees and encourage them all to participate in finding solutions. Set a period during which they can contribute their suggestions, then select the best ideas and send these to experts for evaluation. The winning ideas will be used and their creators will receive credit.

(d) Do not focus on getting one perfect idea. Encourage people to generate more than one solution and assess the input in its variety. A range of ideas are usually combined to find the best approach and achieve the highest level of innovation.

(e) Be there to listen to people who want to share innovative ideas with you. If you are always unavailable, they may think you are uninterested and will stop trying to get your attention. If it is not a convenient time, schedule another appointment when the person can do the pitch to you.

(f) When innovative solutions for a particular issue are needed, create an innovation taskforce with creative thinkers from different disciplines.

(g) Let a consultant facilitate a creativity workshop at which employees can learn to explore different ways of thinking. Ask a human resources representative to research some options for you.

(h) Keep the workplace playful and flexible. Ask your employees whether their environment fosters creativity. If not, what do they suggest? Rearranging the office space, adding colors on the wall, more flexibility in schedules, dress codes? Discover the things that your employees really believe matter and make a difference.

(i) Clients are a great source of innovative ideas. Use surveys, special focus groups or even informal calls or e-mails to solicit new ideas.

2 | I encourage people to generate ideas but often do not act on them or there is little follow-up

Rethink

The generating of ideas is a first, important step towards innovation, but like any other process an idea is only useful once it has led to planning and implementation.

Many great ideas fall by the wayside or are less effectively used than they could have been, not because they are impractical or unworkable or perhaps not revolutionary enough, but because of insufficient support and weak implementation. A culture like that discourages people who generate ideas and wastes resources and time.

Not every idea is worthy of implementation or must result in action but ensure you reward creative contributions.

React

(a) Do not let an idea remain on the shelf for too long. You will lose momentum, energy and even the interest of those involved. Create a team or taskforce to look at an idea's feasibility and report on it within a reasonable timeframe.

(b) If you decide to go forward with it, be thorough in your process planning. The plan should be no different from that of other projects you have, with goals and milestones identified.

(c) Ensure you can assign sufficient resources to carry the plan through. It may be a great idea, but a new direction often means withdrawing resources from elsewhere. Your time is a resource that will have to be redirected as well.

(d) Ensure you have addressed internal politics and have the approval you need from the relevant authorities. Many great ideas fail to be implemented because they did not have the support of the right stakeholders.

(e) If you approve the implementation of a new idea, ensure you monitor the process more closely than you would any other. By their nature, new ideas encounter obstacles as they are rolled out.

(f) Have a change management plan ready. New ideas can have an impact on people's roles and the way they have been conducting business. Communicating the need for change and allaying people's fears will increase the likelihood of a successful roll-out.

(g) If an idea has been scrapped, inform people of the reason. They will understand a lack of resources or competing demands, but will be less inclined to understand why a good idea gets no support.

3 | If the idea is not mine, I tend to be less interested in making it happen/Other people cannot add much value

Rethink

Are you the most creative person you know? It works like this: an idea pops into your head. You get excited. You embrace the idea. You think about it some more, do a little tweaking, name it ... and your brilliant idea is ready for roll-out.

You have not consulted others except to share the exciting news. You do not pay much attention to feedback unless it is supportive. Alternative options are simply not as good. Your head is always filled with great thoughts and innovative ideas, and there is little room for others' contributions. However, employees may work in a stimulating environment, but if their innovation is not valued, they will run into walls every time they try to take a step in that direction.

Do not make it difficult for employees to communicate their ideas to senior management. It demoralizes people and stops them from getting excited about contributing and being part of change in the organization. People feel more like contributors than hired hands when they are encouraged to originate and develop ideas. It gives their work meaning, helps them to make it their own and motivates them in a fundamental way.

React

(a) If you have a new idea, ask for feedback to improve what you have originated, not to get approval or consent.

(b) Take on a greater mentor or teacher role and encourage others to bring you their ideas, then use your expertise to lend a hand to their contributions.

(c) Assume that every idea presented to you could potentially have a positive impact on the business.

(d) Be positive, interested and really listen when a new idea is pitched to you. Respond with questions that explore the idea properly, for example, "That sounds interesting. Can you tell me more?", "How do you imagine your idea will benefit others?", "How does your idea fit with our strategic vision?", "What would the next step be?"

(e) Allow the idea's originator the chance to think out loud and enough time to explain their idea. The longer you listen, the more likely you will see threads of possibility and visualize ways to integrate it with existing ways or processes.

(f) Do not assume a junior person has less to contribute — their particular experience or insight can shed new light on a problem. Welcome and actively seek fresh perspectives. Even people who are unfamiliar with your business may have valuable perspectives to offer.

④ | I do not have the time or resources to bring new ideas to fruition

Rethink

There is a tendency to think of business innovation as solely related to exciting new high-technology products, measured by the number of patents a company has and the percentage of company income that came from such products in recent years. Innovation like that can be costly and resource intensive and less glamorous innovative progress is just as necessary. It involves the improvement of business processes and practices which, for example, cut costs, improve the efficiency of operational processes, decrease waste and lowers the price of product manufacturing. During an economic slowdown, this kind of innovation is preferred. But whatever the focus, true innovators must be prepared to challenge excuses and concede resources, be it people or time, in order to improve the status quo. They never allow any environment to define their reality.

React

(a) Innovation can take the form of small changes, and often does. Start with ideas that are less demanding on resources.

(b) Consider business processes that can be improved through a fresh approach.

(c) Identify the ways in which collaboration and partnerships, both internal and external, will let you pool resources to move an innovative initiative forward.

(d) You do not have to recreate the wheel to be innovative. Take a look at the ideas your competitors have rolled out and focus to simply improve those or provide more creative options.

(e) Spend enough time on the brainstorming and planning phases to address details and select appropriate solutions upfront. This is critical to maximize the possibility of success and ensure that resources are not wasted.

(f) Plan ahead for innovation by setting aside money for resources in your budget.

5 | I prefer sticking with the tried and tested/The risk of failure is too high

Rethink

The management of innovation is like any other process that requires careful study and planning. For an organization trying to remain competitive the consequences of falling behind in innovative thinking and practices are greater than those of dealing with missteps taken in their pursuit. Leadership requires that you make courageous decisions which bring about change. Without it, you risk passing up growth opportunities for both you and the organization.

React

(a) Treat failures and mistakes as experiences that teach you invaluable lessons. Do not feel discouraged if your time and resource investment does not generate success the first time. If you consider experiments as learning opportunities, your time and effort are well spent.

(b) Focus on the big picture instead of the short-term cost. Understand the benefits a successful new idea will generate. It is hard to argue with well-researched numbers.

(c) Get support from someone else in the company who is more adept at risk taking. They can give you a fresh perspective.

(d) List the drawbacks of doing business as usual. What are the problems with the process, product or service as it is now? Nothing is perfect and sometimes we are just more comfortable with established patterns than new approaches.

Overdeveloped

Research has shown that strengths can become weaknesses because you can, in fact, do too much of a good thing. You cannot become less good at a competency in which you excel, but you can balance the behavior by developing a few Stabilizers to tone down an excessive strength.

Stabilizer	Overdeveloped
40 Market Aware	Invests in innovation too much or misreads the market's readiness for new ideas
17 Demonstrates Good Judgment	
56 Technically Competent	
30 Global Thinker	
34 Listens Well	
48 Plans Work	
29 Focused on Priorities	
1 Achiever	
31 Improves Processes	
53 Strategic	

Instructions

Read the definition. If it applies to you, choose a few Stabilizers and develop them by selecting the relevant chapter and following the Strategies for Action.

For more instructions see the How To Use This Book section.

37. Manages Negotiations

> *"In business you don't get what you deserve, you get what you negotiate"*
> Chester L. Karrass

Well Developed
Achieves a win-win outcome even when there are conflicting interests and limited resources

Underdeveloped
Appears unwilling to reach a compromise or consider alternatives to satisfy all parties

Overdeveloped
Is seen as shrewd or cunning and leaves others with a feeling that they got a bad deal

Instructions

Read the definitions on the left. If the Underdeveloped definition applies, go to the Strategies for Action section.

If the Overdeveloped definition applies, go to the end of the chapter.

Test Yourself

True	I can reach a compromise when negotiating during negotiations
True	I usually arrive at outcomes that benefit both parties
True	I manage to find a resolution when there are conflicts of interest
True	When the negotiation is over, both parties usually feel positive
True	I am well prepared before going into negotiations
True	I do not hesitate to negotiate when I see the opportunity
True	I remain composed and even-tempered when negotiating
True	It does not bother me to ask for what I want

Note

Are you sure you need to develop this competency?

If the answer is "True" to most of the statements on the left, you probably do not need to develop this competency.

Strategies for Action

Most ineffective behaviors have an underlying thought or emotional pattern. By identifying these patterns, you can understand the impact they have and design strategies to counteract them.

(1) I struggle to manage the high level of emotion involved in negotiations

(2) I do not believe in win-win situations; somebody always loses in negotiations

(3) I do not know negotiation techniques

(4) I do not like to negotiate/I tend to give in

(5) I have not had experience in preparing for tough or high-risk negotiations

Instructions

1. Read and select one or more of the ineffective ways of thinking/feeling to the left.

2. Find the corresponding number below that will help you to rethink this pattern and identify specific and practical actions that you can take.

1 | I struggle to manage the high level of emotion involved in negotiations

Rethink

Competing needs are at the core of negotiations. This can give rise to emotionally charged discussions, particularly when values, beliefs and differences in culture are also at play.

Learn to recognize when your or others' emotional reaction is working against you. It can derail great opportunities and create unnecessary stalemates. Excessive or inappropriate displays of emotion undermine the rational basis of a negotiation and can also bring manipulation into any discussions.

React

(a) Work on your style and approach: stay composed, do not raise your voice, restate what the other person has said and acknowledge their point of view.
Such an approach is critical to maintain a productive discussion — loud displays or outbursts will always work to your disadvantage.

(b) If talking about people's emotions is important to clear the air, do so but manage the conversation carefully. The goal is to address feelings but get to the business of discussing facts as quickly as possible.

(c) Allow the other party to vent their frustrations so that they feel they have been heard. It will probably reduce volatility during the discussions.

246

(d) If discussions between you and another person heat up, speak to them as if they are not upset, regardless of their reaction. Focus on your response, not their reaction.

(e) Try to be empathetic when a situation is emotionally charged. Why does the other party feel so strongly about a position?

(f) Be quiet at the right moments. When people become anxious, it is a natural human reaction to try to fill the silence with meaningless noise, especially during conflict. During negotiations, anxious people tend to say things that erode their positions. Bide your time by asking questions.

(g) Are you giving away your emotions inadvertently — do you roll your eyes, look away impatiently, fidget? Be conscious of the signals you send.

(h) Do not get pulled in by others' threats, blame or games. Remember, these tactics can rattle you, so do not let them.

2 | I do not believe in win-win situations; somebody always loses in negotiations

Rethink

A successful outcome in negotiation is a solution acceptable to both parties that leaves everyone feeling as if they have gained something. Styles of negotiation depend on circumstances. In some cases, you do not expect to deal with people ever again and do not need their goodwill, so it may be effective to play hardball — seeking to win a negotiation while the other person loses out. This works when purchasing a house, for example, which is why it can be a confrontational and unpleasant experience.

When a great deal is at stake, people often adopt a win-lose approach. But when negotiating, consider the importance of preserving relationships for the sake of now and the future. A win-lose approach is never good for resolving disputes involving people with whom you wish to continue a relationship. Resorting to any lengths to win, such as using threats and manipulation, undermines trust. You may feel as if you have left a negotiation having successfully gotten your way, but if the other party feels unfairly treated or has not gained anything from the process, you can expect them to be uncooperative in honoring your agreement.

React

(a) Only consider a win-lose negotiation if you do not need an ongoing relationship with the other party. A party that gains no benefits from a negotiation will be reluctant to maintain a relationship with you.

(b) Consider honesty and openness before manipulation and let common principles of ethics and fairness guide you when negotiating.

(c) Avoid coming to the table with inflexible black-or-white positions. There is always room to consider other options if you really listen to what the other side has to say.

(d) Refrain from using threats to get your way. Threats are unproductive and only serve to put the other party on the defensive.

(e) Before negotiating, think carefully about the points you could concede and keep those for leverage. Even if you have the advantage, conceding to some points establishes goodwill and allows the other party to walk away with some sense of gain.

3 | I do not know negotiation techniques

Rethink

Skilled negotiators draw on common techniques, regardless of the issue or stakes involved. Negotiations can range from informal discussions about sharing resources to high-stakes matters affecting many people. You will be faced with many opportunities to negotiate throughout your career.

React

(a) Start negotiations by establishing an environment of cooperation. Allow people to have a short period to mingle informally and engage in small talk, arrange the seating to not differentiate sides, have breaks and encourage people to talk among themselves.

(b) Allow parties to verbalize their goals for the meeting.

(c) Always listen to the issues and underlying interests of the parties involved and try to understand them. It is surprising how many negotiations fail due to the issues being misunderstood. Ask as many questions as possible to clarify people's motives and key concerns.

(d) Take steps to ensure that all parties actually hear each other. Rephrase what a person says during a discussion if there is any doubt. Summarize the major points made as the conversation progresses.

(e) Use language that clearly indicates your willingness to solve a problem in a mutually beneficial way and work together. Use sentences such as "What if we try this?" or "What do you think about the two of us taking this approach?"

(f) Use non-verbal communication to let the other party know you are listening and open to discussion — maintain eye contact and nod when you understand. Avoid a posture that says you feel defensive or threatened, such as crossing your arms, scowling, shaking your head or leaning back in your chair as if you have disengaged.

(g) Think about the other party's personal style. Do they tend to be diplomatic, or are they more frank and lay everything on the table upfront? Adapt accordingly as you negotiate.

(h) Consider the negotiation points that are of little value to you and highly valued by the other party. If you have to give in, it is important to know what these points are in advance.

(i) Make any progress and agreement as visible as possible. Document success throughout the discussions by writing the agreed-upon points on a flipchart or board. When frustration is high, refer to the progress that has been made.

(j) Utilize comparable or precedent-setting transactions as a benchmark for negotiations. The information can help you to gauge the type of outcome you might expect and understand the points to which the other party will likely be willing to agree.

248

Rethink

If you are involved in negotiations, someone has chosen to conduct business with you. You are in a negotiating position because you are perceived as trustworthy or an adequate problem solver, or because you possess something of value. The act of negotiating is a careful exploration of your and another person's positions, with the goal of finding a mutually acceptable compromise that gives both of you maximum benefits. And although it may not seem to be the case initially, people are rarely as fundamentally opposed to your position as they may act. In an ideal situation, you will find that the other person wants what you are prepared to trade, and that you are prepared to give what the other person wants. It is fair on your part to negotiate some form of compensation for what you give up.

React

(a) Consider all your interests before negotiations begin. You may have to concede some points, but be clear about the ones you absolutely cannot concede. If you cannot negotiate a win-win solution, what is the least acceptable scenario? Knowing that will help you to stick to your guns.

(b) If the other party has adopted the role of tough negotiator, find ways during the process to commend them on their toughness and recognize that they drive a hard bargain.

(c) If you cannot agree on everything, work on the points that are critical and focus on them for now. Agree to address the other points later, but try to set a precedent for a successful negotiation experience.

(d) If you have reached a stalemate, consider engaging an arbitrator acceptable to both parties instead of conceding.

(e) Be prepared to walk away rather than give in. This may not be the best time to negotiate and there may be another way to get what you need. Walking away when you do not stand to gain anything is perfectly acceptable.

Rethink

The importance of preparation for complex negotiations cannot be overemphasized. A clear understanding of the purpose and goals is the first, critical step. Many negotiations get off to a bad start because the parties involved have not taken the time to define clearly the issues about which they disagree. If there is no real understanding of the issues at stake for both sides, agreement will be difficult.

The time you invest in preparing and asking yourself the right questions before the negotiation starts will be evident in the outcomes, and probably have an impact on its success.

249

React

(a) Consider the negotiation's goals. What do you want from it? What do you think the other person wants?

(b) Consider possible solutions and alternatives. If you do not reach an agreement with the other party, what are your alternatives? Are they good or bad? How much does it matter if you cannot agree? Does failure to reach an agreement eliminate future opportunities? Which alternatives could the other person have?

(c) Consider relationships. What is a relationship's history; could or should it have an impact on the negotiation? Are there any hidden issues that could influence the negotiation and how will you handle these?

(d) Consider the consequences of you winning or losing this negotiation. and what they mean to the other person.

(e) Who holds what kind of power in the relationship? Who controls resources? Who stands to lose the most if agreement is not forthcoming? What power does the other person have to satisfy your needs?

(f) Never make a false statement or assertion, and collect as much accurate information as possible before any negotiations.

Overdeveloped

Research has shown that strengths can become weaknesses because you can, in fact, do too much of a good thing. You cannot become less good at a competency in which you excel, but you can balance the behavior by developing a few Stabilizers to tone down an excessive strength.

Stabilizer	Overdeveloped
58 Trustworthy	Is seen as shrcwd or cunning and leaves others with a feeling that they got a bad deal
35 Manages Conflict	
53 Strategic	
17 Demonstrates Good Judgment	
30 Global Thinker	
7 Collaborative	
26 Ethical	
28 Fair	
29 Focused on Priorities	
54 Takes Accountablity	

Instructions

Read the definition. If it applies to you, choose a few Stabilizers and develop them by selecting the relevant chapter and following the Strategies for Action.

For more instructions see the How To Use This Book section.

38. Manages Underperformance

> "An ounce of prevention is worth a pound of cure"
> Henry de Bracton

Well Developed
Confronts underperformance quickly when individuals fail to meet expectations and takes corrective action

Underdeveloped
Allows underperformance to continue too long or is unwilling to enforce performance standards

Overdeveloped
Is too quick to confront and does not give people a chance to prove themselves, or fails to take circumstances into account

Instructions

Read the definitions on the left. If the Underdeveloped definition applies, go to the Strategies for Action section.

If the Overdeveloped definition applies, go to the end of the chapter.

Test Yourself

True	I feel comfortable to give corrective feedback when needed
True	I manage non-performance issues in a timely manner
True	I understand the underlying behaviors related to underperformance
True	I can quickly detect non-performance issues
True	I coach those who report to me to improve their performance
True	I adapt my style of feedback to the needs of the person I am addressing

Note

Are you sure you need to develop this competency?

If the answer is "True" to most of the statements on the left, you probably do not need to develop this competency.

253

Strategies for Action

Most ineffective behaviors have an underlying thought or emotional pattern. By identifying these patterns, you can understand the impact they have and design strategies to counteract them.

① I do not know how to manage a discussion about non-performance effectively

② It takes a long time for me to deal with signs of non-performance

③ Non-performance is not my problem/ The employee will face the consequences

④ I do not know what is causing an employee's non-performance

⑤ I am uncomfortable with the level of emotion or conflict that accompanies the management of non-performance

Instructions

1. Read and select one or more of the ineffective ways of thinking/feeling to the left.

2. Find the corresponding number below that will help you to rethink this pattern and identify specific and practical actions that you can take.

---

1 | I do not know how to manage a discussion about non-performance effectively

Rethink

The goal of having a discussion with an employee about non-performance is to give them a timely opportunity to increase their self-awareness, and to assist them in being successful in the organization. These conversations can be easy if the person is willing to accept feedback and has already acknowledged that a problem exists. But managers often find this is one of their most challenging responsibilities.

Reviewing the principles provided can help to guide you through an effective discussion about non-performance.

React

(a) Start your discussion by pointing out some positive aspects of the employee's performance.

(b) Always treat the employee with professionalism, dignity and respect, even if their performance has had a negative impact on you and your team.

(c) Check the person's level of understanding of their job description to ensure that you both have the same expectations of their role.

(d) Prepare corrective suggestions before you meet with the employee, but allow them to express themselves. There may be factors of which you are unaware or have not considered that will affect the recommended action. People also must have the opportunity to feel that they have been heard.

(e) People tend to engage in inappropriate problem-solving techniques — blaming, accusing, defending etcetera. Ensure you recognize and manage such behavior, otherwise it could distract you from reaching a solution.

(f) Encourage the employee to suggest solutions to their non-performance. Employees are more likely to accept and support the need for change if they can solve their own problems.

(g) Do not get distracted by other work-related items that also need attention during a performance discussion; save them for another conversation. Mixing different issues lessens the impact of the conversation.

(h) Be as specific as you can about the issue. Avoid generalizations, opinions and comparisons, and provide evidence to support your point of view.

(i) Emphasize the consequences of the employee's non-performance. Highlight the impact their performance has on the rest of the team or organization and the consequences should the employee's performance not improve, for example, opportunities to grow in the company will be limited.

(j) Ensure the person truly has understood the impact of the problem. Signs that they have not could include that they continue to use excuses, accuse you of being unfair and so forth. If this happens, redirect the conversation by saying: "I would like to talk about that later; right now, I would like to stay focused on what you can do." At this point you may need to tell the employee what you think the best solution is.

(k) Remind the employee that strong performance is non-negotiable.

2 | It takes a long time for me to deal with signs of non-performance

Rethink

Managers often recognize non-performance issues but do not deal with it systematically or in a timely manner. They may hope the problem corrects itself, or believe that non-performance does not need to be addressed unless it is truly disruptive.

Competing demands are often at fault for non-performance landing at the bottom of a manager's long list of priorities. But addressing non-performance should never be left for last.

Most non-performance issues can be resolved at an early stage when the impact to the team and the individual's career is minimal.

It is unfair to the team to allow one person's non-performance to continue. It is also unfair to the individual who, quite possibly, is unaware that they do not meet expectations and is caught off-guard during formal performance reviews. Take the necessary steps to deal quickly and effectively with non-performance issues.

React

(a) Address non-performance immediately. Do not wait until the year-end review or other formal assessments if you see a change for the worse or feel worried about a person's performance. Even if the employee is a consistently good performer, a brief discussion about their challenges and how you can assist can prevent the performance from deteriorating.

255

(b) Understand how well an employee's talents match their job requirements. Determine the competencies required for the position and which gaps exist. If possible, use a talent management system such as the PeopleTree Talent Manager™ to analyze the shortcomings between a person's talent, position and the context of that position. It will allow you to measure the existing shortcomings and prioritize development items that will maximize performance.

(c) Schedule a meeting with the employee to discuss how their role can be improved in a way that benefits them, their boss and the business. State which part of their performance must be improved — be specific and cite examples. Be clear about the level of expectations you have and the need to perform at this level consistently. Identify the support and resources you will provide to assist the person in being successful. Set the measurements you will use to evaluate progress. When you finish your meeting, summarize the solution and express confidence in the employee's ability to implement the solution. Finally, document the meeting.

(d) Involve the employee in setting their own goals so that these are fully supported.

(e) Set short-term improvement goals for a person. A 90-day period is ideal, because it allows ample opportunity to monitor progress and experience success on a regular basis.

(f) Decide at the outset how a person will communicate their progress — will it be weekly, once a month? The intervals should be frequent but not burdensome.

(g) Assess whether the person will be able to improve their performance without additional assistance from, for example, a mentor, another team member, coach or technical expert.

(h) Ensure your employees' ability to improve their performance is not hindered by external factors beyond their control, such as political barriers, bureaucracy or an uncooperative internal client who withholds information. Be proactive in paving the way for their success.

(i) Investigate whether non-performance problems are due to motivational issues and not a lack of skill. Understanding these issues and creating some incentives may be all that is needed to manage non-performance.

3 | Non-performance is not my problem/The employee will face the consequences

Rethink

It is a manager's responsibility to take timely action to protect the company when non-performance issues arise, because considerable damage can be done to relationships within the organization and even with customers. Non-performance also has a negative impact on the organization's profitability.

Managing non-performance is about managing return on investment and the bottom line. Managers are paid to improve their employees' performance and this could involve direct intervention.

If you were the coach of a sports team, you would expect your players to perform at their peak. Team members would also expect you to encourage peak performance from all the athletes. It would be unfair to the group if one player was allowed to perform at a sub-standard level. Conversely, why should any individual give their best if the rest of the team is not required to do it?

256

When managing non-performance, remember that you are responsible for the performance of your entire team. Allowing a lack of performance to go unaddressed penalizes others. Employees count on you to have honest conversations with everyone who needs it to help to improve individual and team performance. In short, it is your responsibility as a manager, supervisor or team leader to ensure that everyone performs according to their potential and meets the expectations set for the job.

React

(a) Regularly monitor employees' work performance and the challenges they face.

(b) Establish a culture of open discussion by making yourself available to your employees — set aside a specific time, if possible every week, for people to talk to you.

(c) Ask the human resources department for information about the cost of hiring new talent. The figure will give you perspective on whether it is worth your time to deal with non-performance issues.

(d) Try to be empathetic. Remember a time when you struggled in your career.

(e) Visualize yourself as a mentor rather than a boss. What would a good teacher do with a problem student? How well can you perform in getting the student back on track?

4 | I do not know what is causing an employee's non-performance

Rethink

The management of non-performance begins with an accurate assessment of its root cause. Nearly all performance problems are based on a lack of competence in one of three categories: work experience, technical skills and behavior. However, motivation issues can also play a role. Use these factors as a framework to analyze a person's performance issues and effectively target the appropriate solution.

React

(a) Analyze whether the person has the necessary experience for their responsibilities or a project. If not, it may be the cause of their non-performance. You can then reassign the person altogether to build their experience level first, keep them on the project but give them tasks with less responsibility, or keep them on the project but let them work closely with someone who has greater experience and can supervise them.

(b) What level of technical or functional expertise does the individual have? Identify the items that must be improved and create a development plan. Put together a plan for technical training to enhance the person's skills set. This can be formal training or through mentorship.

(c) Unskilled behavioral competencies are best addressed through feedback discussions and coaching. A 360° feedback process based on behavioral competencies is effective to define the performance issue.

257

(d) Motivation is often the culprit behind reduced performance. Explore whether the person is content with their work situation and address incentives that would help to engage the person again. An employee may not feel comfortable to honestly discuss their issues with you, so offer that they can talk to a human resources representative.

(e) Employees may have personal problems that interfere with their work, such as family illness, death or divorce. Try to provide solutions to help the person through these difficult times and encourage them to use professional support available through the company.

(f) Use a Talent Management system such as PeopleTree's Talent Manager™ to accurately assess an employee's suitability for a position. Is the person in the wrong position given their interests and talent? Does the person have a problem with their manager or the different work styles among the team members? The answers to these questions will provide valuable insight to help you determine the root of non-performance.

5 | I am uncomfortable with the level of emotion or conflict that accompanies the management of non-performance

Rethink

It is never pleasant to manage poor performance. Supervisors who provide feedback can place too much emphasis on how the employee might react, and often avoid important conversations with their subordinates to escape the emotional spillover of non-performance discussions.

Criticism is never easy to take, even if it is constructive, but it is impossible to develop and grow professionally without feedback. People who react defensively, or too emotional, are the ones most in need of learning to receive and accept feedback. Individuals who are excessively emotional when given feedback set themselves up for failure. They are either handled with kid gloves or left in the dark about their behavior or performance. Do not allow such a person to manipulate you.

Non-performance is not a personal issue and should not be treated that way. Step in and manage non-performance, even if it leaves a bruised ego in the process.

React

(a) Focus on the problematic behavior, not the problematic employee. You are seeking a solution to weak performance, not a weak personality.

(b) Avoid catching a person off-guard with feedback — it is likely to make them defensive. Give the person notice that you want to have a discussion about certain points and conduct the discussion promptly to avoid raising their anxiety levels.

(c) Allow the employee to react and do not respond defensively — it will only add emotion to the situation. Behave the way you expect them to behave.

(d) Let the person know you understand why they are upset, but that you cannot work out a solution unless they are composed.

(e) Expect the individual to try to sidetrack the conversation by blaming, denying, acting angry and so forth. Remain objective at all times.

(f) If the person does not calm down despite your attempts, tell them you will give them time to collect themselves and hold the meeting when they are ready to listen. Schedule another appointment before parting ways.

(g) Ask a human resources mediator to facilitate the conversation if the person is too difficult to engage in conversation.

Overdeveloped

Research has shown that strengths can become weaknesses because you can, in fact, do too much of a good thing. You cannot become less good at a competency in which you excel, but you can balance the behavior by developing a few Stabilizers to tone down an excessive strength.

Stabilizer	Overdeveloped
4 Approachable	Is too quick to confront and does not give people a chance to prove themselves, or fails to take circumstances into account
24 Empathetic	
35 Manages Conflict	
20 Develops People	
28 Fair	
22 Diplomatic	
34 Listens Well	
43 Motivates People	
47 Patient	
51 Recognizes Talent and Potential	

Instructions

Read the definition. If it applies to you, choose a few Stabilizers and develop them by selecting the relevant chapter and following the Strategies for Action.

For more instructions see the How To Use This Book section.

39. Manages Time

Moderate

Easy

Difficulty to LEARN | Difficulty to CHANGE

"Time is the most valuable thing a man can spend"

Laertius Diogenes

Well Developed
Has a high level of productivity and uses time well to get work done

Underdeveloped
Uses time unproductively and does not complete the expected amount of work

Overdeveloped
Is inflexible and unwilling to compromise schedules or deadlines to adapt to changing circumstances. Is pushy and demands too much

Instructions
Read the definitions on the left. If the Underdeveloped definition applies, go to the Strategies for Action section.

If the Overdeveloped definition applies, go to the end of the chapter.

39 Manages Time

Test Yourself

True	I do things as soon as I can and do not procrastinate
True	I can juggle multiple projects or tasks
True	I invest the appropriate amount of time in my various priorities
True	I am realistic about how much work I can get done
True	I use scheduling to make the best use of time
True	I do not make unrealistic commitments and can say no
True	I try to do my best but I do not try to do everything perfectly

Note

Are you sure you need to develop this competency?

If the answer is "True" to most of the statements on the left, you probably do not need to develop this competency.

Strategies for Action

Most ineffective behaviors have an underlying thought or emotional pattern. By identifying these patterns, you can understand the impact they have and design strategies to counteract them.

① I delay doing unpleasant tasks/I always leave certain things until the last minute

② I do not know ways to manage my time more effectively

③ I need to make sure things are right and that takes time/I like my work to be perfect

④ I tend to act quickly/I spend more time doing and less time planning

⑤ I find it difficult to say no to people

⑥ I can manage my time; other people's demands on my time cause the problem

Instructions

1. Read and select one or more of the ineffective ways of thinking/feeling to the left.

2. Find the corresponding number below that will help you to rethink this pattern and identify specific and practical actions that you can take.

---

1 | I delay doing unpleasant tasks/I always leave certain things until the last minute

Rethink

You procrastinate when you delay something that should be focused on right now, usually in favor of doing something more enjoyable or which you feel more comfortable doing. Procrastinators can become overwhelmed by work and neglect to complete tasks instead of addressing the problem in a timely manner.

Some people even enjoy the pressure, especially the adrenaline generated by trying to fix things at the last minute. Do you regularly put off doing tasks because you feel overwhelmed or dislike your assignment, or because you are waiting for the right mood to inspire you?

Procrastination may be a coping mechanism, but it is ultimately ineffective and undermines optimal productivity. Procrastinators work as many hours as other people, but they invest their energy in the wrong places. If this behavior is not addressed, it tends to become chronic behavior in a career. However unpleasant it is to begin a task in which you are uninterested right now, think how unpleasant the consequences will be if the project is not completed in time or done poorly because of a lack of time.

React

(a) Become familiar with the signs of procrastination and make a list of them. Add any symptom you have noticed in yourself or others. Refer to the list at the beginning and end of a day to serve as a reminder. Some common examples include filling your day with low-priority tasks, sitting down to start a high-priority task and almost immediately taking a break, making a cup of coffee or checking your e-mails while letting too much time pass by, leaving a priority on your to-do list for a long time without addressing it, and committing yourself to helping others instead of tackling your own work.

(b) If a task or project is overwhelming, set small milestones which you can achieve every day or week, and reward yourself.

(c) Develop your action list based on specific, well-defined activities rather than outcomes. Slowly but surely you will reach your goal.

(d) Ask someone to check on you and measure the work you do on a specific task. It helps to know that you will be held accountable.

(e) Calculate the cost of your time to your employer. How much are you getting paid per day or hour? If you procrastinate and do not focus on the right things, you do not deliver value for money.

(f) Concentrate on results, not busy work. Monitor how long you spend each day on unimportant things that do not really contribute to your success. Do you know how much time you spend on reading junk mail, talking to colleagues, making coffee or surfing the Internet? Are you aware of when in the day you check your e-mail, write important articles or do your long-term planning?

2 | I do not know ways to manage my time more effectively

Rethink

High achievers are excellent time managers. Conversely, people who manage time poorly never seem to have enough of it.

Sound time management has numerous benefits. It gives you greater control of your life. It helps you to manage your stress and energy levels. It makes you more productive. You are better able to maintain a balance between your work, personal and family lives. You work within your schedule, not others'. Time management is one of the least challenging competencies to develop.

We all do some form of time management, but few people approach it as methodically as they could in order to take full advantage of its benefits.

React

(a) Delegation is a tried-and-tested time management technique. Ensure you delegate effectively to your team. Which tasks are you doing that others could do instead? If you delegate poorly, you will always be pressed for time.

(b) How organized are you? Organized people create systems and routines that help them to manage information. They do not waste time to look for lost files on their computers or information that definitely was on their desks somewhere.

(c) Try to minimize the number of times a day you switch between different types of tasks. It wastes time. For example, read and reply to e-mails once in the morning and once in the afternoon. Do your other tasks in-between.

(d) Use a calendar to schedule work and personal activities one to two weeks in advance. It will force you to consider and prioritize what will fill the next two weeks, and you will always be aware of the time available for you and your personal activities. It will also give you control over your schedule, instead of putting it in others' hands.

(e) Take advantage of any technology available to automate processes which cut into your time unnecessarily. For example, online scheduling software allows you to manage meetings efficiently without sending e-mails back and forth, because you can gauge people's availability immediately.

(f) Every once in a while you will have to deal with personal matters during work hours. Be sure to limit these and do them during lunch or come in earlier to handle them.

(g) Keep e-mails unrelated to work to a minimum. They can go back and forth and before you know it an hour has passed without doing any work.

(h) The lower your energy level, the easier it is to waste time by working inefficiently. Most people's energy levels fluctuate during the day. It may be related to the amount of sugar in your blood, the length of time since you last took a break, stress, boredom and so forth. Keep a log for a week to analyze when you are most productive. Be conscious of the type of activities you schedule during times you tend to feel tired versus energetic. If possible, schedule your activities accordingly. For example, if you are most alert in the morning, schedule activities that require greater focus then. You will accomplish more. Leave calls for mid-afternoon when your energy levels are lower.

(i) The Internet is a great resource but it can also waste too much of people's time. Be cautious not to go off on time-wasting cyber tangents. Use the Internet for relevant work-related purposes only.

(j) Ensure you do not abuse the amount of time spent on activities such as making coffee or using the copier or fax machine.

(k) There are many resources to help you to improve your time management skills. Read books such as *The Seven Habits of Highly Effective People* by Stephen Covey.

(l) Most organizations offer some course in time management. Ask your human resources department about the options.

(m) Ask colleagues who manage their time well for tips.

3 | I need to make sure things are right and that takes time/I like my work to be perfect

Rethink

Perfectionism can be defined as an attempt to attain impossibly high goals. Perfectionists get caught in a trap — they never think their work is good enough, and it wastes time. They are rigid about their performance and if it is not perfect, it is not acceptable.

Ironically, the procrastination, paralysis and changes that result from too high standards mean perfectionists often take too long to complete assignments. Or they wait until it is too late then rush to finish a task and achieve less-than-stellar outcomes.

Realists who are more relaxed, however, can manage their time and leave enough room for subsequent changes that will improve the final product. If perfectionists hold others to the same unrealistic standards, they cannot share or delegate work comfortably.

It is important to be aware of the negative impact perfectionism has on time management.

React

(a) Ask for help or delegate. Having assistance on a project can help you to stay focused. You can spend more time on reviewing work and making sure it is up to standard.

(b) Consider spending money on outsourcing key tasks.

(c) Keep your expectations in check. Replace all-or-nothing thoughts with realistic thinking, for example: "It may not be perfect but it doesn't have to be and I'll finish on time."

(d) Ask others, especially your manager, for feedback about the quality of your work so far. They can help you to gauge whether you put undue effort into a task.

(e) Try to adapt your expectations to the circumstances. Many factors over which you may have no control will determine the outcome of an assignment: the amount of resources assigned, due date, complexity of work, previous experience you have had on similar projects etcetera.

(f) Focus on other benefits you gain from working on a project and not just doing it perfectly, such as the learning involved, having fun and the satisfaction of completing something.

(g) Set strict time limits on each of your projects. Move on when the time is up and attend to something else.

(h) Learn how to deal with criticism. Perfectionists often view criticism as a personal attack and respond defensively. Concentrate on being more objective about the criticism and yourself.

(i) Seek the help of a professional coach.

4 | I tend to act quickly/I spend more time doing and less time planning

Rethink

Planning is one of the best ways to manage your time and others'. If you are inclined to act and value getting things under way, you may neglect planning or forego it altogether. To draw from an everyday example, a savvy homemaker will plan meals to prepare for the week, then make a grocery list and take one trip to the store. A homemaker who ignores this small planning step will be forced to return to the store several times to buy items for each night's supper. Doing the latter has no earth-shattering consequences, but it wastes time better spent elsewhere or on something more rewarding. Apply this example to your work environment, where time demands are great and efficient work is critical. Action-focused individuals are vulnerable to impulse and often misinterpret the difference between urgent and important tasks.

React

(a) Use more logic and less emotion to make a decision, then act.

(b) Before taking action, always question whether tasks are absolutely necessary and whether they could be delegated or trimmed to take up less time.

(c) Attend a project-management training program that will familiarize you with the principles of planning and relevant software.

(d) Plan a tentative schedule for the week ahead. It can always be adjusted if necessary and gives you a chance to consider your priorities ahead of time. Be sure to address high-priority, urgent items as well as maintenance tasks that cannot be delegated or avoided.

(e) Plan for contingencies. The more unpredictable your job, the more time you need for such eventualities. Constant interruption is a reality of managers' work. Studies show that, on average, some managers work uninterruptedly for as little as six minutes at a time.

(f) Make time for responsibilities for which you will be assessed, for example, if you manage people, schedule time for coaching, supervision and planning. Similarly, you must allow time to communicate with your boss and the key people around you.

5 | I find it difficult to say no to people

Rethink

People who are too accommodating are taken advantage of by others. Work they should not be doing is dropped on their desk, or they agree to help others when they can barely manage their workload.

Accepting a legitimate responsibility is different from being overburdened because of an inability to say no. Some people cannot turn others down because they believe it will reflect poorly on them or empathize with a colleague's plight too much. If you recognize this pattern, give yourself greater consideration and the empathy you would give others. You also have deadlines, and letting others know that is perfectly acceptable. It takes practice to become better at saying no if you are not used to setting boundaries. But remember, your agenda is no less important than the other person's, and other people's obligations are not your concern. Taking them on could result in you managing your time

React

(a) Never agree to take on more responsibility if you have critical items to deal with that have not been addressed.

(b) Ensure you know what you are getting involved in. The task may seem easy, but things always take longer than expected.

(c) Before agreeing to help someone, consult your supervisor about whether it is realistic and feasible to take on the work. If your supervisor disapproves, it gives you a legitimate reason to say no.

(d) You may find it difficult to manage your supervisor's requests. Clearly communicate to your boss when added work will have an impact on other priorities. For example, if your boss wants your help in a crisis, you may have to put plans on hold. However, negotiate the items that will be put on hold.

Rethink

Do not allow other people to waste your time. If they do, you are at fault for letting them.

Most people are unaware of how their requests encroach on your time, so do not assume they will respect it. You will always have to set boundaries if you expect to manage your time well. Fortunately, there are many ways to send the correct message to others and politely take control of your time.

React

(a) Keep your office door closed if people routinely drop by just to chat. Open it when you can or want to interact. If people still do not get the message, it is perfectly acceptable to politely let them know it is not the best time for you. If they want to talk about work but it is not urgent, schedule a time later that works for both of you. If it is personal, offer to hold the conversation over coffee or during your break.

(b) Whether making or receiving a call, be upfront about keeping it short and to the point. Remind the person if necessary.

(c) Answer phone calls and e-mails at times that make sense to you instead of trying to respond immediately.

(d) Be selective about the gatherings you attend. Do not attend meetings just because you are invited — are they really necessary? Can someone go in your place, represent and brief you? It is a great way to extend staff's experience.

(e) Inform meeting hosts that you can stay for a certain period of time and will be leaving promptly thereafter. It helps you to manage your time and forces others to comply.

Overdeveloped

Research has shown that strengths can become weaknesses because you can, in fact, do too much of a good thing. You cannot become less good at a competency in which you excel, but you can balance the behavior by developing a few Stabilizers to tone down an excessive strength.

Stabilizer	Overdeveloped
8 Comfortable with Uncertainty	Is inflexible and unwilling to compromise schedules or deadlines to adapt to changing circumstances. Is pushy and demands too much
4 Approachable	
24 Empathetic	
35 Manages Conflict	
2 Adaptable	
17 Demonstrates Good Judgment	
34 Listens Well	
43 Motivates People	
30 Global Thinker	

Instructions

Read the definition. If it applies to you, choose a few Stabilizers and develop them by selecting the relevant chapter and following the Strategies for Action.

For more instructions see the How To Use This Book section.

40. Market Aware

"Knowledge removes the darkness of ignorance and thus helps even the most ignorant man to become knowledgeable"

Sam Veda

Well Developed
Knows how business works and remains informed about trends and changes in the marketplace

Underdeveloped
Does not have a proper understanding of business and lacks up-to-date knowledge of trends or changes in the marketplace

Overdeveloped
Pushes the business to adapt too frequently to trends and changes in the marketplace

Instructions

Read the definitions on the left. If the Underdeveloped definition applies, go to the Strategies for Action section.

If the Overdeveloped definition applies, go to the end of the chapter.

Test Yourself

True	I regularly read periodicals and literature from my business field
True	I ensure that I attend events such as conferences and network to stay in touch with new ideas
True	I ensure that I am included in meetings that can help me to gain a better understanding of the business' players and parts
True	I can speak comfortably about many aspects of my business
True	I am knowledgeable about current and future trends in my business

Note

Are you sure you need to develop this competency?

If the answer is "True" to most of the statements on the left, you probably do not need to develop this competency.

Strategies for Action

Most ineffective behaviors have an underlying thought or emotional pattern. By identifying these patterns, you can understand the impact they have and design strategies to counteract them.

(1) I have focused more on my specific role than on the business in general/I have little exposure outside my function

(2) It is more important to build on what you have than to keep up with the latest trends/I focus on our strengths instead of our competitors

(3) I do not have access to market information

Instructions

1. Read and select one or more of the ineffective ways of thinking/feeling to the left.

2. Find the corresponding number below that will help you to rethink this pattern and identify specific and practical actions that you can take.

---

1 | I have focused more on my specific role than on the business in general/I have little exposure outside my function

Rethink

Many professionals work hard to gain knowledge specific to their profession or functional area, but they lack knowledge about the broader environment in which they operate.

Strong skills and knowledge specific to your profession will ensure you can handle shop talk, but can you hold your own when discussing wider business matters? Lacking a broad enough focus can leave you with a very limited perspective. Being aware of the market helps you to understand the priorities on which you should focus as well as the reason why the organization has committed to a particular path. For example, it may not make much sense to scrap a product on which your division has been working, until you understand that a bigger market opportunity now exists, in a different consumer region that is unlikely to use your product at all. Being market savvy also determines how effective you are in relating to both internal and external customers, whose decisions are based on different drives.

React

(a) Be proactive and show interest in assignments that could expose you to areas of the business other than yours.

(b) Register for after-hours or weekend courses that will increase your knowledge about different aspects of business. Ensure you are exposed to information pertaining to customer service, the financial side of business as well as marketing and sales.

(c) Participate in initiatives beyond your regular scope, such as total quality management (TQM) and international standardization organization (ISO) projects.

(d) Read business case studies and learn what worked or failed in different companies. You can find this information in the library and on the internet.

(e) Read your company's annual report and ensure you can interpret it. Which trends are affecting your company's growth? Do you understand the financials? Ask a financial advisor to point out the important factors.

(f) Get a feel for your company's strategic plan. Discuss with your boss the reasons for the particular direction your company has chosen. What drives the business? How are the priorities determined?

---

② | **It is more important to build on what you have than to keep up with the latest trends/I focus on our strengths instead of our competitors**

Rethink

Chasing the latest trends can dilute a company's resources and focus. But organizations must manage the fine line between keeping abreast of trends and becoming obsolete. For example, the US automobile industry maintained a decades-long monopoly on car sales in the country until the oil crisis in the '80s made gas-efficient, compact Japanese cars an appealing alternative for the American consumer.

Although it may not have been possible to predict the rise of gas prices, General Motors, Chrysler and Ford obviously underestimated the value of their competitor's offering and quickly lost their market share. No matter how successful a product or service, it is always vulnerable to market changes and is only as good as the competitor's weakness.

React

(a) Know your competitors: their products, strengths and weaknesses, market share, how they reach their customers.

(b) Consider your customer base carefully and thoroughly. Understand exactly who your customers are: their demographics, needs, patterns and preferences, as well as how your company reaches them and the trends which may affect them in the future.

(c) Compare your company's financial report to those of others in the same market.

(d) Think about strategic partnerships that could let you take advantage of trends with less risk or investment on your part, or strengthen your business in an area in which your competitor enjoys a bigger market share.

3 | I do not have access to market information

Rethink

Being aware of the market can build your self-confidence and your credibility among others, especially if you are new to the business. If you are knowledgeable about changes in the marketplace and how business works, you can ask intelligent and pertinent questions, even with little experience behind you.

Market information is readily available — the challenge is to make accessing it a priority. Like any long-term approach, integrate it into your daily schedule to become an integral part of doing business.

React

(a) Identify one or two relevant topics each month and become knowledgeable enough about them to converse intelligently. Try to understand the causes and consequences of an issue.

(b) Stay informed. Read trade magazines and business books. Ask your peers and boss to recommend books or websites to read.

(c) The media provides numerous ways of getting information. Watch or listen to the many business channels and programs available on television or radio. Listen to business news on your way to work and so take advantage of your commute. Subscribe to well-respected business newspapers and magazines such as the *Wall Street Journal*, *Fortune 500* and the *Harvard Business Review*.

(d) Regularly have lunch with people in the company who are experts in their field, and ask them questions.

(e) Meet people and get to know what they do. You will be surprised how much information you can gain from a casual conversation about issues and trends that have an impact on others' line of work.

Overdeveloped

Research has shown that strengths can become weaknesses because you can, in fact, do too much of a good thing. You cannot become less good at a competency in which you excel, but you can balance the behavior by developing a few Stabilizers to tone down an excessive strength.

Stabilizer	Overdeveloped
17 Demonstrates Good Judgment	Pushes the business to adapt too frequently to trends and changes in the marketplace
56 Technically Competent	
48 Plans Work	
29 Focused on Priorities	
1 Achiever	
31 Improves Processes	
15 Customer-Centric	
48 Plans Work	
51 Recognizes Talent and Potential	

Instructions

Read the definition. If it applies to you, choose a few Stabilizers and develop them by selecting the relevant chapter and following the Strategies for Action.

For more instructions see the How To Use This Book section.

41. Modest

> "Don't worry when you are not recognized, but strive to be worthy of recognition"
>
> Abraham Lincoln

Well Developed
Recognizes the contribution of others and acts humbly about strengths and achievements

Underdeveloped
Does not give recognition to the contribution of others and is perceived as arrogant about achievements or strengths

Overdeveloped
Can be too self-effacing, reserved or shy to champion an issue

Instructions

Read the definitions on the left. If the Underdeveloped definition applies, go to the Strategies for Action section.

If the Overdeveloped definition applies, go to the end of the chapter.

Test Yourself

True	I let others know when their contributions have made a positive impact on my work
True	I share the credit of a joint effort with my collaborators
True	I encourage others to take credit if it is important to them
True	I believe how well my team does is as important as how well I do
True	I can feel good about my accomplishments without others recognizing them
True	I do not exaggerate my accomplishments

Note

Are you sure you need to develop this competency?

If the answer is "True" to most of the statements on the left, you probably do not need to develop this competency.

Modest

41 Modest

Strategies for Action

Most ineffective behaviors have an underlying thought or emotional pattern. By identifying these patterns, you can understand the impact they have and design strategies to counteract them.

① When I do most of the work I should get most of the credit

② I can or should act differently now that I am successful/I would look weak if I were to be a humble leader

③ I want to promote my accomplishments/I want to ensure I get recognition

Instructions

1. Read and select one or more of the ineffective ways of thinking/feeling to the left.

2. Find the corresponding number below that will help you to rethink this pattern and identify specific and practical actions that you can take.

---

① When I do most of the work I should get most of the credit

Rethink

Is there a risk in taking credit for your hard work? That depends on how considerate you are of others' contributions. Almost no accomplishment is achieved in isolation, and you may be perceived as selfish or narcissistic if you do not recognize this fact. In addition, sharing credit has many benefits.

As a leader, it is critical to be able to motivate people. One of the most effective ways to do it is to actively recognize others' accomplishments, regardless of how much greater your contribution might have been. It makes people feel valuable and more confident about themselves.

Modesty requires you to take as much pride in others' contributions as you do in what you have accomplished. Also, know that your praise and recognition of employees are infectious. When others see their peers being recognized, it inspires them to work to gain recognition as well.

React

(a) Regardless of the size of their contributions, make it a point to thank the people who worked on a project during and after completion. Do this formally in a group e-mail or meeting.

(b) Let a person know when their contribution has improved your work. Admit openly that your work would be more difficult without their assistance.

(c) Regularly recognize the efforts of the person reporting directly to you. Make this a routine part of your management practice at meetings and in the office.

(d) Compliments let employees and peers feel appreciated, and it is an easy way to make people feel valued. The compliment does not have to be related to your work specifically. A simple affirmation of someone's pleasant demeanor, for example, lets them know you recognize a special quality.

(e) Focus on "we" and not "me". Approach every project as a team effort that could not be accomplished without the contribution of many people. Rarely is only one individual involved in an assignment. Promote the team's efforts by circulating e-mail messages and memos that recap your team's performance. Forward customer praise to your supervisor.

2 | I can or should act differently now that I am successful/ I would look weak if I were to be a humble leader

Rethink

Changing your relationship with others because you have experienced success at work may make you seem inauthentic and self-important. Who you are is not altered by a new position or title.

Leaders who do not forget where they came from remain accessible to everyone and connected to the issues they have experienced along their career paths. It does not make you a weak leader to be humble about your accomplishments and even talk about your weaknesses. It will not be seen as a lack of leadership skills, instead, people will think of you as self-confident.

React

(a) Do not forget the people who supported you during your rise to the top. Make their names public and encourage others to do the same. It allows you to be modest about the part you played while gaining the respect of supportive staff.

(b) Encourage people to treat you the same way they did before you became successful. Show former colleagues as well as family and friends that the relationships you share continue to be important.

(c) Be authentic. You have not changed simply because your position or level of authority has. Maintain the friendships you had prior to becoming successful.

(d) Resist the urge to be flashy, show off or live beyond your means. Refuse to obtain possessions or be involved in activities that only serve the purpose of drawing attention to you.

(e) Accept praise from others graciously. Show genuine gratitude for admiration of your success, but change the topic when people talk about your achievements too much. Turn the conversation to others' accomplishments and qualities.

I want to promote my accomplishments/I want to ensure I get recognition

Rethink

You recently completed a successful project and you want to ensure your accomplishment is recognized by your peers and other relevant people. How do you do it? With modesty and sensitivity.

Self-promotion is important to help to advance a person's career. Many rewards are associated with recognition, including feeling good about ourselves. But while your accomplishments may be exemplary, you risk alienating people if you promote yourself too aggressively or do so at others' expense.

You want to be recognized, but for the right reasons and not because you are a self-proclaimed success. If you have performed well, people around you will be well aware and credit could be solicited without much fanfare on your part. Also remember that different cultural norms will dictate how much self-promotion is acceptable. This can vary across company divisions, the leadership styles of your superiors, even countries. If you are working in sales, for example, it may be appropriate to make sure everyone in your division knows you surpassed your group's annual target. But this information might not be appropriate to share with a Japanese counterpart who lives in a culture that places value on teamwork and modesty.

React

(a) Ask relevant people who are important to you to provide consistent feedback about your work. Some of us require more reassurance and recognition than others. Do not assume your peers or superiors know or can read your needs.

(b) Work on self-praise. People will not always be available to recognize your hard work, so ensure you have a private reward system that relies on what you think of yourself, not what others think of you.

(c) Be humble about your strengths and achievements. Relish your accomplishments privately and build on them. Instead of boasting about a job well done, use the knowledge gained from its success and move forward.

(d) Find a balanced place from which you draw your sense of accomplishment. List the things of which you are proud in addition to your achievements at work. You may be a great parent, friend or highly skilled at a hobby, for example. It is not just your work that defines your accomplishments — look for recognition in other areas of your life as well.

(e) Ensure that you do not overstate your accomplishments and exaggerate your success to gain greater praise or attention. Be truthful and authentic, or you will appear fake and your real accomplishments will be lost in the noise.

(f) Develop a reputation for quietly striving for success instead of chasing praise.

(g) Ensure you are not spending more time grandstanding than getting work done. Colleagues and customers will quickly become frustrated and resentful.

(h) A modest person believes in working hard without expecting repayment. Do not expect recognition for your work. You are more likely to be praised once your peers see that you are modest about your achievements.

(i) Do not make assumptions about the cultural norms in your work environment. Identify them correctly and act accordingly.

Overdeveloped

Research has shown that strengths can become weaknesses because you can, in fact, do too much of a good thing. You cannot become less good at a competency in which you excel, but you can balance the behavior by developing a few Stabilizers to tone down an excessive strength.

Stabilizer	Overdeveloped
1 Achiever	Can be too self-effacing, reserved or shy to champion an issue
13 Courageous	
11 Composed	
12 Confident	
8 Comfortable with Uncertainty	
9 Communicates Well (Verbal)	
27 Experimental	
5 Balances Personal Life and Work	
21 Develops Self	
49 Politically Astute	

Instructions

Read the definition. If it applies to you, choose a few Stabilizers and develop them by selecting the relevant chapter and following the Strategies for Action.

For more instructions see the How To Use This Book section.

42. Monitors Work

Moderate

Easy

Difficulty to | Difficulty to
LEARN | CHANGE

> "Accuracy of observation is the equivalent of accuracy of thinking"
>
> Wallace Stevens

Well Developed
Puts useful and meaningful measures in place to monitor work processes

Underdeveloped
Has no measures in place to monitor progress and does not act on it

Overdeveloped
Can be overly controlling and stifle initiative

Instructions
Read the definitions on the left. If the Underdeveloped definition applies, go to the Strategies for Action section.

If the Overdeveloped definition applies, go to the end of the chapter.

Test Yourself

True	I set milestones for each significant target in a process
True	I consult my team members for their input and perceptions about how the work flow is progressing
True	I provide regular feedback to all team members so that adjustments can be made throughout the process
True	When necessary, I recalculate schedules and reset milestones as outcomes dictate
True	I believe it is as important to monitor work progress as it is to have a plan

Note

Are you sure you need to develop this competency?

If the answer is "True" to most of the statements on the left, you probably do not need to develop this competency.

Monitors Work

42

Strategies for Action

Most ineffective behaviors have an underlying thought or emotional pattern. By identifying these patterns, you can understand the impact they have and design strategies to counteract them.

(1) I do not like to micro-manage/People can manage their own work

(2) I have competing priorities/Monitoring takes up time I could use to complete other work

(3) I am not experienced in establishing good progress measures/My work environment does not value the monitoring of work

Instructions

1. Read and select one or more of the ineffective ways of thinking/feeling to the left.

2. Find the corresponding number below that will help you to rethink this pattern and identify specific and practical actions that you can take.

---

1 | I do not like to micro-manage/People can manage their own work

Rethink

Many managers are reluctant to monitor work progress because they believe it sends the message that they do not trust their subordinates' abilities.

Confidence in your team and process plan is important, in fact, it should be one of a manager's goals. But checking a process's status is not the same as micro-managing.

A highly capable, determined team and a proper plan are only two components of a successful process. Monitoring the process is as important and serves a critical function. Strategic monitoring allows you to manage, in a timely and efficient manner, any modifications necessary.

Plans are based on assumptions, which can change quickly. The earlier problems are identified and remedied, the more likely the process is to conclude successfully. Plans can look quite different at the end of a process than when they were originally created.

Overconfidence in a plan or a reluctance to remain involved in people's work can cause unnecessary repetition and leave your team feeling unsupported. It can also be more demoralizing than if you had been too involved. An effective manager can strike the appropriate balance between empowering others and allowing them to get on with their work, and establishing and participating in effective monitoring practices.

React

(a) Develop a communication plan for regular dialogue with your team regarding the process's status and necessary modifications. This can take the form of weekly updating e-mails, formal meetings or informal conversations, shared folders for pertinent documents etcetera. Regular feedback ensures that people have direction along the way.

(b) Look for less obvious signs of problems in the process. For example, people may be meeting deadlines but feel undue stress, or lack essential resources, which can be demoralizing and cause burnout.

(c) Post and distribute a progress report, using a Gantt chart, project management evaluation and review technique (PERT) or critical path method (CPM) to set milestones. A visual representation gives your team a quick, measurable way to monitor progress.

(d) Be sure to monitor processes more closely at the beginning of a project, until you are comfortable that everyone understands their roles and has clear direction.

(e) Verify that milestones are achieved and that tasks are on schedule and budget.

(f) Ensure that people are honest about the status of their tasks — ask them to show you the work they have completed so far. People may be reluctant to tell you their work status if they have fallen behind. Trust your instincts. You may discover that your team needs more resources or better clarification of tasks.

(g) Arrange a debriefing to document and discuss lessons learnt so that people know how to work more effectively in the future. Share these lessons with others in your organization as well.

---

2 | I have competing priorities/Monitoring takes up time I could use to complete other work

Rethink

Although it takes time to check the status of tasks and discuss issues with your team, it is far more time-consuming and potentially damaging to correct problems identified late in the process.

How many examples exist where, if you had paid a little more attention, you would have saved yourself much time and effort? We can draw many examples from our daily lives: expecting the car to perform without problems but never taking it in for maintenance work, not attending parent-teacher meetings and getting an unpleasant surprise when report cards arrive, foregoing an annual doctor's examination only to need expensive medicines later.

The point is that few processes are sustainable on their own without some time invested in monitoring efforts. Time invested now reduces time required later.

React

(a) Nurture an environment in which you are regularly informed. Let people know it is important that they keep you up to date with their status without you having to solicit the information. For example, ask people to routinely send you brief status e-mails.

(b) Set up systems that facilitate quick monitoring, for example, utilize shared project management tools to quickly review online the status of milestones and budgets.

(c) If monitoring is difficult to manage on your own, delegate different aspects of the process to the team and hold debriefing meetings regularly.

(d) Invest more time in the beginning of the process, when more direction is needed, so that less of your time is required later.

(e) Limit the amount of time you spend with people who are giving you a status update. Do not let them ramble on or talk about irrelevant issues.

---

3 | I am not experienced in establishing good progress measures/My work environment does not value the monitoring of work

Rethink

You may not have been trained or had an opportunity to monitor processes. Some company cultures do not require or value the structure that monitoring places on processes — this often happens in highly creative environments. Nevertheless, it is widely recognized that a project's success is contingent on the quality of its monitoring.

Effective monitoring requires both interpersonal and analytical skills, which need to be continuously improved. There is no risk involved in taking it on yourself to practice this competence, even if, at first, it is unfavorably received. The benefits will soon become clear.

React

(a) Become involved in an assignment that involves planning and offer to work with your boss or other team members to establish milestones and progress measures.

(b) Do research and evaluate best practices for monitoring processes and their improvement.

(c) Become familiar with tools available to you, such as progress reports or charts (Gantt, PERT or CPM). Once you are familiar with options, introduce them to others so that they can see the value of utilizing them.

(d) Utilize non-threatening methods of monitoring at first, such as debriefings, and then introduce more structured practices when people will accept them more easily.

(e) Find a respected person in the organization who will share their lessons in both successful and unsuccessful workflow monitoring with you. Although it is not a substitute for personal experience, it is useful to listen to what others have experienced.

(f) Document the lessons learnt from your experiences for use in monitoring future processes: what should have happened, could have been avoided or done differently?

Overdeveloped

Research has shown that strengths can become weaknesses because you can, in fact, do too much of a good thing. You cannot become less good at a competency in which you excel, but you can balance the behavior by developing a few Stabilizers to tone down an excessive strength.

Stabilizer	Overdeveloped
4 Approachable	Can be overly controlling and stifle initiative
51 Recognizes Talent and Potential	
25 Empowers People	
20 Develops People	
34 Listens Well	
43 Motivates People	
7 Collaborative	
59 Unifies People	
31 Improves Processes	
33 Inspires a Future	

Instructions

Read the definition. If it applies to you, choose a few Stabilizers and develop them by selecting the relevant chapter and following the Strategies for Action.

For more instructions see the How To Use This Book section.

43. Motivates People

"Motivation is the art of getting people to do what you want them to do because they want to do it"
Dwight D. Eisenhower

Well Developed
Creates an environment that brings out the best in others and knows what motivates different types of people

Underdeveloped
Has no means to energize others or could even demoralize people, albeit unwittingly

Overdeveloped
Takes too much responsibility for motivating others instead of creating the right conditions for people to motivate themselves

Instructions

Read the definitions on the left. If the Underdeveloped definition applies, go to the Strategies for Action section.

If the Overdeveloped definition applies, go to the end of the chapter.

Test Yourself

True	I search for and can see signs of a lack of energy in people
True	I realize everyone needs motivation once in a while
True	I have talked to each of the people reporting directly to me about what motivates them
True	I remain energetic and motivate others even when I am going through a difficult time
True	I am careful not to make negative statements about the organization in public
True	I consider the impact of my statements on morale before I make them
True	I have planned to retain my best performers

Note

Are you sure you need to develop this competency?

If the answer is "True" to most of the statements on the left, you probably do not need to develop this competency.

Strategies for Action

Most ineffective behaviors have an underlying thought or emotional pattern. By identifying these patterns, you can understand the impact they have and design strategies to counteract them.

(1) I think my attitude or personality do not motivate people (too quiet, distant, skeptical, critical, perfectionist)

(2) I am more concerned about tasks or results than people

(3) I do not understand what motivates people/ I cannot tell when something is wrong

(4) People should motivate themselves/I do not have the time to motivate others

(5) Our company culture does not prioritize motivating others

(6) I do not like to create false or high expectations that are difficult to manage

(7) I struggle to motivate myself, much less other people

Instructions

1. Read and select one or more of the ineffective ways of thinking/feeling to the left.

2. Find the corresponding number below that will help you to rethink this pattern and identify specific and practical actions that you can take.

---

1 | **I think my attitude or personality do not motivate people (too quiet, distant, skeptical, critical, perfectionist)**

Rethink

Managers' personality and attitude play a large role in how motivated their subordinates are. Research shows that, more than any other reason, people leave their jobs because of dissatisfaction with their bosses.

Would you remain encouraged and energized if your boss was highly critical of everything you did, or so distant that you never received feedback about your work?

Everyone has weaknesses that can serve to make people feel unmotivated, as well as strengths that can do the same, if excessive. Imagine, for example, a supervisor who is highly creative. Although the person may be innovative and energizing to some, they may be demoralizing others when they cannot focus on critical details, thorough planning or provide sufficient direction.

Raise your awareness of possible barriers you create for others. People are seldom aware of the negative impact their behavior has on others, but a simple change in your acts or attitude can make all the difference to the people working with and for you.

React

(a) Participate in a 360° feedback process that will provide honest feedback from your peers, clients and even manager about your behavior. Remember that feedback is not useful unless you are willing to accept it and make the necessary changes.

(b) Engage a coach to help you pinpoint the aspects of your personality that affect your ability to motivate others. For example, being empathetic, listening well, patience, empowering others, delegation skills, informing others and being open.

(c) Observe people in the organization who are good at motivating others. Which personality traits enable them to do it?

(d) Realize that your motivation stems from a different place than others'. It is based on personality types. You may like to work on your own and need a structured work environment. Another person may enjoy working in teams, sharing ideas, and gets motivated by a flexible environment.

2 | I am more concerned about tasks or results than people

Rethink

If you value action and results above everything else, stop and think again. Results are achieved by people, so having them motivated makes it more likely that you will achieve your goals.

You may think things happen faster when you ignore the human issues, and it may be the case in the short term, but they will not disappear and will only grow if not addressed.

As a manager, you must strike a balance between getting results and getting them done in a sustainable manner that empowers and energizes your team. It takes far more time and energy to replace a dissatisfied person who has left the organization than to keep existing talent motivated by acting concerned about their personal and professional lives. Also consider that a motivated person produces more results in less time than an individual who lacks energy and feels demoralized.

React

(a) Spend the time necessary to get people motivated about a project. People remain inspired when they form a connection with a bigger vision, rather than a task.

(b) Balance your need for action with praise for what has been accomplished so far.

(c) When pointing out mistakes or an area that needs to be improved, always mention the things that have been done correctly as well.

(d) Check in with people periodically to monitor both their progress and their feelings and concerns.

(e) Consider carefully which results really need to be perfect, how aggressive deadlines must be and how realistic your standards are. You can place undue pressure on people with tasks that actually require less accuracy or could be finished within a more forgiving time period.

(f) Do not use a "one size fits all" approach with people. Ensure you understand the different incentives individuals need and use that to get your results.

3 | I do not understand what motivates people/I cannot tell when something is wrong

Rethink

A decrease in performance often follows a loss in motivation. But many clues about a person's motivation level are present well before their performance declines. An observant manager who is well placed to read these signs can intervene in a timely manner.

Some people are naturally gifted in picking up clues from those with whom they interact, but if you are not, you will want to invest time to develop a heightened sense of people's motives and underlying emotions.

React

(a) Look for clues that point to decreased motivation — negative statements, withdrawal from the group, a drastic change in work style, lagging behind in work, consistently missing deadlines, an unusually short attention span, irritability or disruptive behavior.

(b) Observe what makes a person become animated. People tend to be more engaged and excited when they talk about or work on things that motivate them. Do not let the opportunity pass to ask people what about the experience, topic etcetera appeals to them. Use the feedback when considering ways to motivate them in future.

(c) If you suspect something is wrong, ask! Trust your intuition. Just knowing you care enough to notice can be a big motivator.

(d) Listen carefully to what people say and do not say. Sometimes, people who are trying to sort things out have not yet discovered exactly what they are unhappy about.

(e) Reading people is not necessarily easy, so get a head start. Numerous assessment tools can give you great insight into people, for example, the Birkman Method focuses on people's hidden needs. Such assessment tools can provide invaluable information about people's motivation. Ask your human resources advisers about available tools you can use.

4 | People should motivate themselves/I do not have the time to motivate others

Rethink

Think about the times you have felt demotivated. Perhaps you were able to simply brush off a bad spell or recover from disappointment without anyone's help, but would it have been valuable if someone was there to inspire you?

Becoming skilled in motivating others does not require a manager's excessive commitment. In fact, small actions go a long way in letting others know you care and are aware of their circumstances.

Employees who feel appreciated and understood are more likely to put in extra effort for their managers and organizations when no one is looking.

React

(a) Be appreciative — it is the simplest way to motivate people. Let people know the value of their work, be generous with your thanks, point out openly how well someone is doing. When was the last time you expressed gratitude to the people you oversee?

(b) Do not let someone struggle too long with an assignment if they obviously need help. Routinely check on their progress, ask whether they need assistance and ensure resources are mobilized to help if needed. To ask for help and not get it can be highly damaging to morale.

(c) Get to know the people who work for you. Create opportunities to share information about each other in an informal setting. Go to lunch with them or attend after-hours events where you can see people interact outside of work.

(d) Actions speak louder than words. Herb Keller, chairman of Southwest Airlines in the US, has occasionally participated in loading luggage or taking tickets at the gate. To show colleagues that you are a real part of the team and know what their work entails is a powerful message.

5 | Our company culture does not prioritize motivating others

Rethink

Motivation is the key to retain talent and all organizations must ensure their managers value and prioritize activities that support the motivation of employees.

Individuals lose interest in their jobs for a variety of organizational reasons — a lack of communication; poor quality of social bonds among people in the organization; low level of investment in their growth and development; little flexibility in practices and policies such as work hours to meet personal needs; low level of demonstrated interest in their personal goals and aspirations; a lack of opportunities to move within the organization and take on challenging assignments; inability to practice new skills without severe risk; low level of visibility to higher management; and a lack of meaningful work and monetary reward or incentives. Simply put, an organization committed to practices and policies that prioritize the motivation of its talent creates a competitive advantage.

React

(a) Consult human resources and your supervisor to learn about practices and policies regarding incentives to employees.

(b) When morale is low or the work environment has been particularly difficult, provide incentives that encourage people to meet specific goals, targets or deadlines. Everyone needs a push sometimes.

(c) Interesting assignments help to keep people motivated. Ensure the people you oversee have realistic but challenging goals and assignments about which they can get excited. Understand the nature of the work on which people spend most of their time. Rotate tasks to avoid burnout. Ask whether a person would like to work on a specific task or project. Surprisingly, employees are rarely asked that question.

(d) Help people to remain enthusiastic about their work by informing them about the bigger picture and the opportunities they have — not just today, but in the future.

(e) When possible, raise people's profile among higher management by communicating their successes.

(f) Do not assume people are content because they have not complained. Let your subordinates participate in a motivation survey. The results could be enlightening.

(g) Wherever you can, ensure that changes in policy are made and put into practice to reflect the feedback from such surveys. If people's opinions have been sought and action does not follow, they will become demoralized.

(h) Ensure you have plans to retain your best performers and those with high potential.

6 | I do not like to create false expectations or high expectations that are difficult to manage

Rethink

Some managers prefer a conservative approach to motivating others — they want to manage expectations and not make promises, in case they cannot deliver.

Perhaps you downplay the possibility of a project's success, or caution that a demand will not be approved. Although this approach may be based on good intentions, it may overstep the fine balance between setting realistic expectations for people and taking away their motivation.

Allowing and even encouraging people to reach for more, even if they do not reach it, is better than creating expectations so low that they discourage people from achieving their goals.

A manager's responsibility is not to promise the sky, but one can promise to help someone to touch it, as and where one can. A habit of pointing out to people all the reasons for failure will surely destroy any motivation they have.

React

(a) Always begin with a positive response to a person's request and act in an encouraging manner, even if you have your doubts.

(b) When discussing a person's goals, outline both the obstacles to success and the reasons why the goal could be achieved.

(c) Approach every situation as if it were new. Previously, others may not have succeeded, but it does not mean that the person in front of you will not.

(d) Do not assume things have to stay the way thery are. Talk to the appropriate people about options and make a case for the individual you are championing.

(e) Ask the person to give you a plan of how they expect to achieve the goal before you judge whether it can succeed or not.

(f) If your team worked diligently on a project and the outcome was not as good as expected, do not dwell unnecessarily on the results. Encourage the team to apply what they have learned to the next project.

Rethink

An invaluable skill of effective leaders is their ability to sustain motivation among employees. But it is practically impossible to do if you have lost interest and lack motivation.

If your energy level is chronically low and your outlook generally bleak, you can be sure that the people you manage will begin to feel the same.

Think how different you feel when you are around someone who is filled with energy, positive and enthusiastic about their work. One can expect one's motivation levels to vary at times, but if a low level has become a chronic state, it must be addressed. Ignoring it will have negative consequences for you, your team, the subordinates and, if you are in a leadership position, the organization.

React

(a) Consider carefully what might be affecting your positive outlook, not just at work but also in your personal life.

(b) Make a list and identify the aspects of your work or life which you can change immediately, in the short term and the long term.

(c) Create an action plan to address these changes. For example, if you are unhappy with your work schedule, mark it as a short-term item that could be addressed by working from home two days a week. Unhappiness with your position is a longer-term item that you can address by developing skills for another position in the organization.

(d) Read inspiring literature. Ask peers to recommend books for motivational reading.

(e) Do not vent your frustrations in front of your subordinates and be mindful of negative talk. They will not be able to change the situation and you risk demoralizing them. Instead, talk about your grievances to the appropriate person — your boss, a human resources representative, your coach.

(f) Even when you are not motivated about your situation, you can still be positive and affirming about others.

(g) Consider seeing a counselor if your negativity is chronic or becomes disruptive at work.

(h) Sometimes, you may have to fake being motivated for a little while until you really feel that way.

Overdeveloped

Research has shown that strengths can become weaknesses because you can, in fact, do too much of a good thing. You cannot become less good at a competency in which you excel, but you can balance the behavior by developing a few Stabilizers to tone down an excessive strength.

Stabilizer	Overdeveloped
13 Courageous	Takes too much responsibility for motivating others instead of creating the right conditions for people to motivate themselves
35 Manages Conflict	
38 Manages Underperformance	
25 Empowers People	
20 Develops People	
23 Directs People	
42 Monitors Work	
37 Manages Negotiations	
29 Focused on Priorities	
48 Plans Work	

Instructions

Read the definition. If it applies to you, choose a few Stabilizers and develop them by selecting the relevant chapter and following the Strategies for Action.

For more instructions see the How To Use This Book section.

44. Networked

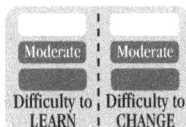

> "Call it a clan, call it a network, call it a tribe, call it a family: whatever you call it, whoever you are, you need one"
>
> Jane Howard

Well Developed
Actively builds and manages social networks both inside and outside the organization

Underdeveloped
Struggles to accomplish much because of limited or non-existent social networks. Does not spend sufficient time to build and maintain relationships

Overdeveloped
Relies too heavily on relationships and networks to accomplish tasks

Instructions
Read the definitions on the left. If the Underdeveloped definition applies, go to the Strategies for Action section.

If the Overdeveloped definition applies, go to the end of the chapter.

Test Yourself

True	I get to know decision makers across the organization
True	I keep in touch regularly with key people
True	I have contacts outside of the organization that are influential
True	I try to meet as many people as I can during events
True	I actively look for opportunities to create partnerships
True	I take advantage of networking tools available through the Internet community

Note

Are you sure you need to develop this competency?

If the answer is "True" to most of the statements on the left, you probably do not need to develop this competency.

Networked

44

295

Strategies for Action

Most ineffective behaviors have an underlying thought or emotional pattern. By identifying these patterns, you can understand the impact they have and design strategies to counteract them.

① I do not like to ask people for favors or bothering them

② I do not have time to network/I do not think it relates to my job

③ I do not know with whom to network/I cannot identify partnerships

Instructions

1. Read and select one or more of the ineffective ways of thinking/feeling to the left.

2. Find the corresponding number below that will help you to rethink this pattern and identify specific and practical actions that you can take.

1 | I do not like to ask people for favors or bothering them

Rethink

It is a common misconception that networking is about asking for favors. People who are good at networking are always trying to expand their circle, regardless of whether they need specific assistance or not. And when the need for assistance arises, they are able to tap into great resources which they have been nurturing well beyond the initial introduction.

The majority of people are happy to be able to help others. Remember, too, that by networking you may be in a position to assist other people either now or in the future.

React

(a) List a few people you would like to meet and think about what you would be able to offer them. Get in touch to offer assistance.

(b) Network with close friends and family first. You may feel more comfortable first doing this with people you know.

(c) Focus on your goal. You would not be asking for assistance if it was not important to you. Share your purpose with the person and make them excited about your cause.

Rethink

Spending time just hanging out is often low on a busy person's priority list, especially if you believe networking is for the sales team, not you.

Networking allows you to build relationships with key people who make isions or control resources. Having just one influential person with whom you have t a strong relationship on your side can positively influence the advancement of your :er or goals.

lost people consider networking a very time-consuming activity, but it is not necessarily case. There are many ways to increase your networking opportunities without too much rruption to your work schedule. An investment of your time today can yield sizeable rns, both tangible and intangible, in the future.

React

(a) Utilize your lunch hour for networking. People lose great opportunities to talk to others because they are married to their desks. Everyone has to eat, and you may as well do it where you have an opportunity to meet others.

(b) Ensure you try to talk to as many people as possible during social gatherings or events. We tend to stick to those with whom we are familiar. You have enough time to talk to your peers and friends, so instead target people you have never met.

(c) Commit yourself to meeting one new person a month in your organization. Become familiar with their function or role in the company.

(d) Attend professional associations which allow you to meet other people in your industry.

(e) Take advantage of Internet-based networking tools such as LinkedIn or even Facebook.

Rethink

Investing time in staying well connected will give you access to information, assistance and guidance that is readily available both inside and outside of your organization.

No perfect script exists as far as networking is concerned. Often, you do not know a potential partnership exists until you start talking to someone.

Even if you do not have a so-called master plan, do not let this prevent you from trying to connect with people. A person skilled at networking is always networking, even when they do not realize that they are.

React

(a) Talk to trusted colleagues or the relevant people about your company's structure and try to get first-hand insight into the perceptions people have of those you identify as important.

(b) Create a list of people both inside and outside of your organization who you think are important to meet. Think about people in the company with influence over how and why decisions are made. Who, in turn, influence them? Identify ways to get in contact with them or, if appropriate, people close to them. Make it your goal to go through your entire list within a given period.

(c) Select a few key professional associations to join that will give you access to experts and influential people in your field.

(d) Spend time to get to know people's skills and abilities — who knows what? Learn who the experts in various fields in your company are. You will know who to call regarding different matters and could ask for assistance, if necessary. An expert can save you much time by identifying the core of the problem and offering solutions that have worked well previously.

(e) Identify people in your company with resources they can share when you need assistance with manpower or time constraints. Having made the effort to establish good relationships with individuals, you will be in a better position to ask for a favor when needed.

(f) Strategic partnerships are an effective way to gain advantage through resources. Networking allows you to get to know who else out there you could consider to gain advantage through your resources, now or in the future. Remain mindful of where those partnerships might exist.

(g) Do not overlook your inner circle of peers, family and friends.

Overdeveloped

Research has shown that strengths can become weaknesses because you can, in fact, do too much of a good thing. You cannot become less good at a competency in which you excel, but you can balance the behavior by developing a few Stabilizers to tone down an excessive strength.

Stabilizer	Overdeveloped
40 Market Aware	Relies too heavily on relationships and networks to accomplish tasks
12 Confident	
17 Demonstrates Good Judgment	
55 Takes Initiative	
56 Technically Competent	
50 Problem Solver	
48 Plans Work	
1 Achiever	
54 Takes Accountablity	
57 Technology Savvy	

Instructions

Read the definition. If it applies to you, choose a few Stabilizers and develop them by selecting the relevant chapter and following the Strategies for Action.

For more instructions see the How To Use This Book section.

45. Open

"We shouldn't be so afraid, because most people really like this contact; that you show you are vulnerable makes them free to be vulnerable"

Liv Ulman

Well Developed
Shares an appropriate amount of personal information so that others can get to know them

Underdeveloped
Is too closed or guarded and unwilling to share any personal information whatsoever

Overdeveloped
Reveals too much or inappropriate personal information, which makes others uncomfortable

Instructions

Read the definitions on the left. If the Underdeveloped definition applies, go to the Strategies for Action section.

If the Overdeveloped definition applies, go to the end of the chapter.

Test Yourself

True	I feel comfortable sharing personal information in the workplace
True	I think about who I am talking to when being open about personal information
True	I spend time interacting socially with people from work
True	My peers and I have open discussions about our personal lives
True	I encourage people to be open with me

Note

Are you sure you need to develop this competency?

If the answer is "True" to most of the statements on the left, you probably do not need to develop this competency.

45 Open

Strategies for Action

Most ineffective behaviors have an underlying thought or emotional pattern. By identifying these patterns, you can understand the impact they have and design strategies to counteract them.

① I will expose my weaknesses/Others will think less of me

② Personal issues should remain at home

③ I am a private person/I am not comfortable sharing private details with people

④ In the past, people were not receptive to my openness

Instructions

1. Read and select one or more of the ineffective ways of thinking/feeling to the left.

2. Find the corresponding number below that will help you to rethink this pattern and identify specific and practical actions that you can take.

---

1 | I will expose my weaknesses/Others will think less of me

Rethink

Whether you disclose personal information or not, people will have their opinions and assumptions about you. Why not ensure that these are based on reality?

Your openness allows others to understand you better and provides a more realistic impression of who you are. Imagine, for example, a manager who is constantly busy and stressed. Subordinates may come to the conclusion that the manager is aloof or disinterested. By being open, the manager is able to share how they are feeling and help the subordinate to understand that they are not aloof, just busy.

Knowing that stress is affecting the subordinate's life, the supervisor, in turn, is in a better position to delegate work and assist the manager. Openness does not expose weaknesses, it provides insight. It takes more confidence and courage to share your vulnerabilities than to hide them.

Sharing your vulnerabilities encourages others to be open with you as well and provides a safe space for people in which to be themselves and trust you. Being open sends a comforting, healthy message to others that weaknesses are part of the human condition.

React

(a) Using humor is a safe way of being open, yet talk about weaknesses. People will usually join in with their own stories.

302

(b) Focus on sharing the positive things in your life, rather than the negative.

(c) Use your openness to help others to learn. Share your personal insight about the good and less positive decisions you have made in your career.

(d) Think about people who are open with you. Do you respect them less because of it?

2 | Personal issues should remain at home

Rethink

Some people do not see the value of openness in the workplace and may believe it is counterproductive. But there are actually many benefits. People who are open tend to be perceived as more approachable, which is an important element of good management and leadership.

Your openness makes people more comfortable to share sentiments and concerns about their work experiences. By being open with others, you are able to make connections with people and, if lucky, even make some friends along the way. Openness also lays the foundation for loyalty and trust. Consider these benefits the next time you doubt whether there is room for openness in the workplace.

React

(a) Take a break or two each day to simply chat with people and tell them something unrelated to work. Make it your goal to make others feel comfortable. Ask personal questions or share a personal story or a smile.

(b) Schedule time in your calendar to attend events, functions, lunches etcetera, for the sake of spending some personal time with people.

(c) Use your openness to help others learn in the workplace. Share your insight about the good and less positive decisions you have made in your career.

3 | I am a private person/I am not comfortable sharing private details with people

Rethink

Everyone has the right to a private life, but being open does not mean you must reveal your most personal and guarded secrets. Simply sharing casual information about your interests, for example, helps to humanize you and provides some insight into who you are. There are many "safe" things people can learn about you that are not private in nature.

If you guard your privacy too zealously, you may come across as cold or disinterested. People admire and respect charismatic leaders with whom they can connect and who they feel are willing to let them in. This is difficult to achieve without a degree of openness.

303

React

(a) If you are uncomfortable with openness, start by sharing information about neutral subjects such as your hobbies.

(b) What would you like to know about other people? If you initiate the conversation and allow the other person to share first, you may feel less guarded.

(c) Try to share something about yourself with someone at work once a week.

(d) How open are you in your private life? Ask your significant other's opinion. It is often easier to practice being more open with your family first, then with your colleagues.

---

4 | In the past, people were not receptive to my openness

Rethink

If you did not have the most positive experience with openness, do not assume it was your fault and give up on it. If people are not used to you acting in this manner, they may be taken aback at first. Most people welcome others being open with them, but there are those who are simply not interested in listening. If you find your openness is often unwelcome, examine how and what kind of information you are sharing and make sure to improve as part of your self-development plan.

React

(a) Start by trying to engage the other person with casual questions, for example, "How did you like that restaurant where we all went to lunch?" or "Do you often go out to eat?" If the person is receptive, continue the conversation.

(b) Ensure you are not sharing information which may make the person uncomfortable. Observe the reaction to what you said. Is there a change in their tone of voice? Do they immediately get quiet, or change their demeanor or the topic?

(c) Observe a respected peer who is well liked and to whom people open up readily. What kind of information does that person share?

(d) Ask a trusted peer whether your comments are appropriate.

(e) Be mindful of people's time and busy schedules. It may be that they want to listen, but perhaps not for that long.

(f) Never share information about yourself that you feel you may regret later. Openness is not confession.

(g) Unless it is a trusted peer, do not share information about yourself which you would want people to keep confidential. It gives them an unfair responsibility to guard what you have told them. It is also likely to make them uncomfortable.

(h) Non-verbal communication is the key when sharing information. Make sure you are sincere about sharing a story and that you come across like that. Make direct eye contact, do not answer your phone during the conversation etcetera.

Overdeveloped

Research has shown that strengths can become weaknesses because you can, in fact, do too much of a good thing. You cannot become less good at a competency in which you excel, but you can balance the behavior by developing a few Stabilizers to tone down an excessive strength.

Stabilizer	Overdeveloped
29 Focused on Priorities	Reveals too much or inappropriate personal information, which makes others uncomfortable
39 Manages Time	
32 Informs Others	
58 Trustworthy	
2 Adaptable	
49 Politically Astute	
52 Self-Aware	
1 Achiever	
17 Demonstrates Good Judgment	
22 Diplomatic	

Instructions

Read the definition. If it applies to you, choose a few Stabilizers and develop them by selecting the relevant chapter and following the Strategies for Action.

For more instructions see the How To Use This Book section.

46. Open-Minded

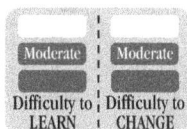

"Minds are like parachutes — they only function when open"

Thomas "Tommy" R Dewar

Well Developed

Is open to different and sometimes conflicting ideas or concepts and willing to change accordingly

Underdeveloped

Appears inflexible and unwilling to consider alternatives, new ideas or different views

Overdeveloped

Agrees with everything and has no opinion or views worth defending

Instructions

Read the definitions on the left. If the Underdeveloped definition applies, go to the Strategies for Action section.

If the Overdeveloped definition applies, go to the end of the chapter.

Test Yourself

True	I do not feel uncomfortable about new or different ideas
True	I am receptive to others' opinion
True	I value the importance of views and beliefs that differ from mine
True	I am open to new experiences
True	I believe there is more than one way to accomplish most things
True	I have, previously, altered my view on a strong personal belief after exposure to a different perspective
True	I think few situations are simply black or white

Note

Are you sure you need to develop this competency?

If the answer is "True" to most of the statements on the left, you probably do not need to develop this competency.

Strategies for Action

Most ineffective behaviors have an underlying thought or emotional pattern. By identifying these patterns, you can understand the impact they have and design strategies to counteract them.

① Being flexible undermines my authority/ Flexibility may be perceived as a weakness

② I think it is important to stick to my beliefs/Some things are simply black and white

③ I have low tolerance for people or experiences that I cannot relate to

④ I know I am right because I understand the issue better/I have more experience than others

Instructions

1. Read and select one or more of the ineffective ways of thinking/feeling to the left.

2. Find the corresponding number below that will help you to rethink this pattern and identify specific and practical actions that you can take.

① Being flexible undermines my authority/Flexibility may be perceived as a weakness

Rethink

When alternatives are offered for your consideration, treat them as opportunities instead of threats. If you feel your intelligence is being questioned or people are being disrespectful, defensiveness will be your natural response. And, if your ideas are not challenged often, it may be because you have created a "yes-men" culture in which people have become conditioned to value authority above creativity and independent thinking. This will not motivate employees, but stifle their output.

An open culture in which individuals feel comfortable to express their opinions and share their perspectives without penalty is fundamental to growth in the workplace. As a manager, it is your responsibility to nurture and utilize others' talents, and it starts with being open-minded. Remember, it may take people some time to trust that they will not be penalized for expressing their ideas.

React

(a) When you feel challenged or tested by someone, take a deep breath and acknowledge your feelings, be they defensive, angry, self-conscious or irritated. Acknowledging your emotions allows you to address your feelings, instead of lashing out at the other person.

(b) Regardless of your feelings, remind yourself your goal is to find solutions, not to be right.

(c) Imagine how you would feel if you wanted to share your opinions and your boss was not receptive.

(d) Ask people what they think before you give your recommendations.

(e) If you suspect you have established a "yes-man" culture, ask trusted peers whether you indeed seem too authoritative.

(f) Establish and foster a culture of open-mindedness — ask others' opinions as a matter of routine, both informally and in meetings; assign people to the role of devil's advocate; provide incentives to those who challenge the status quo; be consistent, supportive and patient with those who learn from you.

(g) People will need to see evidence that you are genuinely open-minded. This means not just paying lip service to it, but actually following through on ideas generated by others.

(h) Be generous and give credit to others' good suggestions, even if they are different from yours.

2 | I think it is important to stick to my beliefs/ Some things are simply black and white

Rethink

For some people, it is practically impossible to let go of deep-rooted belief systems or values they have developed throughout their lives. In some cases, this can be a good thing, but certainly not if those beliefs or values are unproductive or incompatible with their work environment. Imagine, for example, managers who strongly believe that only employees with advanced degrees are qualified to move into management. It would be hard for them to recognize talented individuals within the company who are just as qualified because of their experience.

Great advancements in our history have been possible only through a change in previously held beliefs — democracy, civil rights, the feminist movement. Fresh values swing the pendulum in the other direction so that new industries and systems can evolve, for example, the green energy movement with its solar energy, bio-fuels and electric cars is driven by a change in values.

Letting go of something in which you have invested energy, be it physical, psychological or emotional, can be hard, especially if it is tied to a sense of identity. It is important to be aware of your values and to redefine them when they are not beneficial to you or others.

React

(a) Be open to others' feedback, ideas and ways of thinking.

(b) Reserve your judgment until you can fully assess the value of a proposal.

(c) Ask exploratory questions instead of lashing out defensively. Sincerely try to understand the other person's position. Use inclusive language, for example, "Let's see how we can improve this idea together", "Can you tell me more?" and "This has been my belief, so how do I justify a change?"

(d) Do you have a reputation for being stubborn? Ask colleagues whether beliefs you may cling to are not serving the team or organization. Be sure to not become defensive when others give you the truth.

309

(e) Do research about the evolution of various products and companies, from their original idea to what they have become. Which changes in belief systems or cultures enabled their advance?

(f) Compare how your current beliefs or values differ from those you held when you were younger. You are likely to find that some have shifted, even if you did not realize it at the time.

3 | I have low tolerance for people or experiences that I cannot relate to

Rethink

There are many ways to improve your comfort and tolerance levels for diversity. Being aware of the way things stand for other people allows you to work with them more effectively. Think of the vast differences between generations, for example. Even if you have not walked in someone's shoes, you can be open-minded about the differences between your generations and the value each adds to the workplace.

Diversity exists in many forms in companies: the perspective of the sales team versus engineers, manager versus subordinate, male versus female. It also exists within various contexts and types of business — emerging versus existing markets, single- versus multiple-language customer bases, hi-tech versus low-tech products, start-up versus well-established business units, privately held versus publicly traded companies.

It is in your interest to operate comfortably in assorted contexts and among diverse groups of people. Opportunities come to those who can adapt to and even flourish in unfamiliar situations.

React

(a) Immerse yourself in things different. Try foods from unfamiliar cultures. Visit art galleries with exhibits you would not normally want to see — swap sculpture for photography, ceramics for abstract art and so forth. Listen to new types of music — classical instead of bluegrass, jazz instead of rap, country instead of new age. Watch movies from genres you normally ignore — documentaries, foreign films with subtitles, animation, suspense.

(b) Commit to learning something new about a culture or lifestyle different to yours each month. Try to experience it first-hand.

(c) Take classes at a community college, attend webinars, listen to podcasts or read articles and books about various unfamiliar topics, for example, nutrition, pop culture, art, history, swing dancing, greening the earth, scuba diving, auto mechanics, cooking, foreign languages, gardening, astronomy, first aid training and more.

(d) Ask for assignments that allow you to work with people from different backgrounds or in completely different markets. Look for similarities between your experience and theirs. Differences exist, but there are also commonalities that bind.

Rethink

Have you not gained the knowledge and experience you possess because you had been able to approach your educational and professional career with some degree of open-mindedness? There is never a point at which you have enough experience to know better than everyone else, or know too much to learn, even if you are an expert in the field. Just think how children say things which make you stop and think!

Your expertise can open many doors for you, but you will not be utilizing your opportunities to their fullest if you enter those doors closed-mindedly. If you are comfortable with what you know, sit back and let others teach you something new.

React

(a) Take advantage of the diverse backgrounds and viewpoints of others when planning or improving processes or solving a problem. Consider feedback from various sources, for example, line personnel, both internal and external customers etcetera.

(b) Establish a "walk in my shoes" initiative during which you and other leaders in your workgroup perform each other's duties for one day or several hours, at least. Choose an unfamiliar job, or one that will provide a better understanding of others' needs. Choose the job of someone who reports to you, for example. Share the lessons learnt and modify your perceptions and processes accordingly.

(c) Do not begin a conversation with the goal of proving your point. Instead, listen for information that could improve or perhaps even trounce your ideas.

(d) Listen first then speak.

(e) Use specialized groups or so-called "tiger teams" to challenge your ideas and recommend change.

Overdeveloped

Research has shown that strengths can become weaknesses because you can, in fact, do too much of a good thing. You cannot become less good at a competency in which you excel, but you can balance the behavior by developing a few Stabilizers to tone down an excessive strength.

Stabilizer	Overdeveloped
13 Courageous	Agrees with everything and has no opinion or views worth defending
35 Manages Conflict	
17 Demonstrates Good Judgment	
58 Trustworthy	
12 Confident	
37 Manages Negotiations	
56 Technically Competent	
29 Focused on Priorities	
50 Problem Solver	
1 Achiever	

Instructions

Read the definition. If it applies to you, choose a few Stabilizers and develop them by selecting the relevant chapter and following the Strategies for Action.

For more instructions see the How To Use This Book section.

47. Patient

"Adopt the pace of nature: her secret is patience"

Ralph Waldo Emerson

Well Developed

Is tolerant with others and knows when to slow down to let them catch up

Underdeveloped

Is impatient with due process or the time it takes for others to fully grasp what needs to be done and catch up

Overdeveloped

Waits too long to act. Holds back, puts a brake on processes despite others' readiness to act. Overestimates how much time people need to be comfortable. Lacks a sense of urgency

Instructions

Read the definitions on the left. If the Underdeveloped definition applies, go to the Strategies for Action section.

If the Overdeveloped definition applies, go to the end of the chapter.

Test Yourself

True	I am patient when others take longer than me to grasp a concept
True	I encourage people who need to catch up or look for ways to help them
True	I treat people with respect, even when I am stressed
True	I can adjust my expectations when things do not go as planned
True	I do things well, even if it takes longer that way
True	I focus on the positive when processes take longer than expected
True	I can curb my impulse to act when the timing is not right

Note

Are you sure you need to develop this competency?

If the answer is "True" to most of the statements on the left, you probably do not need to develop this competency.

47 Patient

Strategies for Action

Most ineffective behaviors have an underlying thought or emotional pattern. By identifying these patterns, you can understand the impact they have and design strategies to counteract them.

① I have high expectations of myself and others/ I strive for results

② I am impatient with certain individuals

③ I become impatient with situations beyond my control/I like to be in control

④ I can do it faster or better myself

⑤ I get impatient with the process/I tend to act impulsively

⑥ I regard patient people as indecisive or lacking the courage to act

Instructions

1. Read and select one or more of the ineffective ways of thinking/feeling to the left.

2. Find the corresponding number below that will help you to rethink this pattern and identify specific and practical actions that you can take.

---

1 | I have high expectations of myself and others/ I strive for results

Rethink

If your motivation is optimizing performance and getting results at all cost, it will be difficult to remain patient with yourself and others when things do not move as quickly as you wanted.

Remember, keeping the bar high is important but quite different from setting unrealistic expectations. Your subordinates need to be challenged, but if the demands are unrealistic, you risk that they become demoralized, frustrated and stressed, which are not conducive to peak productivity. You also risk becoming impatient with them. People's ability to produce results varies greatly and depends on their skills set, experience and personality. Someone with less experience or new to a position, for example, cannot be expected to meet your optimum standards immediately.

People will learn better with patient guidance than under stress. Contemplate the big picture: are you measuring success only by the final results? Consider all the other, perhaps less tangible measures of success that patience yields, such as having mentored people, the development of new skills and experiences, the discovery of new ideas as well as strong alliances and friendships forged.

React

(a) Face reality. Have you overestimated what a person or even you can do? What can you reasonably expect a person to know and be able to produce based on their experience? Is this person the right resource to use in this project, given their skills set? If not, it may really be beyond their control if they cannot succeed.

(b) Be clear about your expectations and in providing direction. Do not leave anything open to misinterpretation. People often hear information selectively and two can interpret the same conversation entirely differently. Make a note of your expectations and review them with the team to ensure everyone is on the same page. Add details such as timelines, milestones, targets etcetera.

(c) Strongly encourage people to voice their objections upfront, if they have any. Managers are often not challenged about their unrealistic goals, which lead to disappointment or frustration when these are not accomplished.

(d) Check routinely how high you set the bar. Are you expecting no mistakes ever to be made? Are your deadlines unrealistic or your timeframes unnecessarily short? Are you overly competitive with peers? Are team members unmotivated? Are you allowing subordinates time to learn? Are they continually trying to leave for other departments? Are they forced to work late hours and on weekends on a regular basis? Ask if you do not know, because these are all clues that your expectations could be unrealistic.

(e) Look for signs that people need time to recharge, and allow them the break. It may slow down the process in the short term, but in the long term you will avoid good talent getting burnout.

(f) Do you become impatient when you compare different people's performance? Do not fall into this trap. No two individuals are the same and they will perform differently in different contexts. Getting impatient with someone because you found them lacking compared with another is unfair and unproductive. Rather try to exploit, in a positive sense, people's strengths and develop their weaknesses into strengths. The latter requires patience but will pay off for both you and your colleague in the long term.

2 | I am impatient with certain individuals

Rethink

You are usually a patient soul, except with one or two particular people who seem to ignite your fuse. In our private lives, this could be a relative, friend of a friend, fellow gym member. The situation is common in the workplace as well. But here, you cannot pick or choose or ignore your peers, and the stress of work can intensify small issues and and cause them explode.

The proof of true patience comes when, confronted by difficult conditions or people, you continue to act fairly and civilly. Remember, it only takes one incident of disrespect, fueled by dwindling patience, to permanently compromise your relationship with a colleague.

React

(a) Try to isolate exactly what about an individual stirs your impatience. Does it have an impact on the person's work? It may be something inconsequential such as their tone of voice, demeanor, the way they dress, an annoying habit. If this is the case, try to overlook or accept their idiosyncrasies, especially if these have no relevance to your work.

(b) If your impatience stems from something that does affect your work, such as a betrayal of trust or irreconcilable work styles, initiate an honest discussion with the person. These conversations are not easy, but ignoring your concerns will not make them go away. They are likely to interfere with your performance and level of comfort at work. Ensure you make it clear that you are having the conversation because you want to improve your working relationship. Try your best to understand the other person's position. If necessary, ask a mediator from the human resources department to facilitate the discussion, especially if the topic is emotionally charged.

(c) Look for the positive traits in people — everyone has some. Which talents does an individual bring to the table? Before interacting with someone who is difficult, prepare by reminding yourself of those talents.

(d) Try to understand the motivation behind people's acts or the particular way they have acted in the past. For example, someone may appear rude but, in fact, may just not be comfortable in certain situations in general.

(e) Are you being disrespectful? A lack of patience breeds disrespect. Ensure you do not treat someone you dislike differently from others, for example, interrupting unnecessarily, raising your voice or discounting their opinion rudely.

---

3 | I become impatient with situations beyond my control/I like to be in control

Rethink

Occasionally, we all have our patience tested beyond our control. Just think of traffic in peak hours, or the frustration of so-called hi-tech devices that let you down on deadline.

You may not be able to control life's inconveniencies, but you can control your reaction to them. These situational setbacks must be handled with patient professionalism, otherwise they will disrupt your work and test your sanity more than necessary.

On any given day, any number of things can take an unexpected turn. If you are prone to overreacting to situations over which you have limited control, you are probably a highly stressed individual and not the most pleasant colleague. Learn to expect and manage the unexpected and, really, be grateful for the things that are going your way.

React

(a) Relax! Try to relieve stress with relaxation techniques such as deep breathing and self-motivation. Many books are available to teach you about relaxation techniques.

(b) Draw on your humor. Stressful things are often funny after the fact, but not at the time. Try to find the humor there and then and laugh — it relieves stress.

(c) Recognize when you are losing your patience and ask a trusted peer with a calming influence to help you refocus.

(d) Focus your energy on solutions to the problem instead of allowing frustrations and impatience to build.

(e) Quick fixes cannot always apply. Sit back and go with the flow, if necessary.

(f) Try to be flexible and spontaneous. Whether at work or in your private life, go along when there is a change of plans. The more comfortable you are with plans changing at the last minute, the more patience you will develop for when thing are beyond your control.

4 | I can do it faster or better myself

Rethink

Lacking the patience to delegate or share work with others because you believe you can do it faster or better is inefficient. In the short run you may get things done quicker but, in the long term, your ability to transfer knowledge and build people's capacity will be limited, and you could be seen as arrogant and controlling.

Whether you can do the task more effectively or not is not necessarily a priority — giving others opportunity to prove themselves is because that is what leaders do and it could yield greater long-term value for the organization.

Patience requires a space in which people have enough room to operate on their terms, to make mistakes, even. Instead of giving in to your impulse to control, try patiently developing a team that can collectively produce quality work.

React

(a) Delegate what you can, even if you can do it quicker yourself. Create a comprehensive list of tasks or projects others can do and commit to let them.

(b) When delegating, allow people enough space and time to work through problems, tasks or answers before you intervene, even if you had the answer early. It will give them the chance to consider the problem and, potentially, they could offer a route you have not considered.

(c) If you are an expert in your field, use every opportunity to be a teacher or mentor. Identify those who struggle and coach them where possible. When your impatience grows, ask yourself what a good teacher would do.

(d) Instead of micro-managing, take on new responsibilities that will improve your ability to monitor processes and keep others on track.

(e) Do not assume your experience of doing something is the only or best way to tackle a task. Someone else may take more time but yield more accurate results or take a more creative approach. Encourage innovative ways of thinking and new methodologies.

5 | I get impatient with the process/I tend to act impulsively

Rethink

Some people are prone to making quick and impulsive decisions because they value the result more than its quality or give up too quickly before understanding the value behind the process.

A fast pace does lead to action, but sometimes it is neither appropriate nor does it pay off. The best decisions are often the result of a complex process that involves numerous stakeholders, careful review, and time.

Understand when the best course of action requires patience and respect for the process. Knowing how to balance the needs for action versus patience is a critical skill which good leaders acquire.

React

(a) Calculate the risk. What are the consequences of taking the wrong action too soon? If it will result in grave and irreparable consequences, allow yourself more time to consider your options and get input from others.

(b) If you feel the need to take action, do so by separating the problem into smaller parts and making decisions on a smaller scale. You will satisfy your need for action but will do so in a manageable way.

(c) Assemble a team to make the decision — do not make it on your own. Ensure the team is well represented with a combination of people with varied styles, including analytical thinkers. Ensure the atmosphere allows for open discussion and that one person does not yield all the decision-making power. Try to reach consensus.

6 | I regard patient people as indecisive or lacking the courage to act

Rethink

History is filled with examples of great leaders who achieved something because they chose perseverance over impulsive action, such as Mahatma Gandhi and Martin Luther King Jr. Often, it requires more courage to practice restraint than act, so be careful not to confuse patience with a lack of courage.

Some individuals require more time to weigh possibilities and they deserve the opportunity to become comfortable with their decisions, even if you have already reached your conclusions.

React

(a) Read about great leaders who brought about change with perseverance and patience.

(b) Support individuals who request more time to consider a proposition or decision.

(c) Pick your battles: not all situations require immediate action, so practice patience when the urgency is self-imposed.

Overdeveloped

Research has shown that strengths can become weaknesses because you can, in fact, do too much of a good thing. You cannot become less good at a competency in which you excel, but you can balance the behavior by developing a few Stabilizers to tone down an excessive strength.

Stabilizer	Overdeveloped
55 Takes Initiative	Waits too long to act. Holds back, puts a brake on processes despite others' readiness to act. Overestimates how much time people need to be comfortable. Lacks a sense of urgency
8 Comfortable with Uncertainty	
13 Courageous	
35 Manages Conflict	
38 Manages Underperformance	
16 Decisive	
27 Experimental	
1 Achiever	
54 Takes Accountablity	
39 Manages Time	

Instructions

Read the definition. If it applies to you, choose a few Stabilizers and develop them by selecting the relevant chapter and following the Strategies for Action.

For more instructions see the How To Use This Book section.

48. Plans Work

"In preparing for battle, I have always found that plans are useless but planning is indispensable"
Dwight D. Eisenhower

Well Developed
Sets definite milestones and actions for achieving goals

Underdeveloped
Does not set clear goals or targets and comes across as unprepared

Overdeveloped
Spends too much time on planning and not enough on implementation. Struggles to adapt or respond when circumstances change

Instructions

Read the definitions on the left. If the Underdeveloped definition applies, go to the Strategies for Action section.

If the Overdeveloped definition applies, go to the end of the chapter.

Test Yourself

True	I assess the amount of time and resources I need for processes
True	I ensure the resources I need are available
True	I identify process milestones
True	I document process plans in terms of milestones, timelines, resource requirements
True	I anticipate process risks and pitfalls to create contingency plans
True	I compare actual results against those predicted to evaluate process performance and record lessons learnt

Note

Are you sure you need to develop this competency?

If the answer is "True" to most of the statements on the left, you probably do not need to develop this competency.

Strategies for Action

Most ineffective behaviors have an underlying thought or emotional pattern. By identifying these patterns, you can understand the impact they have and design strategies to counteract them.

① I do not have the time to plan adequately/I am not a detail-orientated person

② I know what the plan is in my head — I just do not document it

③ I do not know what to consider when planning/I am not familiar with planning techniques

④ My work culture places a higher value on action than planning/My organization will not invest in planning

Instructions

1. Read and select one or more of the ineffective ways of thinking/feeling to the left.

2. Find the corresponding number below that will help you to rethink this pattern and identify specific and practical actions that you can take.

---

1 | I do not have the time to plan adequately/I am not a detail-orientated person

Rethink

Many managers are skilled at generating innovative ideas and promoting them to the relevant constituents, but they fail to consider or participate in the details necessary to prepare an initiative.

A lack of time to plan is a typical challenge faced by most managers, as well as others who tend to be more creative. Global thinkers, too, can struggle to find the motivation to sift through details. But planning is an essential responsibility of managers.

Good plans save time by optimizing resources and identifying potential risks so that one can provide for contingencies. Planning also eliminates unnecessary work and redundancies that have an impact on your employees. "The devil is in the details" certainly applies to the art of planning. Even the best of ideas can fail because of critical omissions

React

(a) You may not have the time to lay out an entire plan in detail, but you do not have to do it that way. Delegate different portions and then use your time to piece the information together. The key is to address the details. In addition to saving you time, team member participation can create increased support for the plan.

(b) Do not recreate the wheel when planning. Become familiar with planning tools available to you that give you a template for addressing details. Also look at similar projects that have been launched in the company.

(c) Manage the plan's scope in increments. Prepare in detail for one or two critical parts of the process and focus your planning efforts on these activities first. Create the plan for the remaining portions later.

(d) Ensure there are a few detail-orientated people in your team who will ask the right questions and help you to remain focused.

(e) Ensure you have a short-term and long-term business plan. Having a plan will force you to consider the details carefully.

2 | I know what the plan is in my head — I just do not document it

Rethink

You may know exactly the course of action, but does your team? A documented plan allows others to see clearly the scope of the process, major task requirements and milestones, which mitigates confusion and redundant work. Without a documented plan, your team may regard you as being unfocused and unprepared, or overconfident.

A well-documented script gives team members a source of reference when questions arise. If your plan exists mostly in your head, you set yourself up as the sole source of information, which will place unnecessary demands on your time, attention and energy.

React

(a) At the beginning of each project, set aside time to document your plan, even if it is a draft and bound to change as the project evolves.

(b) Documentation can be as basic as ink on paper, however, a documented plan in an electronic format such as word processing, spreadsheets or project management software is easy to modify and access via e-mail, shared folders etcetera.

(c) During the initial brainstorming and development of your plan, ask someone to act as scribe and take down notes and details which can then be transcribed.

(d) Always send out follow-up correspondence after an initial meeting to summarize each team member's role and responsibilities and the first action items. Documentation in the initial stage of a process is critical to provide clarity.

(e) Be sure to send out written correspondence detailing any changes to the plan to all parties involved. Doing so ensures everyone has instructions in writing and no one is inadvertently left in the dark.

Rethink

Even the best planners can benefit from taking lessons or adopting new practices from those who have succeeded before them. There is no universal method of planning; every project and its circumstances are different. Get to know your options and integrate a few best practices into your plan.

React

(a) Develop various planning methods by researching best practices.

(b) Ask for input in the plan early in the process, not after it has been formalized or resources have been committed.

(c) Identify key people in the process who have a vested interest in the plan's success and invite them to be in your planning team.

(d) Define the goal of the process, and then draft a list of all tasks that must be completed, followed by who should complete each task.

(e) Identify tasks that can be performed concurrently with others, and those that cannot be started until one or more tasks have been completed.

(f) Determine the required resources, for example, personnel time, funding, equipment, materials, software and space, as well as the person who can authorize the use of each resource in the process. Can you secure all your necessary resources, including each staff member's time? Are these people and other resources available at the intervals required by the plan?

(g) Identify any risks, for example, bottlenecks, competing projects, scheduling issues and scarce resources, and plan for contingencies.

(h) Determine milestones and define how you will measure the process' success.

(i) Evaluate your actual results against your goals, for example, being on time and budget, quality checks, resource allocation and so forth.

(j) Discuss, document and share lessons learnt with your team and others who could benefit. You and your team's experiences can help to save planning time, improve resource estimations and make more accurate predictions of potential future risks for your organization.

(k) Celebrate accomplishments with your team and give praise, if appropriate.

(l) Find a person in the organization who you respect and who will share lessons from both successful and unsuccessful work or planning experiences. It is invaluable to listen to what others have been through.

Rethink

Some work environments are more reactive than proactive. Quick action and decision making is imperative for most businesses, but so is thought and good judgment, which tend to increase the likelihood of a quality decision being made.

Planning requires patience and an impatient environment can create pressure to cut corners just to reach to an outcome. Industry-leading companies cite countless success stories that were based on process planning, as well as failures because of its dearth.

It is better to have a positive outcome that took longer to achieve than a negative, fruitless outcome that was quick and easy to reach.

React

(a) If you are in a leadership position, reward and encourage individuals who are good at planning.

(b) Personally investing time in planning will set an example and send a strong message to others that it is valued in the organization.

(c) Support project management training for your employees.

(d) Discuss with your boss and other team members the benefits that were realized by having planned properly.

(e) Talk to your boss about your need for a plan. Everyone has different work styles and some managers will assume you are comfortable to operate without one if you do not speak out.

(f) Be persistent in discussions and meetings about details that have to be considered. Present them in a way that makes a good business case. Even if they are overlooked, you have used your insight to provide valuable information.

(g) Keep notes of lesson learnt throughout the process, and ask your team to do the same. This practice can be communicated during an initial meeting or via an e-mail and supported by e-mail reminders to your team.

(h) Formalize debriefing sessions, if possible, and share lessons learnt with others in the company so that these are considered before others forge ahead on their projects. Compare your plan's goals against the actual results, for example, budget, timelines, milestones, resource allocation, quality etcetera.

Overdeveloped

Research has shown that strengths can become weaknesses because you can, in fact, do too much of a good thing. You cannot become less good at a competency in which you excel, but you can balance the behavior by developing a few Stabilizers to tone down an excessive strength.

Stabilizer	Overdeveloped
8 Comfortable with Uncertainty	Spends too much time on planning and not enough on implementation. Struggles to adapt or respond when circumstances change
2 Adaptable	
55 Takes Initiative	
39 Manages Time	
12 Confident	
50 Problem Solver	
27 Experimental	
46 Open-Minded	
29 Focused on Priorities	
53 Strategic	

Instructions

Read the definition. If it applies to you, choose a few Stabilizers and develop them by selecting the relevant chapter and following the Strategies for Action.

For more instructions see the How To Use This Book section.

49. Politically Astute

"I think a more modern version of how people get promoted in most organizations reflects a broader reality: It's what you know, whom you know and who knows you"

Joan Lloyd

Well Developed
Is aware of and can manage the dynamics of power within an organization

Underdeveloped
Is unaware of the role personal influence plays in accomplishing goals or unwilling to get involved in the organization's politics

Overdeveloped
Is overly concerned with company politics and too interested in promoting a personal agenda

Instructions

Read the definitions on the left. If the Underdeveloped definition applies, go to the Strategies for Action section.

If the Overdeveloped definition applies, go to the end of the chapter.

Test Yourself

True	I know who the obvious and less obvious people of influence are in my organization
True	I adapt my tactics based on a particular situation or person
True	I can foresee who may be opposed when I push an agenda
True	I understand the dynamics among higher management
True	I seldom, or never, get others in trouble because of what I say
True	I know which information to share with whom
True	I let others defend their position without interrupting them

Note

Are you sure you need to develop this competency?

If the answer is "True" to most of the statements on the left, you probably do not need to develop this competency.

Politically Astute

49

327

Strategies for Action

Most ineffective behaviors have an underlying thought or emotional pattern. By identifying these patterns, you can understand the impact they have and design strategies to counteract them.

① Organizational politics is shady/I do not want to get involved in it

② I do not know who to influence or how to do it

③ My hard work should be enough to accomplish my duties

Instructions

1. Read and select one or more of the ineffective ways of thinking/feeling to the left.

2. Find the corresponding number below that will help you to rethink this pattern and identify specific and practical actions that you can take.

1 | Organizational politics is shady/I do not want to get involved in it

Rethink

The word "politics" has a negative connotation for many people. It conjures up images of dishonesty, corruption and the circumvention of established procedures. Of course there are people who use politics to manipulate situations to their advantage, for example, to excuse poor performance. But inherently, politics is not a bad thing.

Understanding the political backdrop of your organization allows you, in many ways, to improve productivity. A keen understanding of the culture and relationships in the organization gives you an advantage when championing ideas and scouting for resources. It also ensures that key people are recognized and rewarded for their performance.

When political resistance is limited, less energy is needed to push your agenda.

React

(a) Observe what enables a respected leader in your organization to use politics to push an agenda. It can help to dispel a stereotype you may hold about the nature of politicking.

(b) Read about politically astute leaders, such as Mahatma Gandhi and Nelson Mandela, who are widely respected and overcame tremendous obstacles by somehow managing the politics of their time. It will provide a different perspective of politics.

(c) Remain genuine and sincere. If your actions are guided by what is best for the organization, rather than what is best for you, you will feel more comfortable.

(d) Make clear to yourself why it is necessary to use politics in the goal you are trying to achieve. Compile a list of ways the "right" people can help you to accomplish your goal more effectively. Does it make sense to do it on your own? Do you believe in your position enough to defend it? On which ethics or values do you really have to infringe to achieve your goal?

(e) Sometimes, as skeptics, we dehumanize people with political power. Attend organizational events that give you an opportunity to talk to key decision makers on a more personal level. Find your common interests, passions and humanity. You will find many respectable, honest people just like you.

2 | I do not know who to influence or how to do it

Rethink

Politically savvy people understand who they should influence and how others can help them to maximize that influence. Influential people are everywhere, but some are more visible than others. Taking time and effort to understand the politics of an organization is thus important, but knowing the who's who is only one step.

Good management of politics has other considerations, such as the right timing and reading a situation correctly. The effort you put into developing this skill will be reflected in your management and leadership abilities.

React

(a) Find a trusted peer or mentor in your organization with whom you can discuss the internal politics. Learn to understand who holds the power to make decisions in different areas, both in theory and reality.

(b) Become familiar with the company's organizational chart and its critical positions. Make it a goal to introduce yourself at least once to everyone in key positions.

(c) Maximize your networking opportunities. Attend receptions, company events and conferences to establish relationships with as many people as possible, not just in your company but also in your field.

(d) Be prepared to succinctly communicate the way your work, project or idea can make a difference. You do not often have the opportunity to discuss your ideas at length, so a well-communicated and convincing speech is important.

(e) Make allies of the relevant people. Keep them informed of the obstacles you encounter, including resistance from people or departments. Together you can develop a strategy to overcome these hurdles and share the task of influencing others.

(f) Try to develop coalitions for maximum influence. Power often lies in numbers and some issues need a coalition to push an agenda.

(g) Are there specific groups with which you have trouble politically, all or most of the time? Look for particular biases you may harbor. You may think they are invisible, but people quickly pick up subtleties in behavior or language that makes them defensive and resistant to your influence.

(h) Timing can make all the difference in garnering support. Sometimes it simply is not the right time to keep pushing. Be sensitive about times you may need to back off in order to keep the door open for later. List the conditions that make this an inappropriate time to introduce your agenda.

(i) Often, it is not that you have reached the wrong people, but your delivery has not been well received. Poor communication or interpersonal skills are a surefire way to lose influence. A 360° assessment is effective for feedback on your strengths and weaknesses, as well as issues on which you can work with a coach.

(j) Read about ordinary people such as Erin Brockovich who, with little political experience, was able to navigate through complex politics and exert great influence.

3 | My hard work should be enough to accomplish my duties

Rethink

Some leaders do all the right things in their roles, yet have little impact on an organization. You may be a stellar performer, but when the time comes to exert influence, you will need to have built your credibility and that people know who you are. Otherwise, you may find it hard to get others to listen.

Visibility and credibility play a big role in politics. Do not assume your hard work will necessarily get that for you. A little self-promotion can go a long way.

React

(a) Forward e-mails of praise from clients or other team members to relevant people.

(b) Keep a list of major accomplishments for your reference during performance reviews. The person doing your evaluation may not remember all your achievements throughout the year.

(c) Ask experts and respected colleagues their professional opinions and advice on a project. It gives you an opportunity to meet influential people and make your work visible.

(d) Become involved in projects beyond your immediate scope that expose you to decision makers. For example, volunteer for a taskforce or committee.

(e) If, at first, you are uncomfortable to promote your talents, talk about your team's accomplishments. It will highlight your achievements indirectly.

(f) Invite key decision makers from other divisions or groups to add value to your meetings and become familiar with your projects.

(g) Your accomplishments may speak for themselves at present, but a former leader in your organization may not have had the same experience with you. Do not overlook previous relationships that may require extra attention or even repair.

Overdeveloped

Research has shown that strengths can become weaknesses because you can, in fact, do too much of a good thing. You cannot become less good at a competency in which you excel, but you can balance the behavior by developing a few Stabilizers to tone down an excessive strength.

Stabilizer	Over Developed
56 Technically Competent	Is overly concerned with company politics and too interested in promoting a personal agenda
35 Manages Conflict	
17 Demonstrates Good Judgment	
26 Ethical	
32 Informs Others	
58 Trustworthy	
13 Courageous	
50 Problem Solver	
1 Achiever	
54 Takes Accountablity	

Instructions

Read the definition. If it applies to you, choose a few Stabilizers and develop them by selecting the relevant chapter and following the Strategies for Action.

For more instructions see the How To Use This Book section.

50. Problem Solver

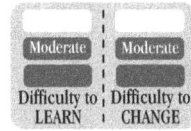

> "We can't solve problems by using the same kind of thinking we used when we created them"
>
> Albert Einstein

Well Developed
Solves challenging problems by using a combination of intuition and analytical thinking

Underdeveloped
Does not follow a rigorous problem-solving process. Has limited ways of approaching a problem and relies heavily on previously used solutions

Overdeveloped
Analyzes issues too much and sees everything as a problem that requires resolution. Does not understand the impact of irrationality or emotion on people's behavior

Instructions
Read the definitions on the left. If the Underdeveloped definition applies, go to the Strategies for Action section.

If the Overdeveloped definition applies, go to the end of the chapter.

Test Yourself

True	I am open to input or feedback from others when trying to solve a problem
True	I seldom have to address the same problem twice
True	I consider multiple solutions for a problem before taking action
True	I can identify problems or challenges that others do not see
True	I understand the nature of a problem quickly, even with little information
True	I use logic and trust my intuition when solving problems
True	I approach problems objectively and keep my personal feelings separate

Note

Are you sure you need to develop this competency?

If the answer is "True" to most of the statements on the left, you probably do not need to develop this competency.

Problem Solver

50

333

Strategies for Action

Most ineffective behaviors have an underlying thought or emotional pattern. By identifying these patterns, you can understand the impact they have and design strategies to counteract them.

① My problem-solving techniques are limited/
I tend to use familiar approaches

② I tend to go with the first thing that comes to mind/I get impatient with processes

③ I need a lot of data when problem solving/
I place more value on thinking than doing/
I do not act intuitively

④ I tend to be influenced by others' agendas/
I do not consider a problem independently and objectively

Instructions

1. Read and select one or more of the ineffective ways of thinking/feeling to the left.

2. Find the corresponding number below that will help you to rethink this pattern and identify specific and practical actions that you can take.

1 | My problem-solving techniques are limited/I tend to use familiar approaches

Rethink

Everyone has preferred methods or a particular style in their approach to solving a problem. Your approach might have worked for you so far, but why not expand your toolbox?

Multiple options increase the number of lenses from which you can view a problem and allows you to adapt to its demands. Being flexible and open-minded creates the optimal mindset for problem solving. Relying only on the approaches you have used in the past limits your creativity and chances to think innovatively. Be careful, too, not to adopt a been-there-done-that attitude to problem solving. No problem or issue is exactly alike.

React

(a) There are numerous approaches to keep in your problem-solving toolbox, for example, SWOT analysis (strengths, weaknesses, opportunities, threats); cash-flow forecasting (testing the viability of a project); risk analysis; unique selling point analysis; MindJet's mind-mapping product (understanding how different factors interact with the use of diagrams); and flowcharting.

(b) Ask peers about their unique problem-solving techniques, as well as people not from your discipline. The marketing department, for example, may have instructive ways to approach a brainstorming session, of which you can take advantage in your field too.

(c) Let others in the team take the lead. Observe their ways of approaching a problem. Which methods could you adopt? What is not working for them?

(d) Contact your human resources department about courses your company has to broaden your problem-solving techniques.

(e) Define the factors that make this situation or problem different from a similar one you have had. Just because they seem alike does not mean the solution is the same.

(f) Consider the resources available to address the problem. You may have a perfect solution or one that was previously successful, but your time or resources at present may be insufficient to facilitate it again. An alternative solution would then be a better approach.

(g) Ensure you include highly creative people in your team. They are effective at introducing out-of-the-box possibilities.

(h) Do not assume you know the answer because you have had a similar experience in the past. It is as important to be aware of what you do not know as it is to draw on what you do know. Be aware of making generalizations based on previous experiences.

(i) When stating information as fact, ensure it is indeed fact and not opinion. Find experts with whom you can discuss the problem to verify your assumptions.

② | I tend to go with the first thing that comes to mind/ I get impatient with processes

Rethink

You may be too impatient or quick to jump to conclusions when solving a problem. And although you may achieve quick results by doing so, you risk overlooking important data available to you. You are likely to cut corners, which could reduce the quality of your decisions.

Many problems are more complex than they appear on the surface — they require analysis and input from multiple sources. Problem solving requires action, but give yourself and your colleagues sufficient time to consider and deal with the process of finding answers.

Getting results is different to solving a problem.

React

(a) Ensure you have ample time to consider and analyze the existing assumptions about an issue. An incorrect premise will set your problem solving efforts off in the wrong direction from the start.

(b) Be sure to properly define the problem. Differentiate between the problem and its symptoms.

(c) Consider the process part of the problem as well as the constraints on it, and work to remove them.

(d) Recognize when a team approach is better than doing it alone. It may take longer this way, but it could be a smart approach that yields better results.

(e) Do not cut corners on problems with important consequences or that could have a great impact on your business. Schedule sufficient time to consider these problems, and do so when and where you have the least distractions.

(f) Divide the problem into components and delegate tasks accordingly. This way, you can focus your attention on the parts where your input is most valuable

(g) People think and work at different speeds. Some will want or need more time than others to consider possibilities and find solutions. Respect and support the time individuals need to contribute to the process.

3 | I need a lot of data when problem solving/I place more value on thinking than doing/I do not act intuitively

Rethink

So-called pack rats are well known, but have you heard of information rats? They are those who place excessive value on data and its collection, instead of taking action. They often waste unnecessary energy on gathering information and evidence, or finding precedents to act as templates for action or to validate their solutions.

Remember, you will not always have the necessary time or resources to explore a problem fully. Effective managers and leaders prove that, time and again, problem solving can be done effectively with limited information, drawing on past experience and a healthy reliance on intuition.

Only relevant information can help you to guard against risk.

React

(a) Set a specific deadline to make a decision. Giving yourself a deadline will help you to avoid prolonged delays in making a decision. Hold yourself accountable to that deadline by setting a date to discuss your decision with your superiors. If you are working with a team, set a date on which everyone will review the information they have gathered and start tackling the problem.

(b) Schedule occasional meetings with your supervisor to discuss the information you have collected and whether it focuses on your priorities.

(c) Do you tend to think too much and complicate things? Use your peers as sounding boards to give you perspective. Look for opportunities to combine or abbreviate processes.

(d) After a project is complete, spend time to consider the information that was important as well as irrelevant. Could you have focused your time and energy in a better direction? Reflection like this is important to process the effectiveness of your problem-solving techniques.

(e) Get in touch with your intuition and learn to trust it. Forget your intellect and logic at some point and ask yourself what your gut feeling says. Practice by working on issues with limited information and little consequence and build up to more important decisions.

Rethink

People sometimes stray from using logic when solving a problem because of their particular biases. If two colleagues dislike each other, for example, they may choose to work on a problem independently, even though their collective efforts would yield a better result.

Others are influenced by authority figures or peers and would rather follow the status quo, instead of considering a problem independently. And, when different stakeholders are involved, people may feel the need to defend their turf to the extent that they insist on an irrational course of action.

Problem solving is always a combination of the subjective and the objective. Ensure that you approach the problem in a logical and sufficiently objective frame of mind.

React

(a) On a scale of one to 10, rate the level of dedication and sensitivity with which you have treated the problem. It is hard to keep an open mind when you are emotional about an issue. If your rating is high, tell colleagues that you care deeply about the issue and ask whether they think you are overreacting to their suggestions. Simply being aware of your level of emotional investment will help you to manage your reactions.

(b) Identify your red buttons — we all have issues or comments that touch our most sensitive spots. Carefully consider why you are so sensitive. Talk to a mentor or coach to get a realistic perspective on your thoughts and for guidance on how to address some of these feelings.

(c) Remain composed when your buttons are pushed during conversation. Do not respond immediately. Instead, count to 10, then ask a question that seeks to clarify the issue. Giving the other person an opportunity to explain and perhaps rephrase what they have said will give you time to consider the comment and compose yourself.

(d) Be honest about your motives. Are you approaching the problem in an ethical manner or are you serving your interests?

(e) Let each team member, including you, contemplate a problem individually before convening to share ideas. It will allow independent thinking and prevent the pack-rat mentality from invading your problem-solving process.

(f) If you know you are overly sensitive or cannot remain objective, remove yourself. Ask someone else to handle the problem and to report back to you. Alternatively, choose only the elements you can deal with objectively. Sharing the weight of an issue can give you the necessary distance to approach a problem more fair-mindedly.

Overdeveloped

Research has shown that strengths can become weaknesses because you can, in fact, do too much of a good thing. You cannot become less good at a competency in which you excel, but you can balance the behavior by developing a few Stabilizers to tone down an excessive strength.

Stabilizer	Overdeveloped
55 Takes Initiative	Analyzes issues too much and sees everything as a problem that requires resolution. Does not understand the impact of irrationality or emotion on people's behavior
24 Empathetic	
8 Comfortable with Uncertainty	
2 Adaptable	
7 Collaborative	
43 Motivates People	
22 Diplomatic	
17 Demonstrates Good Judgment	
4 Approachable	
34 Listens Well	

Instructions

Read the definition. If it applies to you, choose a few Stabilizers and develop them by selecting the relevant chapter and following the Strategies for Action.

For more instructions see the How To Use This Book section.

51. Recognizes Talent and Potential

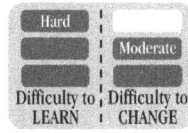

Hard

Moderate

Difficulty to | Difficulty to
LEARN | CHANGE

"Mediocrity knows nothing higher than itself, but talent instantly recognizes genius"

Arthur Conan Doyle

Well Developed
Accurately identifies strengths, weaknesses and potential in people with relatively short exposure to them

Underdeveloped
Needs too much time with people before accurately identifying their strengths and weaknesses

Overdeveloped
Can be blind-sided by the unpredictability of people's behavior under certain circumstances

Instructions

Read the definitions on the left. If the Underdeveloped definition applies, go to the Strategies for Action section.

If the Overdeveloped definition applies, go to the end of the chapter.

Test Yourself

True	I give people a chance to take on assignments even if they are inexperienced
True	I look for opportunities to put people's talents to the test
True	I have been successful in choosing good employees
True	I use tools such as 360° feedback to better understand the talent in my group
True	I am knowledgeable about interviewing and hiring best practices
True	I know who is ready for promotion
True	I can usually get an accurate reading of people in a short time
True	I use all information available to make judgments about people

Note

Are you sure you need to develop this competency?

If the answer is "True" to most of the statements on the left, you probably do not need to develop this competency.

Strategies for Action

Most ineffective behaviors have an underlying thought or emotional pattern. By identifying these patterns, you can understand the impact they have and design strategies to counteract them.

① When assessing or hiring talent, I look for people who fit a specific mould/I rely on my gut feeling

② I base my assessment of people on their past or current performance

③ My assessments are sometimes biased because of organizational pressure

④ I am not really a "people's person" and I cannot read others well

⑤ It is hard for me to change my opinion or perception of someone once I have made a judgment

1 | When assessing or hiring talent, I look for people who fit a specific mould/I rely on my gut feeling

Rethink

Do you have preconceptions about the type of person you want to hire or assign to a job? Perhaps you have had experience with a certain kind of person that has worked out well, or vice versa. Be careful not to interpret talent too narrowly or apply a cookie-cutter approach.

It is normal to look for people who are similar to you when assessing talent, or follow your gut feeling when choosing the best candidate, but this is a biased approach. Performance is subject to numerous influencing factors, including an individual's blend of behavioral competencies, work experiences and technical skills. Additionally, people's success is influenced by the specific context of their jobs, for example, how well they fit with their bosses, teams, companies' culture and types of assignments.

In their book, *The Leadership Pipeline,* Ram Charan, Stephen Drotter and James Noel discuss the impact of organizational level on a person's success. To consider as many variables as possible when assessing talent improves your ability to recognize potential, reduce bias and make better hiring choices.

React

(a) Consult with the human resources department to ensure the behavioral competencies, technical skills and experience needed for the job have been clearly and accurately defined.

(b) Broaden your perspective of how well a person will suit a position by considering how they will fare within its context.

(c) Examine results from assessments such as 360° feedback, which can provide fresh insight into people. It will give you an understanding of a person's strengths and weaknesses. Talk to HR about other feedback tools you can use.

(d) Research shows behavioral interviewing is the most effective. Learn about this method of interviewing and talk to HR if it is not yet used in your company. Read about effective interviewing skills.

(e) Ensure your team is balanced by recruiting people with diverse talents.

(f) Become involved in the actual hiring process. It will help you to gain valuable experience in sharpening your intuition about people and understanding how to ask effective questions that reveal strengths and weaknesses.

(g) Ensure that, during hiring, rigorous processes, techniques and standardized structures are applied.

2 | I base my assessment of people on their past or current performance

Rethink

Current performance is definitely a good place to start when assessing someone, and in the absence of other observations it is often the only indicator you can use. But performance only does not provide a complete picture. As a manager, it is important to also understand people's potential and consider other skills sets which the person has not had the opportunity to prove.

Someone who is new to a position may struggle as they learn new skills and adapt to the new challenges of a position, and may need time to prove themselves. Great talent is often missed or not properly invested in if managers are unwilling to look beyond performance scores or test their subordinates in new ways.

React

(a) Give people who are new to assignments enough time to adapt within their new context before making judgments.

(b) Discover others' knowledge about an employee through 360° feedback or other multisource assessment tools. It is especially useful if someone is a new recruit or has just been assigned to you.

(c) Talk to your human resources department or a PeopleTree Group consultant about the 9-Cell Matrix, which helps to predict performance. This process provides clues about how people are likely to perform in an organization.

(d) Encourage subordinates to be honest with you. People who are given the opportunity and a safe environment to do so will share information that can help you to understand their interests and strengths better. Ask about projects they have worked on previously and why these were successful or not. Enquire about experiences and skills they may have of which you have been unaware. Ask open-ended questions about what they find the most challenging or rewarding.

(e) An effective way to get to know someone's strengths and weaknesses is to give them assignments that challenge them in a variety of areas. Rotate people among assignments until you understand their talents and flaws. Avoid repeatedly using the same person to do a particular set of tasks.

(f) Collect feedback from other managers with whom an employee has worked in the past. What is their perspective of the individual's strengths and weaknesses? It can give you some idea of the person's performance in different contexts.

3 | My assessments are sometimes biased because of organizational pressure

Rethink

At times, managers may be expected to assess someone based on others' opinions, which they may not believe to be accurate. For example, an individual who has risen through the ranks could be a favorite among a certain circle due to strong networking, but could lack the necessary skills or experience. Giving such a person a less than stellar assessment may be frowned upon, unpopular or even upset the CEO.

Alternatively, managers may feel threatened by a rising star and be tempted to assess that person less favorably. Assessments never take place in a vacuum and are often associated with pressure, be it perceived or real. However, judging someone's talent inaccurately is harmful to both the individual and the organization in the long term.

Accurate assessments dictate the development an individual needs to make the best contribution now and in the future. It also ensures that appropriate resources are assigned to projects and that the team is treated equitably. And, it allows an organization to plan its leadership succession based on talent, not favoritism.

It will require some courage to challenge pressures that may be involved, but your honesty and sincere interest in the welfare of the organization are prime reasons to stand your ground.

React

(a) Encourage an open culture in which people feel comfortable to be honest during assessments.

(b) Reward self-awareness and development efforts in those you manage so that they are more forthcoming about their flaws and willing to work on them.

(c) Keep accurate records of a person's performance and behavior so that you can back up an unpopular assessment with facts, rather than opinion.

(d) Consult your manager or human resources department for support and advice if you are worried about a particular assessment you have to conduct.

(e) Ensure you have set clear goals and objectives for subordinates. You will be able to use these as a reference to discuss whether they have been met.

4 | I am not really a "people's person" and I cannot read others well

Rethink

It is worth the effort to engage meaningfully with your colleagues. Otherwise, you risk being seen as unapproachable or distant, and it makes it difficult for you to observe and get a good feel for those around you. Reading others well requires that you become a student of people's behavior, which is not really possible if you remain aloof.

React

(a) Do not stay at your desk or in your office all day long. Take time throughout your workday, even if only for a few minutes, to interact one on one with subordinates or peers.

(b) Take advantage of meetings and staff get-togethers to observe how people behave. Note differences in how individuals interact in a group versus alone.

(c) Question your understanding of your peers or those you supervise. Try to describe the role that each person plays in your work life, for example, coordinator, follower and leader. Write down exactly what you know about each person. Six months later, revisit the description to see if it differs now that you have observed it further. Did you notice something that confirmed your opinion or changed your mind?

(d) When possible, spend time with colleagues in informal and social settings. People are often guarded at work, which makes it difficult to get to know them.

(e) Volunteer to work on a team project that will allow you to interact with others regularly.

(f) Go to lunch with colleagues. Leave your desk.

(g) Become an active observer of people — do some "people watching". Humans have nuance that assessments cannot detect. Spend enough time with colleagues to be able to get a feel for the subtleties that make them unique. If possible, make time to get to know them outside of work. Have coffee or attend company functions together, for example.

5 | It is hard for me to change my opinion or perception of someone once I have made a judgment

Rethink

Be careful not to let first impressions or limited observation influence your assessment of a person permanently. Labeling people can affect their career negatively for a long time and ignore changes they might have made. People can behave quite differently depending on the context and circumstances. For example, introverts may come across as aloof if they keep to themselves during meetings, but they may simply be uncomfortable in the setting. Or, you may have met a colleague for the first time on a day that they were particularly stressed and less amicable as a result.

343

The point is, until you get to know a person well enough or have observed their behavior in different contexts, it is better not to make assumptions leading to labels. Stereotyping draws on few real facts about an individual and general, simplistic models of how you perceive people. Withholding judgment can be hard, but it is worth it. Always look beyond first impressions.

React

(a) Give people a chance. Meet with them several times before you judge.

(b) Measure your impression of someone by asking others what they think. You may be surprised to hear quite different opinions.

(c) Get to know the people you find the hardest to read. What makes them a particularly difficult challenge? If they do not talk much, for example, invite them to a setting where they can feel more comfortable to express themselves, say, lunch or a round of golf.

(d) Undertake an exercise to compare people you know well now with your first impression of them. What is different? What do you know about them now that you did you not notice at first? Did you read them right the first time? If not, why not?

(e) Express in writing how someone might read you. Ask peers their first impression of you and if and how it has changed.

(f) If you find it difficult to discard a first impression of someone, make a list of all the positive attributes the person has, such as skills and experiences they add to your team.

Overdeveloped

Research has shown that strengths can become weaknesses because you can, in fact, do too much of a good thing. You cannot become less good at a competency in which you excel, but you can balance the behavior by developing a few Stabilizers to tone down an excessive strength.

Stabilizer	Overdeveloped
23 Directs People	Can be blind-sided by the unpredictability of people's behavior under certain circumstances
8 Comfortable with Uncertainty	
34 Listens Well	
17 Demonstrates Good Judgment	
18 Detail-Orientated	
24 Empathetic	
59 Unifies People	
20 Develops People	
46 Open-Minded	
49 Politically Astute	

Instructions

Read the definition. If it applies to you, choose a few Stabilizers and develop them by selecting the relevant chapter and following the Strategies for Action.

For more instructions see the How To Use This Book section.

52. Self-Aware

"What is necessary to change a person is to change his awareness of himself"

Abraham Maslow

Well Developed

Is open to feedback and aware of strengths and weaknesses

Underdeveloped

Avoids or reacts adversely to feedback and appears unaware of personal strengths and weaknesses

Overdeveloped

May be too introspective or critical, to the extent that self-esteem suffers

Instructions

Read the definitions on the left. If the Underdeveloped definition applies, go to the Strategies for Action section.

If the Overdeveloped definition applies, go to the end of the chapter.

Test Yourself

True	I know what my best qualities and my weaknesses are
True	I habitually ask for feedback
True	I do not become defensive when given constructive criticism
True	I routinely question my motives, values and opinions
True	I read literature about human behavior and psychology

Note

Are you sure you need to develop this competency?

If the answer is "True" to most of the statements on the left, you probably do not need to develop this competency.

Self-Aware

52

347

Strategies for Action

Most ineffective behaviors have an underlying thought or emotional pattern. By identifying these patterns, you can understand the impact they have and design strategies to counteract them.

① I often feel defensive when given feedback

② I am not the sensitive or touchy-feely type

③ I already know myself well enough

④ I am not concerned about others' opinion of me

Instructions

1. Read and select one or more of the ineffective ways of thinking/feeling to the left.

2. Find the corresponding number below that will help you to rethink this pattern and identify specific and practical actions that you can take.

---

1 | I often feel defensive when given feedback

Rethink

It is difficult to get to know yourself if you remain closed to other opinions about your behavior or work. Research shows self-perception is the least accurate assessment. As such, it is to our advantage to remain open to others' observations of us and not place too much value on our own conclusions.

Just think how much more you could learn about yourself if everyone gave you proper feedback. Granted, not all feedback is 100% valid or correct, and some of it will be useless. Nonetheless, there is always some truth to what others have to say.

React

(a) Participate in a 360° feedback evaluation. It is the most effective way to get collective results from your peers. The PeopleTree 360° methodology uses a forced ranking method that reduces rater bias and assesses your relative strengths and weaknesses.

(b) If you find yourself becoming defensive or hostile when receiving feedback, you may be tempted to give an emotionally charged response. Practice stress-management techniques such as deep breathing. Take time to let the feedback sink in and repeat it in your mind several times, each time followed by the words "self-aware". This allows you a moment to consciously defuse anger or hostility and helps to put things into perspective.

348

(c) Do not get caught up in trying to defend yourself. Let the person know that you will take their suggestions or feedback into consideration. If you are not too emotional, ask for concrete examples so that you can better consider what they have said.

(d) Be approachable. People avoid giving feedback to those who have little time for them or do not listen. You make it clear that you are open to feedback through your body language and facial expressions, and because you encourage it, of course.

(e) Not all feedback is 100% accurate but, if you pay attention, there is always something revealing about either yourself or the other person. You will not be able to detect these nuances if you are being defensive. Even if you disagree with the feedback, it is being given for a reason. What do you think the reason is? What can you learn about yourself and the other party?

(f) If more than one person is giving you the same feedback, chances are there is some truth to it. You would be wise to pay attention to it.

2 | I am not the sensitive or touchy-feely type

Rethink

Nurturing self-awareness is often difficult because people are not interested in who they really are or do not want to appear vulnerable in front of others. The typical work setting places a greater premium on so-called hard skills and less on soft skills. But research shows effective leaders must have both — and maintain a healthy balance between them. Much work has been done on the importance of emotional intelligence, which is rooted in our ability to be keenly sensitive to other people's underlying motives and needs, as well as our own.

Unless you are able to examine and understand your own behavior, it will be difficult to understand and manage that of other people. Know that self-awareness is a legitimate competency, which has great impact on your career success.

React

(a) Meditation describes a state of concentrated attention focused on an object of thought or awareness. It usually involves turning attention inwards to a single point of reference. It is a good technique to tap into our inner motives and emotions. Choose from the numerous meditation techniques available and add them to your daily routine.

(b) Single out someone in the company who is both successful and well liked. Which soft skills would you attribute to that person? Use them as a role model for your behavior.

(c) Consciously try to be more open with people. It may be awkward and difficult at first, but being comfortable enough to share personal information helps you to practice communicating your feelings.

(d) Put yourself in the other person's shoes when presented with problematic situations. How would you feel in the same position? How would you like to be treated?

3 | I already know myself well enough

Rethink

If you believe you know your inner workings completely, it is a quite reliable sign that you have a lot to learn. The human mind and our emotions are infinitely complex.

What you know about yourself may have stood you in good stead thus far, but strengths can become weaknesses and derail our careers if we do not continually and objectively examine ourselves.

Self-awareness is a never-ending journey and should be considered a life-long practice. The need to improve and better understand ourselves never ceases.

React

(a) Challenge your values. Read about practices, religions or philosophies with which you are unfamiliar and see if you find more admirable values, perhaps.

(b) If you are reluctant to discover yourself, try to discover the world. Expose yourself to completely different people, experiences and hobbies. You will learn a great deal about yourself in the process.

(c) Create a self-awareness library and schedule time at least once a week for self-development in a variety of areas. There is a world of interesting reading available.

(d) Numerous psychological assessments are available to effectively assess people from a variety of angles. Try a different angle. Ask the human resources department for a recommendation.

(e) Self-analysis is the key. Always ask yourself questions: Why did you make the decision you did? Why are you really feeling a particular way? What would have been the consequences of a different choice? Do not obsess, just ask.

(f) Meditation is a proven, effective way to tap into inner motives and emotions. Meditation techniques include breathing and mantra exercises as well as yoga. Research the options and make meditation a part of your daily ritual.

(g) Share what you do know or think about yourself with others. Compare your self-assessment with their feedback and find your blind spots and hidden strengths.

4 | I am not concerned about others' opinion of me

Rethink

Be careful that your self-confidence does not become arrogance. Being aware of others' opinions can give you invaluable feedback to improve your relationship with colleagues, in fact, it will improve your overall management skills.

Studies show self-perception is the least accurate assessment, so being open to other opinions means you can target areas for improvement and identify strengths on which you can build. Many careers are derailed by behaviors that begin as strengths but develop into weaknesses.

Concern about others' opinions has many benefits and sends a message that you are willing to improve in any way necessary. Remember, too, that people will be more receptive to your feedback if you have been respectful of their opinions about you.

React

(a) Make it a habit to stay in touch with your behavior by soliciting feedback from others when appropriate. Ask: What am I doing well? What can I improve? What do I need to change?

(b) Participate in a formal 360° evaluation process. It is a great way to gauge how people really perceive you.

(c) Engage a coach who can help to you interpret the results and understand the benefits of changing your behavior.

Overdeveloped

Research has shown that strengths can become weaknesses because you can, in fact, do too much of a good thing. You cannot become less good at a competency in which you excel, but you can balance the behavior by developing a few Stabilizers to tone down an excessive strength.

Stabilizer	Overdeveloped
1 Achiever	May be too introspective or critical, to the extent that self-esteem suffers
13 Courageous	
11 Composed	
12 Confident	
8 Comfortable with Uncertainty	
9 Communicates Well (Verbal)	
27 Experimental	
5 Balances Personal Life and Work	
49 Politically Astute	
21 Develops Self	

Instructions

Read the definition. If it applies to you, choose a few Stabilizers and develop them by selecting the relevant chapter and following the Strategies for Action.

For more instructions see the How To Use This Book section.

53. Strategic

"When you're prepared, you're more confident. When you have a strategy, you're more comfortable"
Fred Couples

Well Developed
Can envision future scenarios based on a combination of intuition, trends and data

Underdeveloped
Is unable to create credible future scenarios supported by relevant information, or appears to have a more tactical or short-term focus

Overdeveloped
Is too focused on the future and seems out of touch with current realities

Instructions
Read the definitions on the left. If the Underdeveloped definition applies, go to the Strategies for Action section.

If the Overdeveloped definition applies, go to the end of the chapter.

Test Yourself

True	I stay informed about trends that affect my business
True	I have experience in strategic initiatives
True	I consider the long-term impact even when following a short-term tactical approach
True	I consider how things interrelate
True	I often entertain possibilities and scenarios for the future
True	I am exposed to people who engage in strategic thinking
True	I am curious about topics outside my area of expertise

Note

Are you sure you need to develop this competency?

If the answer is "True" to most of the statements on the left, you probably do not need to develop this competency.

Strategies for Action

Most ineffective behaviors have an underlying thought or emotional pattern. By identifying these patterns, you can understand the impact they have and design strategies to counteract them.

① I tend to focus on immediate gains or needs that require quick fixes/I have to deal with today's problems

② One cannot predict the future/I do not believe that strategic planning is useful

③ I focus on the here and now/I am practical and not inclined to theorize

④ I do not get involved in strategic thinking because my focus is deeply technical

⑤ I have not had the opportunity to do longer-term strategic planning/I am not familiar with strategic planning models and techniques

Instructions

1. Read and select one or more of the ineffective ways of thinking/feeling to the left.

2. Find the corresponding number below that will help you to rethink this pattern and identify specific and practical actions that you can take.

---

① I tend to focus on immediate gains or needs that require quick fixes/I have to deal with today's problems

Rethink

You may well be a strong strategic thinker, but if you are always putting out fires it will harm your performance as a strategist. Do not let today's problems distract you from focusing on accomplishing your strategic goals. You may get a sense of accomplishment when you resolve this week's crises, or find reward in keeping both hands on the operational deck, but it can be exhausting — and should you really be steering the ship when you are supposed to be planning its course?

Most organizations aim to build sustainable success, which requires thinking of ways to make it happen in the long term. The value you add to strategic initiatives is greater than your input in tactical issues, so ensure your value is exploited properly.

Seeing long-term horizons is critical for organizations and individuals; it is arguably one of the most important concepts in organization theory. Despite organizations' acknowledgement of the need for strategic focus, the average manager rarely leads in ways that contribute to a company's long-term success.

React

(a) Learn to delegate effectively: check carefully exactly what you can pass on to others to diminish distractions to your focus on strategy, and hand it over.

(b) Develop strong, effective teams with the authority to act. You must trust them to make decisions and they must be able to help you to run the business effectively.

(c) Ensure you allocate equal time to tactical concerns and strategic meetings or discussions.

(d) Ensure you have included strategic goals in both your work plans and those of peers or relevant staff.

(e) You must have a well-defined vision for you and your team that has been clearly articulated to all of you. Where are you heading in one or five or 10 years? If you do not consider this question regularly, you will easily revert to the here and now only.

(f) Understand your own time horizon: are you working on projects with a one-year horizon, or five or 10 years? You should also know the time horizon of your supervisor and their boss.

(g) Get a business or strategic plan in place that answers in detail where you are now, where you are going and how you will get there.

(h) Review your strategic position regularly. Use a SWOT plan, which stands for strengths, weaknesses, opportunities and threats. These four components are necessary to assess your or a company's strategic position: you want to exploit strengths, improve weaknesses, capitalize on opportunities and identify threats.

2 | One cannot predict the future/I do not believe that strategic planning is useful

Rethink

Business futurists such as Faith Popcorn and John Naisbett dedicate themselves to the prediction of future trends, and they have been so successful that their books have influenced many people, business leaders included.

Businesses make critical decisions based on projections about the future, however accurate they may be. Whether it is a three-year or 20-year business plan, data is based on forecasting — projected revenues, operating costs, demographics etcetera.

Whatever you do, the future has an impact on your business today. We have enough information available, whether it stems from historical data, experience, surveys or technology, to allow people to work with reasonable assumptions about the future.

If they want to survive, companies must make informed decisions about how to strategically position themselves today, based on predictions about tomorrow. Although it is impossible to predict the future, it is just as difficult for a business to thrive without making informed decisions about the future, and making provision for adjustments along the way. Being unable to exactly define events in the future cannot excuse a lack of strategic thinking or plans.

React

(a) Know the competitive advantage that makes your success sustainable. You must recognize what makes you stand out against your competitors, then create an advantage that remains competitive over time. What do you do best? What makes you unique? What can your organization do better than any other now and in the long term?

(b) Hold futurist sessions regularly and discuss nothing but the future. Brainstorm with your team to identify the major factors that will influence your business in the next five to 10 years. What are the possible scenarios? What will the market look like in five or 10 years?

(c) Review previous business plans and projects' outcomes. Which assumptions about the future were flawed and why? Are you making the same assumptions now? Which data was consulted and was it useful or misleading?

(d) Professional futurists can provide invaluable insight. Look for available seminars or consider contracting a futurist to work with you or your team.

(e) Many books about future trends and their influence are available. Two popular futurists among businesspeople are Faith Popcorn and John Naisbett.

3 | I focus on the here and now/I am practical and not inclined to theorize

Rethink

Every now and then, we all need a metaphorical journey into the future to entertain what our world possibly could look like then. Strategic thinking demands that you be creative too, and even a bit impractical. If your thinking is based only on the way things stand or work now, you limit yourself to today and its parameters.

People who can visualize future scenarios always consider both the here and now, and the future. They are comfortable to speculate and are, in fact, attracted to and energized by propositions that may scare other people, or which generally get dismissed.

Strategic thinkers explore ideas which do not fit and may even defy current views. Your work will definitely benefit if, from time to time, you let yourself imagine the impossible.

React

(a) Allow yourself to follow your hunches and intuition without editing your thoughts or judging yourself harshly.

(b) Find creative people with whom you can share out-of-the-box ideas and feel safe to do so.

(c) Be more playful. Ensure you have activities and people outside work that allow you to laugh and relax.

(d) Do something completely impractical, just because you can. Consider the consequences afterwards. Were they nearly as bad as you expected?

(e) Play devil's advocate with yourself. Challenge yourself with questions such as "Why does it have to be like this?" and "Why not try it their way?"

Rethink

Even specialists who choose to forego an executive or management path must remain strategic in their thinking. Understanding the trends that will have an impact on current technology allows you to remain innovative in your field of expertise.

The head of an engineering department, for example, must think strategically about the impact the retirement of older engineers will have because of difficulties to find young engineers to replace them. Anticipating a shortfall allows the department head to mitigate this risk by supporting mentorship programs, creative recruiting strategies or even the corporate sponsorship of a local university program. Kodak was in the business of selling film, but the advent of digital cameras and the ability to download pictures has rendered this technology all but obsolete. The company had to change.

Regardless of how technical or discipline-specific your responsibilities are, thinking strategically plays an important role in keeping you abreast of trends and provides invaluable perspective.

React

(a) Be aware of what happens in the rest of the world. Read news magazines and articles from other professions too.

(b) Consider how change in the political climate may affect government policy related to your field.

(c) Make use of rotational opportunities that can expose you to other business functions.

(d) Make the time to get away from your desk and talk to people in other departments about their work and possible changes that could affect them.

(e) Attend interdepartmental meetings when possible.

(f) Always look for unusual connections between your job and what people do in other fields.

(g) Take advantage of conferences that will expose you to new trends and peers in your field.

Rethink

For long stretches of time in your career, you may find yourself focusing on tactical work rather than strategic issues. From the individual contributor to the manager-of-managers level, the focus is typically short term and operational.

It can be difficult to make the transition from thinking tactically to working on projects with a long-term focus, say, five to 20 years.

Strategic thinking is vital as you progress up the career ladder to managing functions or businesses. But it is never too soon to begin thinking strategically and show your capability as a strategic thinker, whether the present position requires it or not. You will be making a key investment in your career by working on this competency.

React

(a) Always ask questions: why was a decision made by higher management, what would the future consequence be if you chose a different tactic today, which assumptions are being made about the future that dictate the nature of your work today?

(b) Consider ways to see things from other people's perspective. Imagine you are the customer, your supplier or the competitor.

(c) Ask your supervisor whether you can attend meetings or sit in on strategic planning calls to get exposure to issues discussed and considered.

(d) Ask for the opportunity to participate in cross-functional projects. Strategic initiatives and planning always involve multiple departments or business areas.

(e) Ask the human resources department about courses or training in strategic-planning techniques you could attend.

(f) Read books or business cases that involve strategy.

(g) Keep abreast of trends and new developments that concern your field, government policy, competitors and clients.

Overdeveloped

Research has shown that strengths can become weaknesses because you can, in fact, do too much of a good thing. You cannot become less good at a competency in which you excel, but you can balance the behavior by developing a few Stabilizers to tone down an excessive strength.

Stabilizer	Overdeveloped
40 Market Aware	Is too focused on the future and seems out of touch with current realities
15 Customer-Centric	
17 Demonstrates Good Judgment	
56 Technically Competent	
50 Problem Solver	
19 Determined	
18 Detail-Orientated	
48 Plans Work	
29 Focused on Priorities	
1 Achiever	

Instructions

Read the definition. If it applies to you, choose a few Stabilizers and develop them by selecting the relevant chapter and following the Strategies for Action.

For more instructions see the How To Use This Book section.

54. Takes Accountability

"He that is good for making excuses is seldom good for anything else"

Benjamin Franklin

Well Developed

Accepts accountability for all areas of responsibility, even the unpopular or tough ones

Underdeveloped

Avoids accountability for certain areas of responsibility and makes excuses for non-delivery

Overdeveloped

Accepts too much accountability personally and does not recognize that other factors determine an outcome too

Instructions

Read the definitions on the left. If the Underdeveloped definition applies, go to the Strategies for Action section.

If the Overdeveloped definition applies, go to the end of the chapter.

Test Yourself

True	I do not become defensive or upset when my mistakes are brought to my attention
True	I admit when I have made a mistake, without being asked
True	I do not make excuses for poor performance
True	I provide remedies for my mistakes
True	I share the responsibility when the team has made a mistake
True	I deliver on my promises
True	I readily confront others who skirts accountability
True	I do not blame outside factors for my circumstances or problems

Note

Are you sure you need to develop this competency?

If the answer is "True" to most of the statements on the left, you probably do not need to develop this competency.

Strategies for Action

Most ineffective behaviors have an underlying thought or emotional pattern. By identifying these patterns, you can understand the impact they have and design strategies to counteract them.

① Too many things are beyond my control

② I find it hard to take responsibility for difficult decisions or those that may reflect poorly on me

③ There are few or no consequences for a lack of accountability in my organization

④ I am very forgiving of myself and my mistakes

⑤ Taking responsibility can limit my career or have other negative consequences

Instructions

1. Read and select one or more of the ineffective ways of thinking/feeling to the left.

2. Find the corresponding number below that will help you to rethink this pattern and identify specific and practical actions that you can take.

1 | Too many things are beyond my control

Rethink

When looking for reasons why things did not work out, some people tend to focus on the factors beyond their control. Research shows men are more likely to blame external factors (it is others' fault), while females are more likely to blame internal factors (it is their own fault).

Typical excuses one hears when someone does not want to be held accountable is "I didn't know", "I wasn't there", "I don't have time", "It's not my job", "That's just the way I am", "Nobody told me", "It isn't really hurting anyone" or "I'm just following orders".

Think carefully before looking further than yourself for explanations, because it often means seeking excuses or someone to blame.

React

(a) Be assertive and take control. Ask for what you need to do your job instead of assuming things will happen automatically. The more proactive you are, the less likely you will have reason to blame others. When necessary, confront situations and people in an assertive style that is straightforward and truthful, without being threatening or overly aggressive. Ask for what you need to do your job effectively, such as information, assistance and support. Also, do not be afraid to say no.

(b) Make a list of the external obstacles you might face during the task ahead and plan how to deal with them.

(c) Differentiate between excuses and explanations and ensure you use the latter. An explanation clarifies the situation without blame or justification. Its goal should be to point out ways to improve in the future, nothing more.

(d) Focus your attention on delivering results. Create solutions for the obstacles, not excuses to avoid them. Approach the unexpected hurdles creatively.

(e) Resist pointing fingers when things get difficult. What will really be gained by spending your time and energy on finding someone or something to blame? Rally together, as a team should, and focus again on the solutions to the problem. Create two columns: in one list the ways other people can improve in future so as not to repeat the same mistakes, and in the other column how you can do the same.

(f) Do not focus on the origin of the problem. It does not matter where a problem stems from, or whether you created or inherited it. The crucial question to ask yourself is: "What can I do about it?"

(g) Be aware of the language you use. If you hear yourself making statements such as "Nobody told me", "I'm just following orders" or "The mistake couldn't have been avoided", be sure to question the honesty and validity of these comments.

---

2 | I find it hard to take responsibility for difficult decisions or those that may reflect poorly on me

Rethink

With increasing responsibility comes having to take more difficult decisions that hold greater consequences, which will draw more scrutiny from others.

So, as you progress through your career, ensure you adopt a healthy approach towards defending your actions, taking ownership for bad decisions, and taking action regardless of the consequences. Guard against indecision — the tougher the decision, the more tempting it may be to walk away from the responsibility to avoid the consequences.

As a positive role model for those you supervise, you cannot expect accountability if you do not practice it yourself. Being accountable is key to earning respect, trust and promotion in your career. And remember, no one ever feels comfortable admitting mistakes, especially high achievers.

Regardless of the nature of your mistake, however, its impact will be less profound on others than your inability to take responsibility when appropriate. People tend to be more understanding of poor performance than poor character.

React

(a) If you are overly sensitive to criticism, ask for feedback when you have done an assignment well. It is easier to accept constructive criticism when you are feeling good about your accomplishments. This will prepare you to be more open to feedback when you have not performed as well. Remember that there is always, always room for improvement.

(b) Understand the reason why you are being held accountable. It is not a punishment or admonishment of you as a person. You are being held accountable for improving your skills or because people trusted you. If you recognize your weaknesses, it will create opportunities to learn about process management, problem solving and quality decision making.

(c) A little humility goes a long way. Admit your mistake and assure your boss or co-workers that you will learn from your mistakes. People are more inclined to have sympathy for your situation when you demonstrate genuine humility.

(d) Getting defensive or angry or feeling insecure may be your first reaction, but it will not improve the situation. On the contrary, it could alienate you from others and make it more difficult for you to accept constructive suggestions. Be aware of your emotional reaction and give yourself time to calm down before responding.

(e) Not holding yourself accountable for your mistakes shifts the responsibility to someone else. Consider the impact on your peers or team members if you are dishonest about the part you played.

(f) Do not pass difficult decisions on to others because you do not want to make them. Get input, if needed, to make the best decision, but then make it and proceed.

3 | There are few or no consequences for a lack of accountability in my organization

Rethink

The amount of oversight structures and procedures in organizations differ widely. Some employees have few checks and balances to adhere to, while others' jobs are governed by them. Some environments may even encourage passing the buck, albeit unwittingly.

The true test of accountability is to act responsibly whether there is pressure to do so or not. Accountability means acting in accordance with whatever improves performance and furthers the goals and vision of the company. It means not just doing your job well enough to get by or look good.

As an individual and leader in your organization, you should have the ability to apply a broader definition to accountability and practice it without having to be monitored.

React

(a) Question whether your behavior and output are positively contributing to the organization's objectives. If not, hold yourself accountable for making improvements. For example, examine how much time you spend on personal issues or talking to peers about things unrelated to work.

(b) Examine the procedures and controls in place to ensure accountability. If the organization lacks such measures, establish a taskforce to address the minimum standards that need to be defined, adhered to and monitored.

(c) Establish a culture of accountability within your group by demonstrating humility and admitting your mistakes. Take ownership of poor decisions and, to show you have considered the matter, inform others how you will do things differently next time. Ensure that there are consequences for a lack of accountability, but that these are fair and administered even-handedly.

4 | I am very forgiving of myself and my mistakes

Rethink

Some individuals live by their own rules of accountability. People in position of power, for example, may believe their standards of accountability are different to others'. Excusing your actions because of the position you hold is dangerous. It often leads to abuse of authority in companies and has brought down powerful businessmen. Leaders must be particularly cautious because they are the positive role models for accountability in their organizations. They cannot have lackadaisical attitudes towards accountability or make their own rules. Accountability must be standard across all positions and all levels of responsibility.

React

(a) Once you have come to an agreement with someone, be sure to respect it. It does not matter whether it is something small, such as a document you have promised to peruse, or something major, such as a merger to which you have agreed. Ensure your word can be trusted or people will lose respect for you.

(b) If you are unable to meet promised deadlines, be proactive and let others know in advance. Do not wait for them to ask you what is going on — it is unfair and demoralizing.

(c) Do not make people wait for your response to their requests. It sends the message that their needs are not important to you.

(d) It is reasonable that your plate may be too full. Be realistic about what you can and cannot do. Do not make promises on which you cannot deliver. It is better to be honest upfront about when you will be able to do things.

5 | Taking responsibility can limit my career or have other negative consequences

Rethink

Taking responsibility for a grievous mistake can indeed result in serious consequences, even dismissal. In some cases, individuals are targeted unfairly as "the fall guy" and forced to leave an organization. In such cases, you should not accept blame for actions that were not of your doing. If leaving is your only option, accept that it will be to your benefit to not remain part of such an organization.

Under sound management and leadership, however, the consequences of taking responsibility are usually not as grave as one might imagine. Instead, the fallout from not being accountable causes the trouble and can limit or derail your career in the long run.

Being accountable and taking responsibility for mistakes allow you to identify your areas of weakness and the opportunities for improvement. More importantly, doing so will gain you the trust and respect of your peers and team members, which are not worth risking for anything.

React

(a) When a mistake has occurred, talk to your superior immediately. Be honest about what has happened and express your concern about the potential consequences. You may be relieved to hear that they are not as bad as you thought, and if not, you will at least know where you stand.

(b) Offer solutions or the options available to address or correct the mistake. It shows a willingness to learn and move forward.

(c) If the company's culture is such that mistakes are unforgivable, you may want to consider working elsewhere. It is difficult, if not downright impossible, to develop and learn where there is no room for mistakes.

Overdeveloped

Research has shown that strengths can become weaknesses because you can, in fact, do too much of a good thing. You cannot become less good at a competency in which you excel, but you can balance the behavior by developing a few Stabilizers to tone down an excessive strength.

Stabilizer	Overdeveloped
4 Approachable	Accepts too much accountability personally and does not recognize that other factors determine an outcome too
60 Works Well with Boss	
8 Comfortable with Uncertainty	
15 Customer-Centric	
49 Politically Astute	
25 Empowers People	
59 Unifies People	
51 Recognizes Talent and Potential	
40 Market Aware	
12 Confident	

Instructions

Read the definition. If it applies to you, choose a few Stabilizers and develop them by selecting the relevant chapter and following the Strategies for Action.

For more instructions see the How To Use This Book section.

55. Takes Initiative

> "Without initiative, leaders are simply workers
> in leadership positions"
> Bo Bennet

Well Developed
Takes initiative and demonstrates a
positive can-do attitude

Underdeveloped
Only does what is prescribed and
seems fearful of taking action

Overdeveloped
Is seen as someone with the
necessary energy but lacks direction
or the ability to prioritize. Struggles to
follow instructions

Instructions

Read the definitions on the
left. If the Underdeveloped
definition applies, go to
the Strategies for Action
section.

If the Overdeveloped
definition applies, go to
the end of the chapter.

Test Yourself

True	I am excited about my work
True	If I see things that must be done, I am proactive and get involved
True	I am proactive about taking assignments that will increase my skills and broaden my experiences
True	I do not wait to be told what work to do
True	I take initiative even if the decision is risky

Note

**Are you sure you need to
develop this competency?**

If the answer is "True" to
most of the statements on
the left, you probably do
not need to develop this
competency.

Takes Initiative

55

Strategies for Action

Most ineffective behaviors have an underlying thought or emotional pattern. By identifying these patterns, you can understand the impact they have and design strategies to counteract them.

① I am not confident that I can get the job done/ I am not the right person for the task

② I do not like to take initiative when it involves too much risk

③ I am not enthusiastic about work/I lack energy

④ I do not feel that initiative is recognized or encouraged

⑤ I will only take the initiative if I am rewarded

⑥ I am not the decision maker/I wait to be told what to do

⑦ I am unaware of or untrained in available resources

Instructions

1. Read and select one or more of the ineffective ways of thinking/feeling to the left.

2. Find the corresponding number below that will help you to rethink this pattern and identify specific and practical actions that you can take.

---

1 | I am not confident that I can get the job done/I am not the right person for the task

Rethink

Many people refrain from taking initiative because they lack self-confidence or do not trust their abilities. If you believe extensive experience or complex technical knowledge should back each initiative you ever take, you are greatly limiting the number of assignments in which you will ever be involved. What is more, taking the initiative exactly because you are not an expert is a great strategy for development. Organizations value people who are willing to learn, and able to adapt to new demands, regardless of their previous experience.

Taking initiative will give you the opportunity to work with new people and develop different skills, and it will certainly benefit your performance evaluation — all worth the effort.

People who are comfortable to take initiative, who allow their strengths and weaknesses to be tested, become key contributors to their teams and organizations.

React

(a) Are you assuming you lack the necessary skills before you really know what an assignment entails? If you lack confidence in your skills, you are likely to make quick judgments not necessarily based on facts. Talk to relevant people about what is really needed. Ensure your expectations of yourself compare with those your superior has of you. If you are usually hard on yourself, you are probably overestimating what you need to know to get going.

(b) If your skills set is insufficient for the task at hand, take initiative by recruiting someone else to work with you. You can learn from this person and contribute your strengths at the same time. Use a suitable, knowledgeable peer as a sounding board for ideas.

(c) Volunteer to do assignments that will challenge and extend your abilities. List the things you are least comfortable doing. Resolve to do at least one task or assignment every month that will help you to develop a weak area.

(d) Formulate an individual development plan with your supervisor or coach to address areas in which you particularly lack confidence. Why wait to address a weakness when you can have an ongoing development strategy designed to improve it?

(e) Remind yourself of other times when you were apprehensive about tackling a challenge. What was the result? Did your level of skill derail the project?

(f) If you do not know where to begin, take the initiative by being resourceful. Find out who can help with particular tasks; investigate the work that was done in similar projects and the reference material available to get you up to speed. Instead of spinning your wheels anxiously, start asking the right questions.

2 | I do not like to take initiative when it involves too much risk

Rethink

Different individuals can tolerate different degrees of risk, real or perceived. The lower their tolerance, the less likely they are to show initiative. Risk-tolerant people will regard a certain decision as an opportunity, but those averse to risk will regard the same decision with trepidation. Neither party has better facts to back their perceptions; they simply view the world through different lenses. People's experience of life and work is ruled by their habitual, predominant thoughts. Be prepared to regard risk as an opportunity and take initiative if you want to progress in your organization.

React

(a) Weigh the likelihood of the situation or decision's complete failure, and the degree of damage should the worst-case scenario materialize. Reality tends to be less severe than perception. Talk to a trusted peer or mentor who can be a sounding board for your concerns. They can help to provide perspective. Do they think the situation is as risky as you do?

(b) Become comfortable making decisions without complete data. Practice trusting your intuition. In his book *Blink*, Malcom Gladwell champions the power of using intuition in decision making. Start with small decisions and progress to ones with bigger consequences.

(c) Get used to making decisions regardless of conventional wisdom or the level of support they enjoy. Taking initiative will sometimes mean paving a new way all on your own.

(d) Pair with someone who is more risk-tolerant and can help you to take initiative in projects beyond your comfort zone.

(e) Identify beforehand the risks associated with your work, business, project etcetera. Having a plan to manage risk, should it become an issue, will give you a greater sense of control.

369

(f) Do reflection after projects, on your own and with your team. Review your incorrect assumptions. What worried you the most? What was the consequence of having done those things or neglecting to do them? What could you do differently next time? Were your worries justified?

3 | I am not enthusiastic about work/I lack energy

Rethink

The more responsibility, the more energy is needed to stay on top of things. Getting through any given work week involves long hours, putting out many fires and facing constant deadlines. Even less hectic environments can be taxing. If this sounds familiar, you understand the importance of finding the energy and enthusiasm to stay engaged in your work despite the daily pressures.

If your attitude towards work is that everything is a problem or a big effort, you are less likely to be willing to take the initiative beyond what is necessary to get the job done.

People with high energy levels show enthusiasm towards all aspects of their jobs and tend to gain energy by taking initiative. Successful leaders not only bring energy to the task at hand, but create the conditions for others to become enthusiastic about taking initiative regardless how daunting the task.

React

(a) Fake it until you believe it. Talk about the assignment or task as if you were truly excited. Identify all the positive results to be gained from taking action. Roll up your sleeves and do it. The reward for hard work is just an initiative away.

(b) Regular exercise helps to relieve stress, builds physical and mental stamina and raises energy levels. Include exercise as one of your tools for creating more energy in your life and work.

(c) Be sure to balance your life with things that bring you happiness. If you are not getting recharged outside of work, your energy will be sapped and your performance will lack luster.

(d) Help others to become excited even if you are not. Try not to sound bored or complain in the workplace. Encourage optimistic discussions about the future. Ask people to share their vision and hopes for their own or the organization's future. Make it a ritual part of your meetings. Ensure you are not hampering others' progress by not, for example, getting work done on which they had counted.

(e) Observe how others do it. Identify people who are energizing and who create excitement about work. Spend time with them and tap into their energy.

(f) If you were once energetic but have lost your enthusiasm, examine what has changed about your situation. Is it work or something bigger? Talk to a mentor or coach who can help you to examine the factors that have led to your frame of mind, and the changes you could make.

(g) Would you feel more energetic if you had different responsibilities? Explore whether your position is suitable and, if not, which one would be. Consider new assignments that will begin a new chapter in your career and help you to tap into new energy.

(h) If your energy level is chronically low and you find it difficult to take initiative in anything, including personal issues, consider consulting a professional counselor or seeking medical advice.

4 | I do not feel that initiative is recognized or encouraged

Rethink

Organizations' cultures will vary in the level of initiative actively encouraged in their employees. You may find yourself in one that discourages crafting your own direction; perhaps it is authoritarian, even. But unless you are strictly prohibited from taking initiative, it is to your advantage to be proactive. It is the best way to develop your skills and prove your abilities.

Do not lose your resolve when others do not delegate properly to you or cannot see the opportunity you do. Someone in the organization is likely to eventually take notice of your initiative. And if they do not, at least you will have gained additional experience and skills for the next job opportunity.

React

(a) Do not wait to be told what to do or a crisis to force an issue. Look for tasks that remain incomplete or projects that could benefit from your participation.

(b) Talk to your supervisor about their expectations. They may feel threatened, or perhaps they are unaware that they discourage you from taking initiative. Try to uncover the reasons instead of making assumptions. You may be unfocused and they may need you to act proactively in other areas. Give them examples of concrete issues instead of generalizations.

(c) Share the credit with others when you can so that no one feels threatened by you taking initiative on your own.

(d) If you feel completely unable to take initiative in your position, consider a reassignment where your efforts will be recognized.

5 | I will only take the initiative if I am rewarded

Rethink

You may be hesitant to take charge if you cannot see a guaranteed or direct reward for your efforts. Every day in the workplace we are faced with the choice to make a difference, and when we stand at that crossroad an instant reward may not be obvious.

But remain aware of the long-term reward of your actions. Invaluable experience and self-confidence can be gained from choosing to take on challenges.

Each time you choose to take initiative, you stand to gain confidence — of your peers, the organization and, most importantly, in yourself.

React

(a) Do not assume you will not be successful. If you lack resources, talk to the relevant people about making them available. If you are convincing enough, you will get the support you need.

(b) If you cannot do it on your own, mobilize others to take interest and share the project with you.

(c) Look for inspiration from within rather than outside. Others may not be motivated to provide direction, so be the one who stands out. The issue may not be a priority for others, but you can see the impact it will have, so remain determined and resilient.

(d) Make a case for the benefits of pursuing the course of action you are suggesting. Your efforts may not receive the appreciation you wanted, but at least you did your best. Perhaps your plan of action will be implemented when the timing is better.

6 | I am not the decision maker/I wait to be told what to do

Rethink

Organizations depend on people who are willing and able to take charge of situations. Waiting for directives from your supervisor all the time will encourage micro-management and will hamper opportunities to make an impact and demonstrate your value.

Your successes will earn you authority and prove you have the skills to be a leader. Think of being commanding as an opportunity to solve the organization's problems and achieve its goals, not just your own.

React

(a) Do not assume you cannot make certain decisions. Find out what your level of authority is and within which parameters you need to work.

(b) Be proactive. If you have ideas about addressing a problem, consult the relevant people and explain how you propose to do it.

(c) Take charge of the situation first then stop at checkpoints along the way to ensure you are moving in the right direction.

7 | I am unaware of or untrained in available resources

Rethink

It is not uncommon for employees to overlook the resources available to accomplish their goals quickly and complete what may seem like improbable tasks. Be resourceful and take the initiative to find these resource opportunities, even with minimal guidance.

React

(a) Spend time familiarizing yourself with the types of tools on which you can rely to do your job. Most organizations have made sizeable investments in resources such as software, trade journals and reference material. Set aside some time after work or during weekends, if necessary, to peruse your reference material.

(b) Ask peers and colleagues what they used to accomplish similar jobs. Conversations like these expose you to resources that may be available but of which you were unaware or never thought to utilize.

(c) If you do not have the resources you need at your disposal, cast the net wider. Look beyond your group or division or even your company to find the necessary ones.

(d) Enquire about training available from your human resources department and schedule time to attend it.

(e) Suggest informal gatherings, at lunch perhaps, where you and colleagues can share your know-how and train others informally.

(f) Immediately tell colleagues if you cannot take advantage of a resource or even use it. There is no shame in not knowing, but shame on you for not asking!

Overdeveloped

Research has shown that strengths can become weaknesses because you can, in fact, do too much of a good thing. You cannot become less good at a competency in which you excel, but you can balance the behavior by developing a few Stabilizers to tone down an excessive strength.

Stabilizer	Overdeveloped
32 Informs Others	Is seen as someone with the necessary energy but lacks direction or the ability to prioritize. Struggles to follow instructions
34 Listens Well	
18 Detail-Orientated	
47 Patient	
19 Determined	
48 Plans Work	
29 Focused on Priorities	
50 Problem Solver	
60 Works Well with Boss	
53 Strategic	

Instructions

Read the definition. If it applies to you, choose a few Stabilizers and develop them by selecting the relevant chapter and following the Strategies for Action.

For more instructions see the How To Use This Book section.

56. Technically Competent

Moderate

Easy

Difficulty to
LEARN

Difficulty to
CHANGE

"Ah, mastery ... what a profoundly satisfying feeling when one finally gets on top of a new set of skills ... and then sees the light under the new door those skills can open, even as another door is closing"

Gail Sheehy

Well Developed
Has the functional and technical knowledge and skills to get the job done

Underdeveloped
Lacks critical functional and technical knowledge and skills to do the work

Overdeveloped
Is too reliant on technical skills and does not think it necessary to develop other people and personal or process competencies

Instructions

Read the definitions on the left. If the Underdeveloped definition applies, go to the Strategies for Action section.

If the Overdeveloped definition applies, go to the end of the chapter.

Test Yourself

True	I have the functional knowledge required to do my job
True	I have the necessary technical skills to do my job
True	I upgrade my skills if and when necessary
True	I routinely utilize relevant training and coaching opportunities
True	I read widely about topics related to my work to increase my knowledge
True	I have a mentor or coach who guides my continual learning and improvement of my expertise

Note

Are you sure you need to develop this competency?

If the answer is "True" to most of the statements on the left, you probably do not need to develop this competency.

375

Strategies for Action

Most ineffective behaviors have an underlying thought or emotional pattern. By identifying these patterns, you can understand the impact they have and design strategies to counteract them.

① My technical skills are too limited/I may need to broaden my knowledge base

② I have not had enough time to develop proficiency in technical skills

③ I am not too interested in becoming a technical expert

④ I get by with strong interpersonal skills/ Technical skills are not that important

⑤ My environment is restrictive and unappreciative of technical skills

Instructions

1. Read and select one or more of the ineffective ways of thinking/feeling to the left.

2. Find the corresponding number below that will help you to rethink this pattern and identify specific and practical actions that you can take.

1 | My technical skills are too limited/I may need to broaden my knowledge base

Rethink

You may already possess some technical skills but have not capitalized on opportunities to enhance and improve them. Do not stop short of your potential. You may not have had the chance, financial resources or time to further your education, but it is never too late to increase your technical knowledge.

Improving your technical skills may be a huge investment you have to make, but the results will be noticed by your colleagues, managers and clients. It will position you to solve increasingly complex technical problems. You will also add value by resolving problems quickly, saving time, and you will not have to ask others to do the job for you.

React

(a) Decide in which field you would like to become a technical expert. Make your choice based on market demand for specific skills, current or future job requirements, your personal strengths and weaknesses and so forth.

(b) Become educated, be it formally or informally. If you can afford the time or money to go to college, do so.

(c) Undertake as much training as you can. It will improve your CV as well as your skills, knowledge and expertise. Pay attention to online classes, distance learning and other training opportunities available through your organization or elsewhere.

(d) One of the most affordable ways to improve your technical skills is by reading books. Visit book sites such as www.amazon.com, search for a book on the topic you wish to learn and check the reviews and ratings.

(e) Read online tutorials. They are accessible, up to date and free. They usually offer additional references, user comments and interactive demonstrations.

(f) Subscribe to printed or online technical magazines.

2 | I have not had enough time to develop proficiency in technical skills

Rethink

It takes time to develop functional or technical skills and the learning curve can be painfully slow, especially when you need the knowledge today. Your career could demand that you get reassigned or rotated numerous times through various business arenas, types of markets, departments and even contexts, such as international versus local postings. At each juncture you will probably have to enhance certain skills. You will eventually gain the necessary expertise through experience, but you can speed up the process by taking certain proactive steps. Be patient with yourself and develop a support system to help you succeed.

React

(a) Identify training and courses available through your organization that can help you to gain knowledge in specific areas.

(b) Ask your supervisor and colleagues to recommend literature to help you get up to speed.

(c) Find a coach or mentor experienced in your field of specialization and follow their instructions. Being mentored or coached is critical to becoming a technical expert, because there are numerous nuances and details specific to different careers that you cannot learn in a classroom.

(d) Spend time in the company of technical gurus. If you observe and engage with them, some of their knowledge is bound to rub off on you.

(e) Tackle your assignments — in the end, hands-on training will give you expertise that textbooks cannot teach you.

3 | I am not too interested in becoming a technical expert

Rethink

Even at basic levels in an organization, it is imperative to have the necessary technical skills required to perform your job. Even if you lack the interest to become an expert, being technically and functionally accomplished puts you in a position to better manage others, understand problems and provide solutions.

Few make it to the top of an organization without in-depth knowledge of how business works. They may not be functional experts in every area of the business, but they have enough technical knowledge in key ones to know the business inside out.

Building technical skills should be an ongoing, never-ending process in anyone's career. Skills must be continuously upgraded and you have to stay on top of changes and developments in your functional or technical field.

React

(a) Discuss your career ambitions and development options with your supervisor, and show your willingness to learn new skills to maximize your performance.

(b) Identify the functional or technical knowledge you need to manage others. Prioritize to gain better knowledge in these areas.

(c) Exploit your experiences to give you technical learning opportunities. Always seek assignments that could develop some of the technical skills you need.

(d) If you enjoy learning in groups, look for college extension courses and other classroom, workshop or lecture offerings in your area. The opportunity to interact with people from varied backgrounds is a key advantage of classroom learning.

---

4 | **I get by with strong interpersonal skills/ Technical skills are not that important**

Rethink

In recent years, much emphasis has been placed on emotional intelligence and the so-called soft skills, such as interpersonal skill, in the workplace. It has somewhat overshadowed the need for relevant, updated technical — hard — skills.

Competence in both behavioral skills and technical expertise is critical for an effective manager and leader. In fact, among a handful of competencies that are the most likely to disrupt or limit careers you will find poor functional or technical skills.

Fortunately, the development of technical skills is within many organizations' reach and they typically have resources available for either formal training or exposure through assignments. The key is to recognize that interpersonal skills are not sufficient to conduct business. People need to trust and be confident that you understand the subject technically and functionally, too.

React

(a) Identify the operational and technical knowledge you need to gain to conduct your business properly. Prioritize to gain knowledge in the areas that will have the greatest impact on your ability to perform business now.

(b) With the help of a coach or manager, formulate a development plan with specific actions aimed at increasing your functional knowledge and requisite experience.

(c) Improve your business acumen by subscribing to relevant publications in your field. Use them to stay abreast of trends and increase your general knowledge.

(d) Exploit your social nature — attend conferences and association meetings to provide new insights and perspectives.

(e) Ask peers to share literature or articles they come across which they find insightful.

(f) Consider your motivation, in other words, how driven you are to grow in challenging areas and achieve goals.

5 | My environment is restrictive and unappreciative of technical skills

Rethink

Regardless of what your environment rewards or encourages, experts must be willing to present, sell, educate or market their credentials to others, including the public. There are several ways to promote your expertise, depending on your budget, personality and profession.

React

(a) Use blogs, newsletters, books, e-books, magazines, articles, whatever resources to present yourself to the world.

(b) Register as a speaker or presenter at conferences or association meetings.

(c) If your schedule permits, consider a part-time teaching assignment at a local college or university.

(d) Volunteer to mentor or train others in your organization to establish yourself as an expert internally.

Overdeveloped

Research has shown that strengths can become weaknesses because you can, in fact, do too much of a good thing. You cannot become less good at a competency in which you excel, but you can balance the behavior by developing a few Stabilizers to tone down an excessive strength.

Stabilizer	Overdeveloped
14 Creative	Is too reliant on technical skills and does not think it necessary to develop other people and personal or process competencies
36 Manages Ideas	
20 Develops People	
31 Improves Processes	
2 Adaptable	
30 Global Thinker	
59 Unifies People	
7 Collaborative	
52 Self-Aware	
53 Strategic	

Instructions

Read the definition. If it applies to you, choose a few Stabilizers and develop them by selecting the relevant chapter and following the Strategies for Action.

For more instructions see the How To Use This Book section.

57. Technology Savvy

"Technology, like art, is a soaring exercise of the human imagination"
Daniel Bell

Well Developed
Quickly realizes the impact new technology can have and finds opportunities to integrate it into the business to create competitive advantage

Underdeveloped
Appears intimidated by technology and struggles to understand how to make effective use of it

Overdeveloped
Places too much importance on technology to solve problems. Is easily distracted by new but marginal developments

Instructions
Read the definitions on the left. If the Underdeveloped definition applies, go to the Strategies for Action section.

If the Overdeveloped definition applies, go to the end of the chapter.

Test Yourself

True	I understand the importance of technology in every business
True	I find ways to integrate technology with existing processes
True	I keep abreast of new technologies that could benefit my business
True	I think technology does not replace the human element of a business but rather complements it
True	I see technology as a way to improve productivity

Note

Are you sure you need to develop this competency?

If the answer is "True" to most of the statements on the left, you probably do not need to develop this competency.

Strategies for Action

Most ineffective behavior has an underlying thought or emotional pattern. By identifying these patterns, you can understand the impact they have and design strategies to counteract them.

① I find technology intimidating or too complicated to use

② The organization is not prone to using new technology

③ Introducing technology causes more problems than it solves

④ Technology is for IT people/I prefer the good old days

⑤ So far, I have not had to use technology extensively to be successful at work/ Technology is not that important in my job

Instructions

1. Read and select one or more of the ineffective ways of thinking/feeling to the left.

2. Find the corresponding number below that will help you to rethink this pattern and identify specific and practical actions that you can take.

① I find technology intimidating or too complicated to use

Rethink

It is normal to resist or fear that which we do not understand. Psychological studies have shown that we tend to fear what we cannot control. This often includes technology, even though automated processes are designed to work more reliably and safely than humans. Aircraft accidents, for example, are caused predominantly by human error and not technological failure.

There is so much technology in the market that it can make one feel at a loss just sifting through what is available. But before giving up or making a judgment about whether to adopt new technologies, ensure that your resistance is well founded and not based on fear or a lack of understanding.

React

(a) Before adopting new technology, do in-depth research about the tool. Ask someone who has tested it and applies it successfully. It will help you to gain confidence about its benefits.

(b) Ask colleagues who are technologically savvy about their experience with a technology and its pros and cons.

(c) Keep gaining knowledge and confidence in technological areas and build on it. Small victories help you to gain the necessary confidence and, as you do, your fear is reduced and eventually it disappears.

(d) Do not become overwhelmed by all the features available. Technology such as web surfing tends to open up many tangential possibilities. Focus on the aspects that will help you to accomplish what you want. It is the best way to make learning pragmatic and uncomplicated.

(e) Ask someone who knows the technology well to demonstrate how it is used. Use resources in the IT department if available.

(f) Divide information about the technology into small pieces — an important concept in learning anything new. For example, it is impossible to learn a new language all at once, but if you learn progressively, word by word and phrase by phrase, you will gradually gain a complete understanding of the language. Technology is the same. Think about technology as just another subject to master.

(g) Set a goal to become skilled in using one or two small technological items, for example, an electronic organizer, a new cellphone or scheduling software. Learn how to use a new feature each week.

2 | The organization is not prone to using new technology

Rethink

Introducing new technology in an organization which does not prioritize it is always challenging. New technologies, be they small or large, can alter existing work patterns, social relationships and even jobs, especially when people are replaced with new technology aimed at increasing efficiencies in the company operations.

People who fear a loss of some kind will resist technological changes. This may lead to unnecessary stumbling blocks or even failure to implement new technology.

Regardless of how effective or well designed the technology solution, it can fail if change management issues are not carefully considered. Be prepared for some short-term upheaval before successful change is implemented. It may take a while before new technology visibly yields greater productivity, or employee satisfaction with the changes is reached.

React

(a) Assess the impact of the technological change on employees. The checklist must consider which positions are likely to benefit, who would be disadvantaged in the change, what compensation there will be for them and whether there is a budget for such compensation.

(b) You will have to develop a strategy to communicate change to your employees. It should include how the technology will work, why it is being adopted and how training and support will be provided.

(c) Identify the people who will play critical roles if the technological change is accepted. Ensure you involve them in the change process.

(d) Be patient. Remember, people adapt to technology at a different pace and anxiety among employees will cause resistance to its acceptance and productive use.

(e) Compensate those employees who have been disadvantaged fairly. Promoters of technological change often argue that everyone is a winner with the implementation of new technology. But losses, ranging from work demotion to termination, do occur. Pay attention to the emotional and financial needs of those who lose their jobs or whose status drops due to technological change. It is a critical investment in the organization and sends the right message to other employees.

3 | Introducing technology causes more problems than it solves

Rethink

Technological innovations are unlikely to succeed if they are not fully supported and integrated with existing business processes. It is not uncommon in organizations for large sums of money to be invested in the latest technology without sufficient consideration being given to how it affects existing technology, systems and processes, and vice versa. This is where many of the headaches originate.

Many technological innovations have been shelved by the same employees they where intended to help because of a lack of user support or integration with the rest of the business.

Protect your investment in technology by ensuring it does not duplicate existing technology and is well supported by the organizational structure, and that you have considered how to build capacity among its users.

React

(a) Ensure you have the appropriate advocates to champion the technology and create acceptance before its roll-out. Executive-level managers are the most effective sponsors.

(b) Develop a clear communication strategy. It should include how the technology will work, why it is being adopted and how training and support will be provided. Determine whether the communication should be formal, such as a CEO announcement, or informal, such as discussion in management meetings. Consider branding options that tie the company's identity to the technology.

(c) Budget for and invest the appropriate resources in quality training. Building capacity among users is critical to the technology's successful application. Also consider periodical refresher courses and training.

(d) Carefully investigate software providers that can help you to draw a variety of applications into a cohesive unit, thereby helping you to align systems and processes more closely.

(e) If you need to grow your business, you may have to consider an application — SAP — which allows real-time access to data, business processes and suppliers.

4 | Technology is for IT people/I prefer the good old days

Rethink

You may find it difficult to see how the world of technology connects with yours. For some people, technology is almost unnatural and they regard it warily and with distrust — it is a threat to old-fashioned values and the simple life. Such people hate those IT types who tinker with technology and blame them for all the unnecessary changes. But technology is no different to music, philosophy or any other product of the human intellect. It has positive and negative effects on people, and it is not going to go away either. So, it makes sense to accept technology as a natural part of modern human activity and a valuable extension of our capacity.

Although your day-to-day work may not involve technology in the way it does for someone in the IT department, your life has invariably been touched by modern technology. It is important that you recognize this. It will make you more curious about technological changes, which will help to improve your attitude towards gaining technological savvy.

React

(a) Consider the positive changes you have experienced in your life that were brought about by technological advances. We are surrounded by examples of how technology has benefited mankind: thermostatically controlled heating and cooling, telephone answering machines, automated assembly lines, knowledge of the universe, medical advancements and many more.

(b) Reflect on the positive outcomes you experience from the use of technology, such as time saved, new business opportunities created, the ability to stay in contact with friends and family.

(c) Make a list of the technologies you appreciate most and without which you could not live. We complain about technology when it does not work, but your lifestyle would be highly disrupted without it. Would you really want to return to no cellphones or e-mail, no automation, poor medical advances etcetera?

(d) If you cannot shake your adverse attitude to technology and your position demands that you do, consider whether you should get another job.

5 | So far, I have not had to use technology extensively to be successful at work/Technology is not that important in my job

Rethink

Even if you have been successful so far with limited or no use of technology, your productivity and the quality of your output could be greatly improved by becoming technologically savvy.

Technology exists to reduce inefficiencies, so why not explore the possibility of working smarter? Once the benefits of new technology are better understood, you will be able to implement technological changes more easily and at a greater success rate. Be aware, too, that younger entrants into the workforce are increasingly skilled in the use of technology. Your ability as a manager to relate to new talent will be greatly improved if you are technologically savvy as well.

React

a) Make a list of how the organization would benefit if all employees were capable of utilizing existing technology to its full extent.

(b) List how your lack of support for technological change would benefit you. Then imagine that you did make the change and it is now five years later. Which benefits do you personally stand to gain from the new technology?

(c) If you cannot find the obvious value that will be added by new technology, do the necessary research to obtain clear information on the returns on investment you can expect.

(d) Try to automate one process and become familiar with that tool. Once the benefits are clear and you are more comfortable with the technology, explore its other available features in which you can perhaps invest further.

Overdeveloped

Research has shown that strengths can become weaknesses because you can, in fact, do too much of a good thing. You cannot become less good at a competency in which you excel, but you can balance the behavior by developing a few Stabilizers to tone down an excessive strength.

Stabilizer	Overdeveloped
17 Demonstrates Good Judgment	Places too much importance on technology to solve problems. Is easily distracted by new but marginal developments
29 Focused on Priorities	
40 Market Aware	
15 Customer-Centric	
36 Manages Ideas	
48 Plans Work	
31 Improves Processes	
50 Problem Solver	
30 Global Thinker	
1 Achiever	

Instructions

Read the definition. If it applies to you, choose a few Stabilizers and develop them by selecting the relevant chapter and following the Strategies for Action.

For more instructions see the How To Use This Book section.

58. Trustworthy

"Few delights can equal the mere presence of
one whom we trust utterly"

George MacDonald

Well Developed
Is trusted by others and can be relied
on to keep promises and protect
confidential information

Underdeveloped
Is not trusted by others

Overdeveloped
Goes too far in order to keep a
promise. Protects confidential
information, even when it may have a
negative impact on others

Instructions

Read the definitions on the
left. If the Underdeveloped
definition applies, go to
the Strategies for Action
section.

If the Overdeveloped
definition applies, go to
the end of the chapter.

Test Yourself

True	People are comfortable sharing information with me
True	I can be counted on to do what I committed to do
True	I am honest with people about my intentions
True	I am consistent in how I act towards different people
True	I am quick to admit when things are my fault

Note

**Are you sure you need to
develop this competency?**

If the answer is "True" to
most of the statements on
the left, you probably do
not need to develop this
competency.

Strategies for Action

Most ineffective behaviors have an underlying thought or emotional pattern. By identifying these patterns, you can understand the impact they have and design strategies to counteract them.

1. My own interests always come first

2. I sometimes share things that should be kept to myself

3. I tend to tell people what they want to hear

4. I overreach in my commitments/I often cannot deliver on my promises

5. I tend to misrepresent myself or my contribution

Instructions

1. Read and select one or more of the ineffective ways of thinking/feeling to the left.

2. Find the corresponding number below that will help you to rethink this pattern and identify specific and practical actions that you can take.

1 | My own interests always come first

Rethink

Sustainable relationships are built on mutual interests being satisfied. Focusing solely on your own interests may seem preferable in the short term, but people will become reluctant to do business with you if, in the end, their needs are not met. Working towards mutually beneficial outcomes builds trust and will serve you in the long term.

React

(a) Write down reasons why the other party's interests should be considered. Are your actions worth the short-term benefits? What are the long-term benefits of a mutually beneficial approach?

(b) Consider creative ways to achieve the same result through fairer means.

(c) Ask yourself if you would do the same to someone about whom you personally care. The same standards should apply to a professional setting.

(d) Are your actions in the best interest of the organization?

(e) Which negative political ramifications might your actions have?

2 | I sometimes share things that should be kept to myself

Rethink

Abusing information can be highly damaging in the workplace. It is a privilege to be considered worthy of confidential information, whether the information is of consequence or not. Respect the fact that someone is willing to trust you. Negative personal opinions about others must also be considered confidential.

Talking behind someone's back encourages unproductive chatter and draws unnecessary participants into matters best handled professionally between you and the other party.

React

(a) If you have a problem with someone, resolve it by talking directly to that person.

(b) Do not try to qualify the information you have received. It is not up to you to decide whether it really must be kept confidential. If you have been asked to keep it confidential, do it.

(c) Resist the temptation to share confidential information as a way to bond with others. You would only lose because you would be compromising your relationship with the one who trusted you. Try to bond with others over positive things you have in common, such as hobbies and work experiences.

3 | I tend to tell people what they want to hear

Rethink

You may be overly sensitive to confrontation or prefer to remain in others' good books. Always telling people what they want to hear is misleading and can cause greater harm in the long run.

People will respect you more for being upfront, saying what you think and taking responsibility, if necessary. If you are concerned about sparing someone difficult news, remember that the news will have to be delivered at some point — if not by you then someone else.

People will appreciate that you take the responsibility and care enough to be honest.

React

(a) Instead of assuming what people may want to hear, focus on what they really need to hear. Use this as a guide when deciding which information you want to withhold.

(b) Honesty is well served with a dose of diplomacy. In the workplace, it is important to be able to manage sensitive discussions, especially because parties often have much at stake. Groom your diplomacy skills to become more successful at communicating difficult information.

(c) Are you less likely to be scrupulous with certain people? For example, are you hesitant to be completely honest with your superior, a particular client or a close peer? Identifying these people will provide clues to your motives. Ask a coach to help you improve your sincerity and openness with these individuals.

4 | I overreach in my commitments/I often cannot deliver on my promises

Rethink

Knowing that you can be counted on to deliver on your commitments is fundamental to building trust among your team and peers. Not only is your performance at stake, but when you cannot deliver on promises, you also have a negative impact on others' performance. Adjustments will have to be made to bridge the gaps in your performance. If people lose trust in your judgment, you will soon see fewer opportunities come your way.

Remember, good intentions cannot excuse your failure to fulfill obligations.

React

(a) Be realistic and honest about what you can get done or to how much you can commit. Explain your situation or commitments to those involved and give them other options if you do not want to make a delivery promise. Perhaps you can make a smaller commitment on which you can deliver that will serve as your contribution.

(b) Be organized and know your workload. Sometimes people commit to too much because they are ignorant of their true workload. Keep an accurate calendar with timelines for other projects due and review it carefully before you commit. Share your calendar with others to raise awareness of your workload and justify why you cannot commit at this point.

(c) Commit yourself, but on the condition that obstacles in your way are removed. For example, perhaps another project can be moved or a co-worker can be assigned to help.

(d) Learn to say no. It really is okay to do so. As long as you can motivate it, you have the right to say no.

(e) Ensure that you fully understand the scope of a project and the resources available before you commit to a deadline.

5 | I tend to misrepresent myself or my contribution

Rethink

Some degree of self-promotion is important in the workplace. Without promotion, the full extent of a person's contribution may go unnoticed.
However, honest self-promotion does not include taking credit for other people's work. This kind of behavior may go unchecked at first, but eventually it creates resentment and mistrust.

Your real achievements could be discounted if people have lost trust in you.

React

(a) Promote your contribution only if you were involved in the majority of the work.

(b) If you were only tangentially involved, praise others' accomplishments without including yourself in the accolades.

(c) Admit your mistakes. You will be perceived as honest and open to improvement.

(d) When taking credit for work done, be sure to include the efforts of your team and everyone involved. Few projects' success is based on one person's contribution.

(e) Is your information based on fact and truth, or your interpretation of the truth? Be careful when walking that fine line. Are you able to back your statements with evidence?

Overdeveloped

Research has shown that strengths can become weaknesses because you can, in fact, do too much of a good thing. You cannot become less good at a competency in which you excel, but you can balance the behavior by developing a few Stabilizers to tone down an excessive strength.

Stabilizer	Overdeveloped
8 Comfortable with Uncertainty	Goes too far in order to keep a promise. Protects confidential information, even when it may have a negative impact on others
2 Adaptable	
13 Courageous	
35 Manages Conflict	
28 Fair	
17 Demonstrates Good Judgment	
32 Informs Others	
46 Open-Minded	
30 Global Thinker	
49 Politically Astute	

Instructions

Read the definition. If it applies to you, choose a few Stabilizers and develop them by selecting the relevant chapter and following the Strategies for Action.

For more instructions see the How To Use This Book section.

59. Unifies People

"One man may hit the mark, another blunder, but heed not these distinctions. Only from the alliance of the one, working with and through the others, are great things born"

Antoine de Saint-Exupery

Well Developed
Recognizes the value of teamwork and can pull people together for a common purpose

Underdeveloped
Prefers working alone and struggles to bring people together and create a cohesive team to achieve a common goal

Overdeveloped
Is too team-oriented and does not recognize individual effort and contribution. Tries to unify groups that are not naturally teams

Instructions

Read the definitions on the left. If the Underdeveloped definition applies, go to the Strategies for Action section.

If the Overdeveloped definition applies, go to the end of the chapter.

Test Yourself

True	I routinely assign projects to teams, not just individuals
True	I clearly define the team's goals and inspire a sense of common purpose
True	I have a good understanding of team members' different work styles
True	I look for a balance of skills in my team
True	I clearly define the contribution that each team member will make
True	I regularly gather the team together to discuss progress
True	I confront individuals who are being disruptive to the team
True	I reward the team effort, not just individuals

Note

Are you sure you need to develop this competency?

If the answer is "True" to most of the statements on the left, you probably do not need to develop this competency.

Strategies for Action

Most ineffective behaviors have an underlying thought or emotional pattern. By identifying these patterns, you can understand the impact they have and design strategies to counteract them.

① I think people become more accomplished by working on their own

② I do not spend time on promoting the team's strategy or purpose

③ I assume people can or will work well together

④ I have not had the opportunity to manage a team/I only have to manage myself

Instructions

1. Read and select one or more of the ineffective ways of thinking/feeling to the left.

2. Find the corresponding number below that will help you to rethink this pattern and identify specific and practical actions that you can take.

---

1 | I think people become more accomplished by working on their own

Rethink

Many tasks have to be completed by individuals, but most initiatives can benefit, in one way or another, from a team approach.

Working in teams pools talent and resources and produces more innovative solutions. It is ideal for dealing with complex systems or products. For many people, working in teams is a great motivator and creates a sense of camaraderie and belonging.

A variety of factors makes a team successful, including the level of trust, the team's ability to take initiative and their skills set. Many of the practices used to manage individuals also apply to teams. In both cases goals must be set, direction provided and processes monitored. The team leader's role is arguably the most critical to the success of the collaboration.

React

(a) Establish a culture that values team participation. Share team accomplishments with both your subordinates and higher management to gain recognition for their efforts. It is an effective way to reward people for their collective work.

(b) Reward and celebrate team goals that are met, not just individual goals.

(c) Consider carefully the scope of the project and whether its quality would benefit from teamwork or one person's involvement.

(d) Find ways to optimize people's input by putting together teams with diverse skills sets to tackle projects.

(e) Clearly define the role of each player in the team. This means highlighting and promoting what each member brings to the team.

(f) At your initial team meetings, establish the necessary procedure individuals must follow: how they will communicate, the decision-making process, details of how work will be done and ways in which conflict will be resolved.

2 | I do not spend time on promoting the team's strategy or purpose

Rethink

Research from the Center for Creative Leadership shows a lack of clarity about a team's purpose is a major cause of its problems and failure.

Challenging, attainable and well-defined goals set a team on course and establish cohesion. Managers make the common mistake of pulling resources together well, but not providing a well-defined approach or goal.

Commitment to the strategy unifies people, so be sure to provide a clear-cut purpose to the team's efforts and a vision of where their work is taking them. The better you are at directing your team, the more successfully you will unify them and get them to work together. But remember, it requires ongoing attention and management.

React

(a) Be sure to create and maintain a well-defined, relevant mission statement.

(b) Allow the team members to participate as much as possible in creating their vision and goals. It will increase their sense of ownership of the project.

(c) Create milestones and concrete measures of success to help team members to stay motivated along the way. Tie measurements to the goals achieved, for example, the number of new clients reached.

(d) Build a sense of camaraderie by celebrating the team's milestones.

(e) Periodically, take the time to articulate to individuals exactly what their parts play in the team's success as well as that of the ultimate goal, and what that goal means to the company.

3 | I assume people can or will work well together

Rethink

Most complex projects require teamwork. Invariably, individual team members will bring diverse skills and work styles to a project. It is risky to assume that a team will automatically work in a collaborative and cohesive manner.

397

Interpersonal dynamics and individual work styles are the key to how effectively a team can achieve its goals, yet managers often overlook the importance of their compatibility.

Any team will represent a variety of working methods and approaches. PeopleTree Group's research has identified and defined numerous common styles, for example, the political positioner, global thinker, idea generator and people motivator. The more diverse the team, the greater the mix of skills on which to draw. But a diverse team also has a greater chance of not maximizing its potential, because interpersonal issues and styles could create incompatibility and hamper its success.

Become aware of your team's makeup beyond their obvious skills — it will maximize your success.

React

(a) Gather all the team members together for an initial face-to-face meeting. It is important to establish the team's identity, build trust among its members and create a sense of unity.

(b) Let your team be assessed for different team styles and facilitate a guided workshop to help the members understand each other better. The Birkman Method® is an effective tool to look at how individual needs affect a team's dynamics. The PeopleTree Group's Team Styles and Individual Talent Analysis reports, available through a consultant at www.peopletreegroup.com, can give managers key insights into individuals in their team.

(c) Ask your human resources department about team-building exercises your team can attend.

(d) Help people to make the vital connection between career advancement and working well with others. Effective interpersonal skills are critical for advancement in any organization. Learn, and teach your team, to develop them.

(e) Be sure to intervene quickly when a team member is being disruptive. Talk to the person privately to assess the challenges they experience. An outside mediator may be necessary if intense conflict arises between individuals in the team. Misunderstandings must be addressed before they assume greater meaning than they should.

(f) Do not assume that team issues can be resolved at once — you may have to address matters again. Remain constantly aware of the group's needs.

4 | I have not had the opportunity to manage a team/ I only have to manage myself

Rethink

Whether your position formally requires the management of others or not, a team member always has opportunities to unify others in pursuit of a mutual goal. Instead of focusing just on your work, broaden your perspective and pay attention to the team's efforts. Although you may not have had the opportunity to manage a team thus far, you can expect that your role, as you progress in your career, will most likely involve managing others at some point. In their book, *The Leadership Pipeline*, authors Ram Charan, Stephen Drotter and James Noel illustrate the progression of competencies needed as individuals advance in their organizations.

Not surprisingly, the competencies necessary to manage yourself are quite different from those needed to manage others. Becoming aware of theses competencies and developing them earlier rather than later will allow a smoother and more successful transition to any new role you may face.

React

(a) If your position does not include managing a team, try taking on the role of motivator in your workgroup. Help your colleagues to stay focused on progress and the positive side of things when morale is low.

(b) If not already in place, try to institute periodic team meetings to review the work status. Offer to facilitate the meeting and, possibly, the discussion.

(c) Talk you your boss about opportunities to take a lead role in a team project.

(d) Join special committees, at work or privately, that expose you to group dynamics.

(d) Become familiar with the competencies required to manage others. Talk to a PeopleTree Group consultant about the 360° assessment process and the company's Individual Talent Analysis, which provide an in-depth view of areas for development.

(d) Read *The Leadership Pipeline* by authors Charan, Drotter and Noel.

Overdeveloped

Research has shown that strengths can become weaknesses because you can, in fact, do too much of a good thing. You cannot become less good at a competency in which you excel, but you can balance the behavior by developing a few Stabilizers to tone down an excessive strength.

Stabilizer	Overdeveloped
13 Courageous	Is too team-oriented and does not recognize individual effort and contribution. Tries to unify groups that are not naturally teams
35 Manages Conflict	
38 Manages Underperformance	
25 Empowers People	
20 Develops People	
23 Directs People	
43 Motivates People	
51 Recognizes Talent and Potential	
28 Fair	
2 Adaptable	

Instructions

Read the definition. If it applies to you, choose a few Stabilizers and develop them by selecting the relevant chapter and following the Strategies for Action.

For more instructions see the How To Use This Book section.

60. Works Well with Boss

"Getting along with men isn't what's truly important.
The vital knowledge is how to get along with one man"

Phyllis McGinley

Well Developed
Has a positive working relationship
with the person to whom they report

Underdeveloped
Has a strained relationship with the
person to whom they report

Overdeveloped
Relies too much on a boss for support
to get things done. Tries too hard to
get on with the boss

Instructions

Read the definitions on the
left. If the Underdeveloped
definition applies, go to
the Strategies for Action
section.

If the Overdeveloped
definition applies, go to
the end of the chapter.

Test Yourself

True	I inform my boss of the status of my work
True	I am honest with my boss about issues
True	I do not get defensive when my boss gives me negative feedback
True	I act respectful towards my boss
True	I can put myself in my boss's shoes

Note

**Are you sure you need to
develop this competency?**

If the answer is "True" to
most of the statements on
the left, you probably do
not need to develop this
competency.

Strategies for Action

Most ineffective behaviors have an underlying thought or emotional pattern. By identifying these patterns, you can understand the impact they have and design strategies to counteract them.

(1) My boss's technical competence does not commandeer my respect

(2) My work style and my boss's are very different/Sometimes our styles clash

(3) My boss is a difficult person/I am intimidated by my boss

Instructions

1. Read and select one or more of the ineffective ways of thinking/feeling to the left.

2. Find the corresponding number below that will help you to rethink this pattern and identify specific and practical actions that you can take.

1 | My boss's technical competence does not commandeer my respect

Rethink

Conflict between you and your boss could stem from a lack of respect for the other's abilities. It is critical to learn to respect a person's strengths as well as working with their weaknesses.

Disrespect gives rise to harmful behavior such as talking behind your boss's back and working against them instead of with them. If you think the person lacks the extensive technical skills you have and expect a boss to have as well, you should realize that different levels require different skills. For example, in a boss a certain depth of technical knowledge is not as important as being able to manage processes or teams well.

Individuals on the executive track often sacrifice depth of technical knowledge for breadth of experience in multiple functional areas or disciplines. Also, someone's talent set is greater than their technical knowledge, so be cautious about using the latter as your competence gauge.

Research shows about 50% of performance is linked to behavioral competencies, not technical skills and experience levels. Even in high-technology companies it is common to see up to a quarter of the management-track positions held by people without a technical degree.

React

(a) Judge your boss by overall performance, not depth of technical knowledge.

(b) Be realistic about comparing your boss with others. You may have worked hard at specializing in an area and developed expertise in it, or previously had a boss who was a technical expert, but it may not be necessary now for your boss to do the job well.

(c) Instead of criticizing or judging, find ways to use your technical knowledge to make your boss and team more successful.

(d) Share literature or experiences that you have found useful in building your technical knowledge with your boss.

(e) Ask your boss to identify technical experts in the company from whom you and your team can get guidance if he or she is unable to answer your questions.

(f) Improve your own technical expertise so that you do not to have to rely on your boss.

(g) Learn as much as you can from the boss's strengths instead of focusing on the weaknesses.

---

2 | My work style and my boss's are very different/ Sometimes our styles clash

Rethink

Your boss may have a work style with which you disagree, or you may have difficulty to adapt to it. For example, your boss may be a micro-manager while you need plenty of room to navigate your own course. Your boss may provide little direction while you work best with a preset plan.

Work styles vary greatly and clashing styles can cause friction, not only between peers but also between bosses and the people they manage. Expecting your boss to be able to read your needs is not a way to manage these differences. Without honest communication matters usually worsen.

In your career, you will likely be assigned to many different managers, each with their own style. Use the challenge as an opportunity to learn from different styles. Do not see them as a hindrance or threat. Remember, too, that a person's work style does not define the whole person. Your boss may be excessively detailed and analytical when managing a project, but relaxed and informal when listening to your problems.

A balanced picture of a person is important to maintain good relationships.

React

(a) Have an honest discussion with your boss about your preferred work style and the guidance you need to perform your best. This type of feedback will help your boss to understand the approach with which you are most comfortable. Be as specific as possible and cite examples of when your boss's style made things challenging for you. The goal is to understand the best way to work together.

(b) Reinforce behavior by letting your boss know what he or she is doing right. Thank your boss for giving you room to carry out a project or, conversely, for taking the time to help you structure a task properly.

(c) Ask your boss what is required of you. What can you change about your work style to improve your relationship? For example, if your boss is constantly micro-managing, perhaps it is because he or she has a need to be informed and you are not providing enough information.

(d) Suggest to your boss that your group or team participates in assessments which probe deeper into the different work styles represented in the group. Assessments such as the Birkman Method and the PeopleTree Team Styles tool explore the differences between individuals and groups.

(e) Get to know the person behind the work style. If possible, try to spend time in a social setting — go to lunch together or attend a social event where you get a chance to converse with your boss.

3 | My boss is a difficult person/I am intimidated by my boss

Rethink

Some bosses come across as arrogant, are intimidating or simply difficult to deal with because of their personality. They may be chronically unpleasant or need to be handled particularly carefully. Such a situation is never pleasant, especially because a boss has the advantage of authority. It is nevertheless in your best interest to work on ways to manage the relationship instead of avoiding it or becoming defensive. Neither of these responses gives a productive working relationship a chance.

We obviously make assumptions about people based on their behavior, but these assumptions can prove to be faulty once we get to know them better or have worked closely with them. Realize, too, that people often react to circumstances totally unrelated to you. For example, extreme stress can bring out the worst in people and most managers are under a considerable amount of stress on any given day. But some characters are just plain difficult. If this is the case with your boss, it is his or her problem not yours — do not let it negatively affect your career. You may not be able to develop a close relationship, so instead focus your attention on performing well despite this challenge and do not take your boss's lack of self-awareness personally.

React

(a) Focus on things about your boss that you respect — tenacity, level of business acumen, ability to make decisions. Do not just consider your boss's behavior, but his or her accomplishments as well.

(b) Observe the context or situations that make it more difficult to work with your boss. Does it always happen, or just under particular circumstances? If it is the latter, what can you do to assist your boss during those times?

(c) Prepare yourself emotionally for the ups and downs that go hand in hand with a difficult personality. A person whose moods are inconsistent is difficult to work with, so be sure not to take a bad mood personally.

(d) Be as open as possible with your boss. He or she may be unaware of the impact of their behavior and, without feedback, are unlikely to change.

(e) Become familiar with behavioral competency language. It will help you to define and communicate which elements of a person's behavior make them difficult, for example, someone is not open, does not listen, is not approachable, patient or fair.

(f) Get to know your boss in social settings. Attend events where you can interact or plan a lunch with your boss, if possible. You may get to know a very different person.

(g) Keep your boss informed. Often, we withhold information from people we do not respect. Keeping you boss well informed ensures lines of communication stay open and encourages dialogue between the two of you.

(h) Relationships are a two-way street — have you thought about what you might you be contributing to the situation? Be honest with yourself. You may have little control over your boss's behavior, but you do have control over yours. Write down things you may be doing that make the relationship difficult. Are you too competitive? Do you expect your boss to behave in a certain way all the time?

(i) Although a strong relationship with your boss is ideal, a person is sometimes just not willing to change. Concentrate on building a good relationship through your performance and not your relationship. The best you can do is to focus on developing your skills to prepare you for a reassignment.

(j) If the relationship with your boss is verbally or mentally abusive, talk confidentially with your human resources representative about your options.

(k) Do you get defensive when your boss gives you negative feedback? Do you hold a grudge about something that happened in the past? Do you talk behind your boss's back?

(l) Manage your expectations. You do not have to like everything about your boss. Are you comparing your boss to someone else?

Overdeveloped

Research has shown that strengths can become weaknesses because you can, in fact, do too much of a good thing. You cannot become less good at a competency in which you excel, but you can balance the behavior by developing a few Stabilizers to tone down an excessive strength.

Stabilizer	Overdeveloped
7 Collaborative	Relies too much on a boss for support to get things done. Tries too hard to get on with the boss
49 Politically Astute	
13 Courageous	
44 Networked	
2 Adaptable	
56 Technically Competent	
1 Achiever	
26 Ethical	
12 Confident	
58 Trustworthy	

Instructions

Read the definition. If it applies to you, choose a few Stabilizers and develop them by selecting the relevant chapter and following the Strategies for Action.

For more instructions see the How To Use This Book section.